Small-Town Heroes

Curt Simmons

Small-Town Heroes

One Community

Two Coaches

Three Championship Paths to Success

Theatron Press
www.ipibooks.com
ipi

SMALL-TOWN HEROES

ISBN: 0-9776954-1-7

Printed in the United States of America
09 08 07 06 1 2 3 4

Theatron Press

An imprint of Illumination Publishers International

www.ipibooks.com

ipi

Dedications

To my two living uncles, Cleo and Cliff, who were a major factor in my father becoming such a great man.

To my mother, Priscilla, who proved once again the ancient addage is indeed true, that behind every great man is an even better woman.

To every high school coach across the country who believes building character is more important than bringing home championships.

And to the memory of my father, LaVerne Simmons, who with so much grace and so little fanfare handed me the tools I would need for happiness and how to be a successful human being.

CONTENTS

Introduction

"Big things come in small packages!"

No doubt many parents have used that familiar phrase to offset the discouragement one of their children felt after comparing a soon-to-be-opened present under the tree with the much larger one destined for a sibling. And certainly a large number of long-shot-to-make-it athletes in every sport have gotten themselves psyched up for greater success on the playing field simply by embracing that motivational saying. But beyond the comfort a kid can receive from mom or dad to help calm their Christmas-morning concerns, and beyond the inspiration an undersized athlete in any sport can derive by making it their personal motto, those six words still have a very important message to communicate to our bigger-is-better and size-does-matter world.

The story you are about to read is one more example of the truth that lies within that opening statement. I gladly offer it to you as a reminder of just how important it is to resist the temptation to think bigger is always better and only things oozing with gobs of glitz and glamour are of any real value. *Small-Town Heroes* contains a story with very little glitz and glamour. The story is a simple, yet inspiring account of events that transpired in one small town in America in the 1950s, then again in 2002 and 2003, and the amazing connection between the two. It's a small-package story I'm confident can teach all of us a number of really big things about the truly important matters in life and how we should go about pursuing our personal goals and dreams in heroic fashion. While much of the actual story within the pages of *Small-Town Heroes* centers on basketball, the entire book will introduce you to a whole lot more than that. It's much more about discovering success in all facets of life. It's a book focused on helping you make sure your day-to-day contributions to the world are positive at the moment and ones you'll be proud to claim whenever you look back upon your time spent on this earth.

Just as the magnitude of this story would barely be measured on the Richter scale of worldwide sport's significance (assuming the long-awaited Red Sox and White Sox victories in the last two World Series were measured at 10.0), the paths to success offered in this book aren't earth-shattering either. For example, while there is some evidence having good looks, being in great shape and making the appropriate apparel choices play a role in improving your odds of making a good impression on those in high places, the paths provided in this story have nothing to do with improving your outward appearance or encouraging you to dress for success. Though earning a good education can perhaps better prepare you to earn a spot on the company team ahead of the guy without one, getting a degree from a respected institution (and the more the better!) isn't included in this story's model for success. And despite the truth knowing the right people (or knowing someone who knows the right people) can often help you get your foot in the door of opportunity, uncovering certain secrets about how to gain direct access to some influential people won't be included as one of the ingredients for cooking up a successful life or sensational career. Instead, these paths are all about achieving your goals and aspirations by having a proper mindset, possessing the right kind of heart and developing the right kind of character, all of which, over time, can greatly enhance your chances of being a successful person.

In line with the story being one of a lesser-known variety, the main characters in this small-town drama will be unrecognizable to all but a few of you as well. There are no big names to drop. There's no key individual in the story who was at one time, is now or probably ever will be someone of considerable note outside of the small towns they represent. But should you decide to follow the example of the ordinary people you'll be introduced to shortly, it will have a profound and positive impact on your life. My hope is you'll not only follow their example, but also recognize and honor all the other little-glitz-and-glamour people who have had a much more positive and long-term affect on your life than any Hollywood actor or Hall of Fame athlete.

For those of you who greatly enjoy playing the game of basketball, if you're hoping to pick up a few pointers to bolster your performance on the court by reading this book, you're in for a major disappointment. While you will be introduced to a team of basketball players who were successful in their on-the-court endeavors, neither those athletes nor their coaches have offered up any tricks of the trade that could, in a skills sense, make you more likely to make the team or sink a free-throw at a critical juncture of the game. On the other hand, (to borrow from basketball lingo) if you're *shooting* for a promotion at work or a particular grade in your most challenging class this semester, this book will be a big help. If you're *passing* through a tougher than normal stage in your life or a tenser than normal episode with your spouse or children, you'll find the information in the remainder of this book quite helpful. And if you're *rebounding* from a disappointing stretch in your life, a difficult divorce or a recently-discovered dysfunction in your immediate family, what you're about to read may be just the thing you need to gain some perspective and understanding about where to go from here.

My deepest and most sincere thanks to all of you who contributed information to help bring this story to print. Your memories of specific events and your moments spent in chronicling them for my benefit is greatly appreciated. Without you taking the time to answer my questions and fill in the many missing pieces of the puzzle, this writing project never would have been completed. And to all of you now embarking on a trip to discover *Small-Town Heroes*, it's a tremendous privilege to share this story with you and boast of another big thing I found in a very small package. I hope the present you're about to open is one you will cherish for the rest of your life.

Curt Simmons
Lisle, Illinois
2006

Section I

The Setting

Chapter One

To Be or Not to Be?

I told the condensed version of this story for the very first time in January of 2004 to an audience of nearly 500 churchgoers in Chicago. It was quite an emotional experience for me that morning as I shared some specific details of how a 46-year drought came to a fitting end, and how tradition, tennis shoes and twelve young athletes converged to bring some much-needed rain to the desert of championship basketball in the small town of Darrington, Washington.

"You should write a book about the whole experience," my wife said to me later that afternoon. While I initially doubted the significance of chronicling events that culminated in the end of arid ways in the Pacific Northwest community, her suggestion kept making more and more sense as each day passed. Soon, that lone spark ignited a flame in my heart to share a story about what I considered to be some heroic activity that took place in Darrington, a tightly knit town seeking to regain pride in their once-storied basketball tradition. It has now been nearly two years since her suggestion and, in that time, I've come to realize the significance of bringing these events to the written page.

Before making a final decision about whether or not to write this book, I found myself vacillating on the issue whenever I asked the following question: "Will anybody really be better off by reading about this small-town sport's story?" I must admit, at first, I was looking for a few reasons why *not to be* involved in writing this book. But each time that question entered my mind I came away with a stronger feeling many people could benefit from knowing the backdrop and basic gist of this story. With those positive thoughts resounding in my conscience on a regular basis, I slowly but surely became convinced the story had *to be* shared. I ultimately came to the conclusion the story had an important message for people in all walks of life about how to achieve real success. And I couldn't help but think how so many people searching for success today are often oblivious to the "Dead End" signs posted on the roads they're taking to get there. I was confident this story could bring some attention to those "turn-around-now" advisories and also provide a few alternative routes to point success-seekers in the proper direction.

To aid me in reaching a final commitment to proceed, I asked myself some other questions about the value of this project, only this time with the purpose of determining if someone's gender, age, race, upbringing, education, economic level or current employment status would change the answer to my initial question. Could this story's main theme for finding success be of benefit to every single person regardless of those differences? For example, would it work equally well for the person using food stamps to pay for their groceries, the multi-millionaire sending a live-in maid to purchase his groceries, the high school senior bagging the groceries, the middle-aged truck driver delivering the groceries, the single mother checking the groceries and the owner of the individual store determining the price of the groceries? Without any reservations, I answered those questions in the affirmative. Continuing on with that type of interrogation, here are a number of other questions I asked about various individuals in all walks of life, should they decide to pursue the paths to success put forth in this story.

Could a CEO of a large corporation improve his chances of bringing stability and stellar sales to his company simply by embracing the success model revealed in this story? And could the employees under that individual's authority gain greater satisfaction in working for their boss just by focusing on what brought about basketball success in the small town of Darrington? Could a commitment to walking on these paths better their chances for a much-desired promotion, perhaps the one they've been unable to secure up to this point in their career? While I'm obviously biased and, no doubt, would love to see many corporate bosses and their employees mulling over the information found in this book, I still had to answer all of those work-related questions in the positive.

Next, I considered the millions of small business owners who blanket our nation's cities and towns. Was this book (and the revelation within it) really going to be worth the time it would take to read for these busier-than-normal individuals? Would there be a good return of investment on the $15 it would cost them to purchase the book and the 15 minutes a day they might commit to reading it? Could an acceptance of this story's success model aid them in taking their businesses to an entirely new level of revenue and respect within their communities? Would they be better in the long-run to hold on to these success principles, even during trying times when similar businesses seemed to be making greater headway without employing them? Again, I concluded none of these small business owners would regret any decision they made to carry out in their workplace what they would learn a few individuals had done in Darrington to bring about success in their small town.

Stepping away from the business world, I asked the same type of questions about a number of other individuals in various areas of employment or emphasis, wondering if I would come away with similar responses. I began in the political arena.

Could this story's simple message of success be of any help in landing a candidate a government position if they applied it during their run for office? And once they were elected and in place for their term of leadership, could adherence to these principles of success help both them and the citizens they represented better enjoy each other's company? If they were to consistently live out these principles, would that bring about positive changes in the areas they governed and ultimately lead to each resident's life being a little bit better than it was before they were elected? Or was it even possible for a candidate or current political office-holder to fully endorse and embrace this story's model for success? Once again, I was absolutely certain, should any politician decide to employ this model, it would be a tremendous blessing for their constituency, whether it was someone benefiting from their President's performance or the resident of a small town enjoying the much-smoother ride of a mayor who finally grabbed hold of the reins of proper leadership.

Moving out of the government arena, I took a trip down the halls of education and asked similar questions about the individuals conducting affairs in that environment. If a teacher applied this story's success model, would students benefit from their mentor's move in that direction? If a school's *principal* allowed these *principles* to penetrate their heart, how might teachers and students in that school benefit as a result? If students at the same school decided to put this story's success model into their own hearts and then into the public arena, how would their parents feel about those changes? Would they be thrilled their children were being educated in such an atmosphere? Would it have any positive affect on their offspring's grade-point-average? I felt not only would they be thrilled with the atmosphere and thankful for the rise in their children's academic status, but other parents outside of that particular school would hear about the education revival taking place there and quickly demand the promotion and practice of those same values at their child's learning institution. I'm convinced when this story's simple model for success becomes a focus in the offices, classrooms, gymnasiums, cafeterias and hallways of any school in the world (public or private, inner city or suburban), administrators, teachers, counselors and other school personnel will be in a much better position to lead the younger generation into successful adulthood. Their students will become smarter, more socially capable and better prepared for life in the real world and the many challenges it poses.

Then I decided to put these all-important questions to the test in the medical field. Could a physician become more valued and respected in his patient's eyes just by consistently modeling these principles for success? Could a doctor's application of this story's success model produce something beyond the blessing of physical healing for his patients? How might the rate of every patient's recovery improve in hospitals around the world if doctors and nurses carried these principles in their hearts while examining medical charts or making regular rounds to check on the progress of the sick? Could their actions even lead to a reduction in the overall cost of health care? Could lower malpractice insurance rates be a by-product of these values being put into practice? Could there possibly be quicker discoveries for some of the still-unconquered diseases if physicians, drug companies and medical research teams lived out these values to the best of their abilities? If someone working in the medical field were to take a break from their hectic schedule, devote a few minutes every day for the next few weeks to finish reading this book, then begin doing their best to incorporate this story's success model into their own lives, would it make a positive and long-term difference in our world today? I concluded, once again, regardless of whether these individuals were in a medical office, a hospital, a lab or a research institution, or whether they worked as a receptionist or a radiologist, a secretary or a surgeon, a nurse's aide or a neurologist, this story's message of finding success was of great value to each of these individuals.

Bringing this story's success model into question in a church environment or religious setting had great significance to me as well. Being a minister, it was important for me to ask these questions and come away with similar answers. Could a congregation of Christians benefit from their minister's emphasis on this story's success model, first from watching him embrace it in his own life and then from hearing him preach about it in the pulpit? Could he lead his flock to greater spirituality, greater numerical growth and greater confidence in their eternal destiny if he modeled these success principles in his life first then encouraged each member to practice them every day in their own? What if the vast majority of people on that church's membership roll decided to make them a way of life? Would that make the minister's job a bit more enjoyable? Would he be inspired to preach deeper and more inspiring messages every week if he knew most of his listener's were way more focused on addressing these areas in their own lives than they were in analyzing the data and delivery of his sermons? Could church attendance begin to swell in his congregation if first-time visitors to their Sunday services saw these principles of success being modeled in the members there? Without hesitation, I had to say a hearty "Amen" to all of those questions!

Since this book would focus much of its attention on the world of sports, I decided to ask the same questions for coaches and athletes alike. Could this story's main message on attaining success benefit them while pursuing their personal goals? Once again, I found the answer to be a positive one for the following participants in the world of sports.

I concluded this story's model for success would definitely help the not-so-gifted players in Pop Warner as well as the best professional athletes in the NFL. It would help a nervous father in his first year of coaching 10-year-olds on the gridiron and New England's Bill Belichick looking to lead the Patriots to their fourth Super Bowl title in five years.

I was confident an application of this story's success model would bring many benefits to basketball beginners who can barely dribble as well as the absolute best college players running the courts during March Madness. It would benefit Meagan's mom on the bench as she's trying to keep her overly excited eight-year-olds from shooting at the wrong basket and Roy Williams while he's manning the sidelines for the North Carolina Tarheels.

It was clear to me following this story's success model would be a huge bonus for first-time hockey players who only recently learned to skate as well as the top point-producers in the NHL. It would provide an advantage for the volunteers who organize practices and games for the local youth hockey club and the very best owners and general managers orchestrating championship runs for the Stanley Cup.

Without a doubt, I knew clinging to this story's principles for finding success would bring great reward to the weekend hacker who spends more time in the trees than on the fairways as well as the incredibly gifted Tiger Woods in his pursuit of another major championship. It would reward the history teacher with a 25 handicap who reluctantly agrees to coach the high school golf team and the well-paid golf guru who helps refine the swings of top professionals on the PGA tour.

I was certain this story's model for success could greatly aid the unpolished, 11-year-old Golden Gloves contestant as well as the 225-pound, chiseled champion at the top of the boxing world. It would help the willing uncle acting as his nephew's first trainer and the highly-experienced corner man shouting out instructions to the 25-year-old welterweight during his first shot at a title.

I was certain if coaches in the amateur and professional ranks planned out their seasons and developed strategies for success with this story's message in mind, they would all be more affective in motivating their teams to play smarter and harder. During the course of a typical season, I was sure these coaches would not only be able to steal a victory or two that looked like sure defeat simply by staying committed to these principles, but also their players would be much more likely to "Win one for the Gipper!" if they saw them leading in this fashion.

I knew if more athletes at all levels decided to adhere to this story's model for success, their individual performances would likely improve and they would certainly be contributing to a much better chance of a much better won-lost record for their respective teams. I concluded a pitcher with a keen eye toward living out this success model would contribute more to his baseball team's success than he would by throwing his hard-to-hit slider, and a running back carrying this model in his head and in his heart on the gridiron would be of greater benefit to his team than the way he carried the pigskin on third and five. I came to believe a highly skilled basketball player's decision to embrace this story's success model would be of greater importance to his team than any of his spectacular slam-dunks and no-look passes for fast-break baskets. And I was absolutely positive any athlete's commitment to this story's success model would greatly increase the odds of their team coming away with positive results in any and all competitive arenas. Along those same lines, I knew the more athletes per team willing to make a similar commitment, the more the odds of victory would turn in their favor.

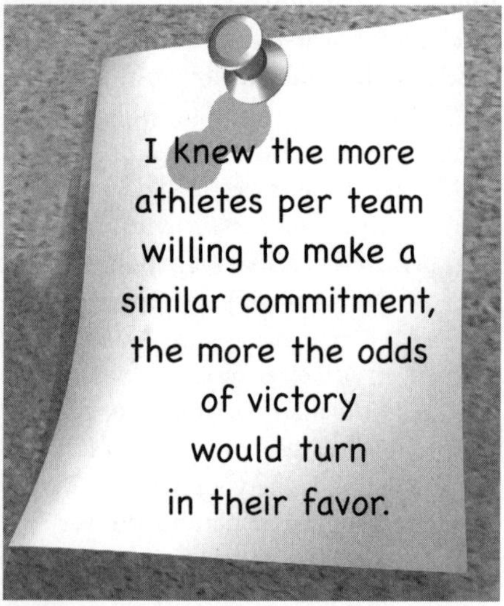

And last, but certainly not least, I put this model for success to the test with a review of my personal life, wondering whether or not I could trace my highs and lows through the years to the adherence (or lack thereof) to these particular principles. Had it been true during my high school days, whether that involved activity in the classroom, having the ability to create and maintain friendships or attaining success on the basketball court and baseball field? Did it prove to be true while I pursued my college degree and finalized my choice of careers? Could I see a huge difference in my marriage when these principles were a part of my overall character? Did my parenting seem to improve when I improved upon putting these principles for success into practice? Did my financial picture come into better focus when I allowed this model to become my focus? Did my work as a minister produce greater dividends whenever I decided to take these roads to success in the spiritual realm? Though I lack the recorded data to indicate the answer to all of these questions is a positive one, my memories of trouble and failure for the past 30 years or so are still clear enough in my mind to convince me I need to make this model for success a model for my personal life until the day I die.

To summarize, I became thoroughly convinced an acceptance of this story's model for success not only ushers in greatness, but also brings a healthy sense of pride and self-worth into a person's heart, whether that individual is male or female, 15 or 50, black or white, educated or a drop-out, rich or poor, in charge or taking orders. This is the type of pride needing to become more prevalent in today's world, as we presently have more than enough of the self-focused and harmful kind. In saying this, I don't believe it's wrong, by any means, for someone to set a personal goal to succeed by becoming CEO of the Year for a Fortune 500 company. And any person should feel awesome if their peers praise them for having successfully perfected a surgical technique that will save countless lives. There's absolutely nothing wrong with someone enjoying the wonderful feeling of satisfaction coming from capably directing the largest school district in the state and, without a doubt, it would be a tremendous experience for any individual to someday be able to hold up a championship trophy due to their athletic accomplishments. It would be fantastic if someone were offered a full-ride scholarship at a prominent university simply because of their extraordinary skill in a particular sport, and there's absolutely nothing inherently wrong with a young man gaining financial security by signing a $10 million-a-year, guaranteed contract with a Major League baseball team. But nothing is more important than finding success in areas of life that matter more than money, man's praise or making headlines in the sport's page.

Now if I failed to mention your vocation or didn't include the area in which you've chosen to devote most of your personal time and energy, don't fret! This story's success model will work for you as well. If you're a garbage collector or a gem collector, it will work! If you're a school-crossing guard or serving in the National Guard, it will work! If you're an airline pilot or an airplane mechanic, it will work! If you're gainfully employed on Wall Street or part-time employed at Wal-Mart, it will work! If you're the president of Starbucks or pouring coffee at Starbucks, it will work! But not only does it work in a corporate sense, a team setting or in the other areas I've already mentioned, this model works in the home quite well. Once you learn more about these simple success principles, try them out on your spouse and see how they react. Go ahead and use them in raising your children and watch how they turn out as adults. Show them off in the presence of your parents on a consistent basis and watch how much they'll be willing to work with you toward a compromise on some of those things you thought would never happen until you were out of the house and off to college. And after you've reaped the benefits of this model in your family life, employ them in your neighborhood and see how many more friendly waves you'll receive. Display them at whatever weekly meeting you attend and see how many more people will want to spend time with you beyond the group setting. Here's the bottom line—this story's model for finding success really works.

In sharing this story with you, I also saw it as a great opportunity to promote small towns and put on display the many fine people who call these towns home across the country. Not only that, I also saw it as a chance to minister to those same people, something I haven't had as my focus ever since I decided to enter the full-time ministry more than 23 years ago. I've worked as a minister in metropolitan areas with populations of 75,000, 150,000, one million, three million, 10 million and 20 million people. I've ministered in two churches that had 2,500 and 7,000 people respectively on their membership rolls, both numbers being much larger than the population of the three small towns I called home from birth until my junior year of college. While I agree with the strategic wisdom of launching an important work in a bigger city then sending people from there to champion that cause in the smaller, surrounding communities, it has always been my concern that smaller towns weren't on the hearts and minds of very many people (self included) within the fellowship of churches of which I am a member. I've pondered many times what strategy would be best suited for getting the word out to these areas, and I had always hoped I could somehow be involved in that plan's implementation, whether leading a church in a smaller town or overseeing others in that capacity. I guess you might say this book is my way of getting reconnected with smaller towns, and perhaps it's the beginning of something that will become more defined in the near future for small-town ministry and my role within it.

While each of the aforementioned reasons helped motivate me to write this book, it surely didn't hurt the cause my father happened to be one of the main characters in the story. I have come to greatly appreciate how he lived out this model for success in the realm of coaching and, looking back on the 43 years I spent with him, I realize now how it described much of his overall life. Unfortunately, my father is no longer alive. He passed away in late 2002 and I suppose this book, in some small way, is an opportunity to thank him for giving me a much better idea of what life should be all about as I grew up under his authority and care. And I firmly believe each of you reading this book can greatly benefit from knowing some of the history of his life and the lives of a few others in one small town who found success in their endeavors.

Chapter Two

True Heroes

Although a lot of excitement was stirring in my heart as I began mapping out plans for the research and writing of this book, it didn't take long before my work led me face-to-face with a few regrets. Most of those regrets stemmed from coming to realize I had only located a few nuggets of knowledge about my father's coaching career prior to his death, all while living for 43 years in a Texas-sized gold mine. So many questions started coming to my mind about that part of his life, and I was disappointed I never bothered to ask them while he was alive.

Why didn't I find out more about his greatest moments and most-vivid memories while coaching high school basketball for 17 years? How did he conduct his practices in the pre-season? What specific things did he do in the off-season to keep himself and his returning players as sharp as possible? What were his practices like after a win, or how about after a disappointing loss? How did he feel after the victories? How did he deal emotionally with the tough defeats? What halftime strategies did he employ to motivate his team when they were trailing? How did he keep his players on the edge when they owned a comfortable lead at the break? What were his relationships like with his players and assistant coaches? Did he ever have to use disciplinary measures to straighten out a player who wasn't taking him seriously? What was the most difficult decision he ever had to make while coaching at Darrington? What was his most satisfying moment as a coach? What was his pre-game ritual before a regular-season game? What was his pre-game ritual before a championship contest? And what did he do to celebrate the championships? Sure, I knew quite a bit about what happened in those glory days before I was even born, but there was so much more I could have known, and only now am I beginning to realize how much.

But those questions didn't seem very relevant to me for most of my adult life. I respected my father for all he had done to be a blessing to my life, and that was more than enough stored information to bring deep amounts of pride and gratitude into my heart whenever I thought about him and his role in my life. And my father was never one to clamor for attention, especially around his own family, nor did the topic of his coaching success get discussed very often unless it was asked of him, and even then he greatly downplayed his accomplishments or tried to quickly change the subject.

Of course, with the information I was privy to, I was always eager to share about the success he enjoyed while coaching with anybody who seemed interested, and I loved talking to my father every now and then about his winning ways in Darrington. And I'm sure I would have welcomed and appreciated any gathering of additional information about his many accomplishments from others who knew him. But, in my mind, that extra enlightenment wasn't really needed to bolster my feelings about my father. You see, regardless of his coaching credentials, he had been a hero in my mind for many years. I didn't need to hear any flattering remarks about him from former players or fellow-coaches to convince me how great he was. I didn't need to read article after article in the sports pages of the past, or look through a yearbook from the high school he represented to prove he was someone special. Sure, most of those hero thoughts about my father came after I moved well past the "he's-my-dad-not-my-hero" stage that ended somewhere around the time I graduated from high school. Since then, however, hero is the most appropriate word that comes to my mind whenever I think about him and his role in my life.

Now, before moving ahead with this story about small-town heroes, I'm in full agreement with those of you who feel the hero label is often bestowed upon those with little or no right to wear it. After hearing so many stories through the years about the valiant men and women who have fought in America's military conflicts, and with nightly reports of heroism being told about our troops in the midst of the current war centered in Iraq, I again have been reminded only certain types of people are truly deserving of wearing the title of hero. In my opinion, Pat Tillman is one of those individuals. Tillman, a professional football player from 1998-2002 with the Arizona Cardinals, was positioned to renew his contract with the Cardinals in 2003, or perhaps gain an even better offer as a free agent with another NFL team, either deal reported to be worth approximately one million dollars per year. Instead, Tillman decided to enlist in the Army, knowing he would receive approximately $25,000 a year for his efforts, all while risking his life in either Afghanistan or Iraq. When asked about his extraordinary and unusual decision, Tillman said the main reason for making that choice was he felt he owed something to his country, especially to all the brave and heroic people of past wars who had fought and died to secure the freedoms he was greatly benefiting from as an American. Contrast that attitude with how a typical professional football player would react if they were asked to renegotiate their multi-million-dollar contract due to their sub-par performance in consecutive seasons and you can see why Tillman should be considered heroic. Sadly, Tillman was killed in Afghanistan in April of 2004 while doing his part to help maintain that same precious freedom for the rest of us in the midst of an increasingly hostile world. Yes, Tillman is a true hero, as are most of the men and women who have served in the armed forces and daily put their lives in harm's way.

What Tillman did is what all heroes have done in the past to become such heralded figures, and it's what they continue to do—they think more of others than they think of themselves and sacrifice their comforts and freedoms to bring benefit to their fellowman. In many cases, their sacrifices bring blessings to men and women they've never met and their selfless acts often secure a better way of life for those yet to be born. Sadly, most of the beneficiaries of this heroism will never express an ounce of gratitude to these individuals for the great deeds wrought on their behalf. Yet, despite being keenly aware of these truths, heroes remain focused on their mission at hand.

With these general thoughts about the heart and character of those in the military acting as my guide for whether it's right to use the term hero in describing an individual, it is my firm belief our country and our world is full of heroes who are not now, and have never been, on the literal battlefield. Though they would probably be the last to ask for it, they, too, are worthy of recognition. They, too, put others above themselves. They, too, are willing to risk their lives, their reputations, their careers and their comforts, simply to do what is right. Those of the past who immediately come to mind are the brave men and women who persevered through some of the most intense episodes in the early stages of the Civil Rights Movement. Whether it was Rosa Parks sitting on a bus that reeked of ignorance and arrogance, James Meredith courageously walking onto an all-white college campus that was forced to accept him or Martin Luther King Jr. confidently standing behind a podium outlining his dream for all mankind, numerous African-Americans displayed true heroism by daringly but peacefully opposing the blatant evils of racism, often amid protest and violent opposition. These individuals stretched themselves and inspired the same elasticity in others. They spent great quantities of time trying to find solutions to life's challenging and unpleasant situations, and little, if any, of their waking moments feeling sorry for themselves. They pushed for justice and equality with great passion, but did so without threatening remarks or putting other people's lives in jeopardy. They set examples for all generations to come of perseverance through pain and endurance amid prejudicial treatment. Where acquisitions and ambitions were involved, these heroes decided upon personal relationship building rather than personal possession building as their primary focus.

While those fighting for freedom and justice through the ages are true heroes in every sense of the word, there are many others in our world with very similar qualities, displaying their heroic character on different turf. They, too, should be classified as heroes. With this broader scope in mind, let's consider a few places where these individuals can be spotted.

A hero could be an elementary or secondary schoolteacher. Many of these trained educators were fully capable of choosing and excelling in a different career path, one that likely would have supplied them with a more substantial income. But they love teaching children and see the long-term value of adequately equipping the next generation, so they're staying put in the lower-paying academic environment.

A hero could be a police officer who patrols the streets and puts his or her life on the line every day. These are courageous men and women who, at times, receive unfair scrutiny, criticism and even punishment for certain life-and-death choices they're called upon to make, decisions often made while hardened criminals lunge at them with knives and murderers with loaded weapons emerge from behind garbage bins to confront them in dark alleys. These upholders of the very laws designed to protect us are usually earning a much lower income compared to others in less-challenging lines of work.

A hero is a housewife who decides to decline a second income option that would bring her family the additional monies needed to purchase a newer and bigger home in the suburbs, a much nicer automobile or the opportunity for longer and more exotic vacations. Instead, she and her husband (also a hero for his support of her decision) have concluded her staying at home with the children and laying a foundation of love and "money-isn't-everything" is much more of a benefit to them (and ultimately to society as a whole) than being able to own a Mercedes, having one of the nicest houses on the block or taking the kids for another week to the time-share condominium on the beaches of Hawaii.

Heroes are the men and women who volunteer to spend some of their free time at homeless shelters, displaying a willingness to sit down beside the drunken and downtrodden and listen to hard-luck story after hard-luck story without making a single judgment.

Heroes are the selfless individuals who sacrifice some, most or all of their Saturday nights just to be ready to talk with one desperate soul who might be calling the suicide hotline center with the hope of hearing compassion in the voice on the other end.

Heroes are the real victims of someone's poor judgment who refuse to do what many Americans are doing in large numbers and sue the erring individual for as much as they can possibly get. The "everybody-else-is-doing-it" justification has never been an acceptable excuse for any behavior according to the philosophy of life they've embraced.

Heroes are those individuals following in the footsteps of people like Helen Keller and Christopher Reeve, men and women who choose to view their physical limitations as a chance to inspire and excel, not as an opportunity to complain or cry out "unfair, unfair."

Heroes are the happy and content individuals in our world who don't get caught up in keeping up with the Joneses.

Heroes are the daring souls who stand by their personal convictions, caring very little about analyzing the latest popular opinion polls just so they can be assured of being in the majority.

Heroes live day-to-day and decision-to-decision acting out what they believe is right rather than doing what is most expedient.

Heroes take action regardless of how many others join them in their cause, steadfastly believing in the power of one.

Heroes don't look for pay or paybacks. Revenue and revenge are nowhere to be found in their dictionaries of daily living.

To simplify, heroes want to use their lives to make other lives around them a little bit better, much like those who have donated their time and money to bring relief to the areas of our world devastated by the tsunami of late 2004 and the hurricanes of 2005. This is their greatest satisfaction whenever they're able to accomplish it, whether that comes at the end of their appointment, the end of their day, the end of their year or the end of their life.

Webster defines a hero as *"one renowned for great strength, courage and daring; someone celebrated for special achievements and attributes."* With this definition in mind, along with the aforementioned portrayals of real heroes, here are a few reasons why I believe my father deserves to be granted this honor, regardless of the many awards he collected while coaching high school basketball.

First, he stayed faithful to my mother for 45 years of marriage, and in today's world of husbands highly likely to commit adultery or choose divorce, my father rose above both and set himself apart from many of his wedded contemporaries. He loved me unconditionally as a son, gave every member of our family way more gifts and get-together time than he really could afford and rarely missed an important event of mine during my growing-up years. Two of his greatest habits were treating people with kindness and turning his other cheek. He openly cried when he was sad, laughed hysterically when he heard something funny and reached out to help others whenever he became aware of a need. He loved life and lived it as full as he knew how. Just one year removed from my graduation from college where I received my degree in Journalism while studying to be a sportswriter, my father refused to express disappointment when I chose my life's vocation of being a minister. In fact, he embraced it, and I always felt he had a sense of pride about my chosen role in life, even though I'm pretty sure he was hoping I would follow in his footsteps, or at least hoping I would end up writing about the game he loved so much. He welcomed my wife, Patty, into his family as if she were his own, did nothing but adore his three grandchildren and made people (sidekick or stranger) feel special in his presence. I never saw him drunk. I never heard him argue with my mother. I came to realize his amazing inner strength as he kept himself together emotionally and guided the rest of our family in the same direction after the death of my brother at the age of 15. I watched with admiration as he courageously quit smoking after 35 years while in his mid-fifties. I personally witnessed his amazing humility at age 60 as he responded to important biblical truths he had been unaware of his entire life—not to mention the new information was being presented to him by the same young man he had taught to tie his shoes and treat the young ladies with respect! And, perhaps more than anything else, I was impressed with how much he enjoyed spending time with me, especially the companionship and corresponding conversations we had during the thousands of cribbage games we engaged in for 35 years, starting at the age of eight when he taught me how to play. He was a tremendous example of what a good husband, good father and good man were all about, and I'm pretty sure there were only a small percentage of people during his lifespan with similar qualities.

Now in saying all that, I am also completely aware my father had his share of weaknesses and was far from being a perfect role model. But don't all heroes fall into that category? Whether it's the aforementioned soldiers or Civil Rights' trailblazers; former presidents such as Abraham Lincoln, Franklin Delano Roosevelt, John F. Kennedy, Jimmy Carter or Ronald Reagan; influential leaders and humanitarians like Mahatma Gandhi, Mother Teresa or Nelson Mandela; athletes such as Lou Gehrig, Jackie Robinson, Roger Bannister, Wilma Rudolph, Jack Nicklaus, Arthur Ashe, Walter Payton or Jackie Joyner-Kersee; aviators and astronauts like Charles Lindbergh, Amelia Earhart, Alan Shephard, John Glenn or Neil Amrstrong; or those who never make the headlines but are heroic nevertheless, like a fireman, your favorite teacher, your first coach or your friend who donated their kidney to you, they all have stains on their hero's cape. And consistent with their hero status, these men and women you so greatly admire have been willing to acknowledge their imperfections.

And if your living heroes are deserving of remaining on that elite roster, they'll often be seen working on those faults and overcoming their personal weaknesses during their remaining days.

Yes, even with his imperfections in full view, my father was a hero in my eyes. I just didn't realize how much of a hero he was to so many others before I had even arrived on the planet. Nor did I know about how he had managed to maintain his hero status in the eyes of hundreds of people in Darrington for so many years, long after his heroic deeds, both on and off the court, were complete. And I certainly didn't grasp how his life and legacy had the ability to inspire another man nearly 50 years later to live in a similar fashion. And I was least aware how the memories of his championship coaching days in the state of Washington could elevate one coach and twelve young men to do something they and many others in their town were beginning to believe could never be done again.

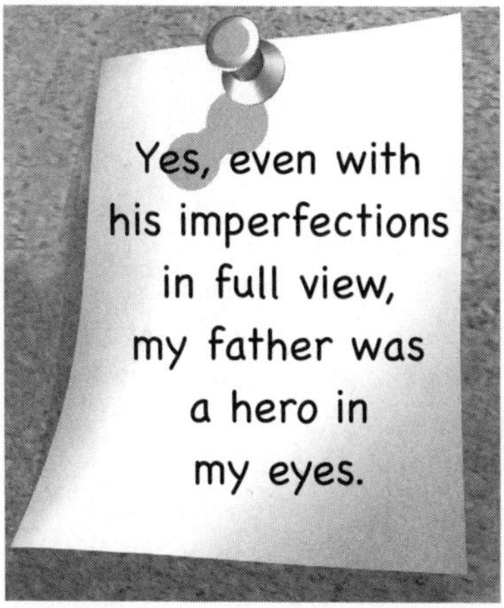

While my father is one of my heroes, Jeff Bryson is on my list as well. I don't know Jeff very well, other than from spending a few hours with him in December of 2003 and the few opportunities I've had since then in gathering information from him to help me finish writing this book. But I definitely look forward to getting to know him much better in the days ahead because he inspires me. Apparently, his actions have the ability to inspire others as well. Now there's no doubt Bryson possesses weaknesses as a human being. Members of his immediate family, his best friends and even those watching him coach during a practice or a game can likely attest to that. Yet he is still a hero in many regards. He lives in the same community as my father did 50 years ago, sits on the same bench in the same gymnasium and barks out similar directions to competitive young men, mostly on Tuesday and Friday nights in small-town America, living out his role as varsity men's basketball coach for the Darrington Loggers. What he and his team did for my family will never be forgotten by any of us. Yet, in many ways, what he did would probably be considered small in the opinion of many people, and, perhaps, even Jeff would see it that way. But a decision, made by this man in November of 2002, was one of the fondest gestures offered on behalf of my father and one I will have firmly embedded in my heart until my final breath. It was also this decision, I believe, that produced some additional motivation to help turn a high school basketball team from perennial hopefuls to powerful champions.

Chapter Three

The Bookstore's Big Void

In many ways, I feel as though I'm writing this book on behalf of millions of people across our great country, each with a similar story to tell about a hero figure in their lives. Perhaps their stories are even more inspiring than the one I'm about to share with you, and perhaps the heroes they've spotted deserve equal or greater recognition. I'm inclined to believe this is the case. If my assumptions are correct, then those individuals are the fortunate ones who've been in the presence of a true hero. If you happen to be one of these lucky people, my encouragement to you is to allow this book to be a simple reminder of just how appropriate it is to let your heroes know how you feel about them. Who knows, maybe this book will plant a seed in your heart and one day you'll transcribe a story about an amazing man or woman who inspires you with their heroic activity. The more books of this nature that become available to the general public, the more likely all of us can keep walking on the real roads to success. It's clear to me we have enough of the anti-hero types flooding our movie screens, magazine stands and minds. A little bit of counter-punching from the truly heroic side is sorely needed in a world that often glamorizes people and performances far from heroic. Besides, it's impossible for me to envision any negative ramifications coming from having more bookshelves in Borders and Barnes and Noble stores around the country fully stacked with true stories about heroic people. Right now, there's way too much non-fiction on the shelves documenting the activities and beliefs of those who fall well short of being the kind of people we should want our children emulating. To help prove this point, let's take a quick trip through the various sections of a typical bookstore and see what's in stock.

Athletes' autobiographies are in full supply, in many cases chronicling immoral accounts of sex, drugs and the high-profile life of professional sports. Yet these books offer little or no information about how to be a true champion, how to rise above the many temptations that come with the territory or what to do once the lights go out and the cheering crowds go home.

Political powerhouses tell us how they've climbed to the top of their profession and then offer practical ways of how to make sure our voices are heard, regardless of the morality we may be espousing. Sadly, a high percentage of people rising to the top of the political world do so because they have the most bucks, not the best character. Do the wealthy people who run much of our country really have that much to say about heroism? Wouldn't a single mother raising three children and working two jobs to provide for their Campbell's Soup today and their college tuition tomorrow be just as capable (or more) of offering us valuable information about how to be a hero? Could her principles and ethics be more valuable for citizens of our country to learn than those taught by the senator who was fed with a silver spoon?

Millionaires tell us how we can become just like them in a relatively short period of time, finally finding true happiness by being independently wealthy, completely detached from the normal, nine-to-five work schedule and our miserable, slave-driving bosses. Can these so-called moneymaking experts really know what all the $25,000-a-year-employees need to find satisfaction and contentment in their lives? What about a book written by the man who puts in 40-45 hours a week at his place of employment, makes $10-15 an hour, loves his job, respects his boss and wouldn't change a thing if he could do it all over again? Aren't there a lot more people needing to hear from him than from the man or woman who managed to be one of the few who made it big in multi-level marketing or another moneymaking venture?

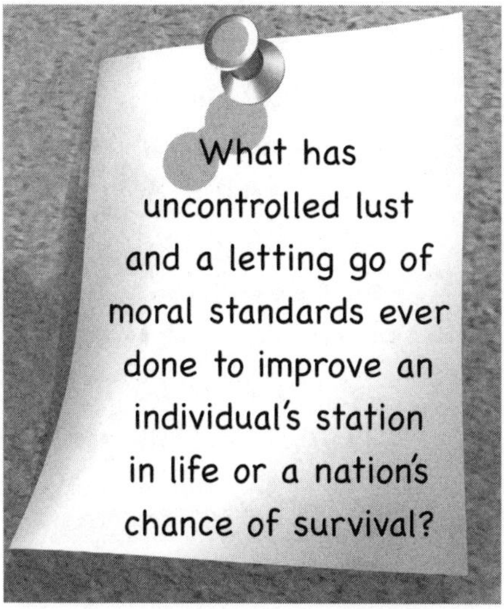

Many psychiatrists and psychologists promote their beliefs in the books they write, doing what they can to remove a heroic quality from many eager-to-learn Americans called personal responsibility. They're telling us, and attempting to prove it with scientific graphs (all of which are supposedly backed up by years and years of disciplined and detailed study), exactly why we don't need to take responsibility for our own actions. Their books are full of information about how most of our problems and failures (and, in some cases, all of them) can be traced back to a genetic flaw, poor parenting or lousy leadership.

Then there are the never-in-short-supply romance novels describing a kind of love that doesn't even exist in the real world, nor should it. What has uncontrolled lust and a letting go of moral standards ever done to improve an individual's station in life or a nation's chance of survival?

Wouldn't it be nice to read a book about love and romance written by someone who still has a great marriage after 25 years, largely due, they say, to a rock-solid foundation of friendship and absolute purity before saying "I do"?

And let's not forget the plethora of "How To" books. These books have plenty of information to keep we interested readers all wrapped up in our own little world, doing something we truly enjoy just a little bit better than before, whether it's gardening, gaining more computer skills or going on the best possible vacations. While these books aren't necessarily harmful or dangerous to read, when was the last time you saw a self-help book on how to be a better friend to somebody, or a book about how to show more respect to your boss? Or one on how to be grateful for what you have a whole lot more than being hopeful for what you don't? Or how to take care of your elderly parents in your own home in the best possible way and avoid the need for a nursing home, how to bite into the big problem of world hunger, how to practically love someone who has announced themselves to you as an enemy, how to avoid being selfish and how to be the best possible neighbor? Our planet would be in a lot better shape if these were the books making the New York Times Bestseller List and the contents within were finding their way into the homes and hearts of millions of readers across the globe.

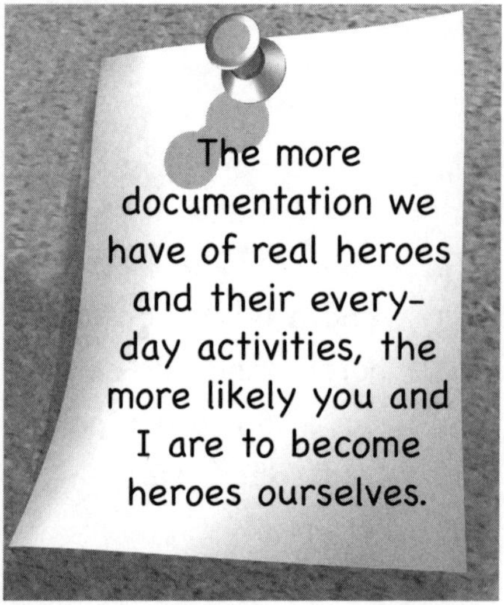

The more documentation we have of real heroes and their everyday activities, the more likely you and I are to become heroes ourselves. Perhaps with enough writing about what really matters, we can convince Borders and Barnes and Noble to create a new section for their stores, simply titled *True Heroes*. Now, if publishing a book isn't a possibility for you, perhaps you can write a short story about your hero and give it to them as a birthday or Christmas present. Before handing it to them, make some additional copies and distribute them to as many of your family and friends as possible. If that seems a bit lofty for your writing skills, why not compose a letter or a short note, put it in the mail and allow them to learn why you consider them a hero. Or, best of all, the next time you see that individual, spend a few moments letting them know what they mean to you. The method of communication isn't the issue here, the expression of gratitude is!

The documentation for this particular story has become available to you primarily because of Kevin Ashe, a long-time Darrington resident. Kevin made sure this specific memory about my father's abiding contributions to Darrington could become part of my life. Without the information I received from him, I couldn't have offered it to you as a story of inspiration, with characters worthy of imitation. Interestingly, the more I researched the information needed for this book, the more I discovered basketball success couldn't have come to Darrington without a very profound and long-term contribution from Kevin himself.

Unbeknownst to him, Kevin has helped me not only to find the inspiration to write this book, but also closure in my father's death. My father's death was the end of a wonderful life—one I was blessed to be a part of for so many years. Yet I later came to realize his death was just the beginning of a true story that mesmerized those 500 first-time listeners in Chicago and motivated them to examine their lives for evidence of heroism and the likelihood of future success.

Chapter Four

"H" is For Hero

Before disclosing this story's model for success, I must warn you none of the paths it will encourage you to choose are easy to navigate. All three are narrow and treacherous, traveled upon by only a small percentage of people on our planet. At times, loneliness gets the best of those brave enough to start walking down these paths and they opt for roads with fuller-volume traffic. At other times, a feeling of missing out on what others appear to be enjoying so much can tempt walkers on these paths to test out other highways. While the temptation to select alternative routes may seem relatively easy to succumb to, I'm convinced, with persistence and a little help from other people wanting to remain on the right roads, you can resist those urges. I say this with confidence because all of us, especially in our younger years, walked primarily on these paths. We rarely walked elsewhere. But somewhere along the way to growing up, we learned about other available paths. These new paths looked fairly safe and easy to travel on, showed great promise for self-promotion and provided numerous fellowship opportunities with countless travelers. Unfortunately, many of us started walking down these paths and it became normal, even comfortable, to walk on them—so much so even the thought of changing lanes, let alone roads, seems frightening and full of negative ramifications.

Although this three-pronged success model I'm about to share with you may be difficult to employ on a consistent basis, it is amazingly simple to understand. Perhaps you've heard all or part of it before in a motivational speech at your school's graduation ceremony or your company's year-end sales meeting, or maybe you've read about it in another book dedicated to the subject of success. If so, I promise you the re-education process will be extremely helpful.

With that in mind, here goes! The three championship paths to success are as follows: *Humility, hard work* and *a heart to help others.* Perhaps I'm over-simplifying in offering you this story's not-so-fancy, three-ingredient recipe for success. But keep reading and responding! Then and only then can you know for sure if this is the case! I think you'll find not only am I not over-simplifying, but consistently walking on these three paths is a lot more challenging than you may have thought.

But it wasn't nearly as difficult when we were younger. Picture for a moment a class of kindergartners going about their many activities on a typical school day. Observe the pride oozing out of their pores and their desperate desire to be noticed. Check out that ugly, unwilling spirit that keeps them from asking their teacher for help. Watch them work stone-faced and slothfully on their finger-painting project. Catch them yawning and looking rather bored upon their entrance to the playground. Then observe each child, one by one, deciding to bypass the monkey bars and giant slide, opting instead to return to the classroom for a moment of reflection. Notice the prejudice in their hearts as they choose to associate with only those of their same size, sex or color. Listen carefully as the many attitudes lodged deep in their hearts spew freely from their mouths while describing the animosity they feel for their teacher and fellow-kindergartners.

Now I'm quite certain what I've just described isn't anything close to what you visualized in your mind about those five-year-olds. Sure, the picture I just painted might parallel some of the thoughts and activities in a class full of college students, many of whom are looking to find the fastest way to a passing grade or anxiously awaiting their final departure from the university so they can begin their quest to get ahead in the world. Or it might describe the atmosphere in a room full of anxious employees during an emergency business meeting where the boss is offering his critique on the reasons for slower-than-normal third quarter profits and announcing specific plans for layoffs as a result. But it certainly doesn't tell the true story of the mindset and movement of most tenderhearted children at that age, the same type of person all of us were on the inside at one point in our lives. Humility was almost second nature to us when we were five. We weren't gunning for valedictorian honors or a free ride to the college of our choice. Among the many reasons for showing up, we loved coming to school for the graham crackers and milk and because we could be as mindless and messy as possible with clay and paint. We weren't afraid to admit we didn't know the answers to our teacher's questions. We knew there was so much knowledge to acquire and we took as much information into our five-year-old brains as possible. Laziness was a foreign concept at that stage of our lives as well. We gave every ounce of our energy to every single activity we engaged in throughout the day. That was the only way we knew how to operate—whether it was on the bus, in the classroom, at the playground or during the time between the final bell and bedtime. And, surely, selfishness wasn't our number one weakness. We wanted as many friends as possible, and we loved the times when we could help a classmate complete a project. We didn't allow the height, weight, color or gender of a classmate to cause us to stereotype them or stay away from them altogether. No, unfortunately we learned to do all of those things in the years to come. And sadly, due to the examples we saw in many of the people a few years ahead of us, the lack of teaching on true success we had access to and our own desires for self-promotion and security, many of us became skilled, even experts, in the areas of pride, laziness and a lackadaisical spirit when it came to the welfare and concern of our fellowman. Simply put, it's time to return to kindergarten!

Before moving on, however, I must issue a strong warning—there are absolutely no guarantees embracing this model for success will result in worldly prosperity or the praise of people around you. Some of the greatest people in the history of the world have chosen to walk these paths, and many of them found very little visible return on their investment, or they suffered greatly as a result. Some were taken advantage of when they humbled themselves. Perhaps they lost a job, a close relationship, a good reputation or even their life. Some worked humbly and tirelessly as slaves in the blistering heat for decades, yet they lived in deep poverty and died in dark obscurity. Some received ridicule from the majority of people in their country, simply because of their outreach and ongoing compassion toward a minority group. Some were imprisoned, beaten, even killed for taking a stance on loving everyone and excluding no one. The greatest man to ever grace our planet was nailed to a cross by his enemies and left to die in shame, even though he lived out these three principles to perfection for an astounding 33 years. So, should you choose to walk on these paths, you may find yourself in similar straits. But remember this: While your level of worldly success will likely be scrutinized and criticized, you'll be able to hold your head high knowing you've found success in the areas of life that really matter in the long run. And I'm confident others in the know will do what they can to make sure your words and deeds are remembered long after you've passed from this world.

Unfortunately, very few people today are choosing to be measured by this success model and not by the world's yardstick. Those who are choosing this model can sometimes be seen rising to the top of their chosen professions and attaining high levels of worldly success (athletes, entertainers, business tycoons and the like). This is a tremendous bonus to our world whenever it happens, because the more individuals in the public eye choosing these three paths to success, the better our chances become for creating a domino effect of heroic living. Thankfully, there are a few rich and powerful people in the national and worldwide spotlight displaying the three qualities of humility, hard work and a heart for others on a consistent basis. Now granted, I don't have all the facts to tell you who they really are 24/7 and what they're all about behind closed doors. But from hearing them being interviewed through the years, having a chance to listen to a few of their speeches in various settings, knowing something about their career highs and lows, understanding a bit about their upbringing and current family situation, having some knowledge of their humanitarian efforts through the years and just watching them as they interact with other human beings, these individuals seem to have embraced these three heroic characteristics and, in my opinion, have reaped the benefits of sowing those seeds of success. Unfortunately, the amount of people in politics, professional sports and the pages of People Magazine living in this fashion is a relatively low number.

While it's great to have a few good examples of people attaining success in places where the general public can catch a glimpse of it, there are hundreds of thousands of others living in similar fashion to those individuals in the limelight, and the vast majority of them receive nowhere near their paycheck or publicity. And more than likely, you'll fall into that low-paying-low-profile category should this story's success model be acted upon in your life.

So now that we're clear the success I'm referring to has little or nothing to do with greater net income, newer homes, a much larger nest-egg for retirement, nice things always being said about you and no problems to face once you start displaying them in your life, let's get down to business. Why do the three paths to success put forth in this model seem so difficult to choose? Why do we often believe, if we were to welcome them into our hearts and then into our interactions with people on a day-to-day basis, we would actually end up missing out a whole lot more than we ever would in making up ground? Here are some of my thoughts about why our first response to walking on these paths is often a negative one.

Let's begin with humility. Here are some common thoughts that fill my head and heart when I consider the need to display humility whenever an opportunity presents itself.

"Most everybody else in the world is looking to be seen, heard and known, and if I don't get involved in some of the same, I'm going to be left licking up their dust."

If I manage to fight off that ugly thought, along comes another nasty notion that causes me to pause instead of putting humility in high gear.

"If I remain humble, most of the people around me are just going to take advantage of me and I'll end up being the laughing stock of everybody."

The third barrier in my mind to walking the path of humility exposes my deep desire to be noticed.

"If I don't promote myself, then who will? If I don't let people become aware of my abilities and talents, more than likely nobody is ever going to notice them.

These are some of the anti-humility poisons that enter my bloodstream, and they do so on a regular basis. I've come to realize, in order to discover true success via the humility route, I must refuse them or have a powerful antidote on hand. Or, to put it in boxing terms, when those type of thoughts enter my mind, I have to hang on for dear life, much like a fighter who's way ahead on points in his match but eerily close to being knocked out by an inferior opponent in the latter rounds. Like him, I must stay standing for whatever time is remaining in the round and protect myself from further "it's-all-about-me" blows, get to the corner for a short rest and a word of inspiration from a trainer, clear my head of the cobwebs of pride and get reenergized for the final rounds—anything except throwing in the proverbial towel.

Humility begins in the mind. To be a humble person, you must train yourself to believe what many others around you will probably consider a philosophy of weakness and immaturity—*"I cannot achieve success without the help of others."* To stay humble, you must also invest a great deal of time repeating the following statements, then do whatever you can to keep them forever lodged in your memory bank:

"I was wrong."

"I'm very sorry."

"There's always room for improvement."

"I got here with the help of many other people and I will continue needing the help of other people if I expect to be successful in the future."

"The more advice I get, the better off I will be."

"I will welcome people into my life to give me their perspective about how I'm doing in certain areas."

"It's not about **me**, *it's about* **us**."

"If someone gives me praise for my efforts, fine, but I will not seek it out."

"Regardless of my position or popularity, I realize I am no better than anybody else."

"All I have learned or accomplished is much more due to those who came before me or those who have helped me than it is to my creativity or ingenuity."

If you're willing to make these statements when the situation warrants, thus winning the battle against your natural tendencies of pride, independence and self-promotion, another enemy of success will be advancing its entire army in your direction, eager to fight you to the finish—laziness! Hard work is the best weapon in defeating it, but it's a weapon that's quite heavy to carry and incredibly challenging to operate. Here are three losing statements I often tell myself when my mind says, "Work harder!" but my heart says, "Whoa Nelly!"

"Nobody is really watching me anyway, and nobody will ever know I'm taking an extended break. Besides, I've seen what my boss does and I know I usually work a lot harder than he does."

In addition to the you're-all-alone-in-the-office-and-nobody's-watching demon who visits nearly every employee almost every day of the week, you'll also be offered some soothing shortcuts to success by a little red creature on your shoulder with horns and a pitchfork, whispering sweet do-nothings in your ear, similar to the following.

"I've worked hard all week and I deserve a break. I make $15 an hour and our CEO makes $15 million a year. Do you think my lack of working hard all day, every day will hurt him in the least?"

And finally, meet the most dangerous of all foes lurking in the ditches on the hard-working road to true success.

"I've worked my tail off so many times, and not once have I been recognized for it. It just doesn't pay to keep on doing it."

Sound familiar? How do you deal with those low-impact and self-focused visitors? Do you fend them off with heroic truth? Are you able to recognize them for what they really are—poor excuses for giving less than your very best? Since hard work has a lot to do with maximizing your available energy, pushing yourself and dealing with unpleasant things like blisters and bad backs, sweat and strain and wrinkles and worn-out shoes, it will be important for you to remember the following heroic truths concerning the labor you engage in:

"I will always put in an honest day's work."

"I will work as hard when I'm all alone as I would if hundreds were watching."

"I will be more into stretching myself than stretching my break times."

"I will push myself physically when I begin to plateau in my performance."

"I will work for my boss, my teacher or my coach in the same manner I would want them to work for me if I were in their position and they were in mine."

"I will not compare myself with the work ethic displayed by those around me."

Now granted, none of these hard-work mottos are easy to incorporate on a short-term basis, let alone day after day, year after year and decade after decade until the day you retire. Since this is the case, is there anyone you know who might be able to help you stay on your hard-working toes instead of on your take-it-easy heels? And when you fail to live up to those mottos, will there be anybody nearby who can help to keep you from becoming discouraged and giving up your heroic fight to do what you should be doing in the workplace? Will you be able to make the necessary changes and work harder at the next available opportunity? If so, congratulations! Now prepare yourself for the third and final enemy of heroism called selfishness, the most dangerous of all oncoming traffic on the road to successful living.

If you're like me, having the thought of helping other people finds its way into your heart on a fairly consistent basis. But the biggest problem I encounter when it visits me is how quickly it leaves, thanks in large part to these three voices of reason that make it feel like an unwanted guest.

"If I choose to focus on looking out for other people before looking out for myself, who is going to be looking out for me?"

If that selfish notion finds no place to nest in your heart, look out for the following excuse trying to lay a few eggs in your brain.

"Thinking about other people's needs, not to mention doing something about them, is so exhausting. It takes energy! I'm so busy trying to survive in my own little world, I don't have any time to get involved."

But the staunchest advocate for selfish living is the one entering your mind with the following justification:

"What impact will my miniscule efforts make with those people anyway? Their problems are way beyond my ability to help, so someone else will just have to make themselves available on this one."

Having a heart to help others begins where we would expect it to begin—in the heart. While most of us can cling to humility and a hard-work mentality for long periods of time with good, old-fashioned self-denial and suffering (we may have to, just to make sure we keep getting a paycheck!), caring for another human being on a deep level requires a softening of the heart in places where perpetual selfishness has done its best to turn it to stone. Here are a few statements you can use to chisel away at the hardness of heart you might be experiencing at the moment:

"Other people's needs are greater than mine."

"Even though I'm going through some rough times right now, I know there are many, many others finding it much rougher than me at the moment."

"There's nothing more important to do in my life than to express care and concern for my fellow human being."

"Caring is much more an action than it is a thought."

"If I were in that person's shoes, what would a typical day be like, and what would I need from others to find greater joy and fulfillment in my life?"

"It is more blessed to give than to receive."

Should these words turn into regular acts of kindness and selflessness in your walk through life, you will be making a profound contribution to our world, one that has nothing to do with dollars and cents, discoveries of newer and greater time-saving devices or dramatic presentations on the big screen millions of people will be talking about for years to come. And even though fame, fortune and power will likely elude your grasp, you will acquire a deep level of respect and gratitude from the very people you serve—everyone from the children who live under your roof every day to the stranger who benefited because you went out of your way to help her fix a flat tire.

So there you have it—humility, hard work and a heart to help others—the three clearest paths to success and a place in the Heroes Hall of Fame. And they're all about your mind, your body and your soul, and doing all you can to put those three components of the human package in their proper places and keeping them there. But beware! Enemies of true success and heroism are lurking nearby each of these paths. They're more than ready to meet you once you start heading down these paths, and they'll urge you to choose an alternative route or stop walking altogether. I've identified a few of the ones I typically encounter on my daily walk toward heroism because it's extremely important for you to be able to recognize similar foes. But it's even more important to realize you can defeat these enemies with good, old-fashioned perseverance and the help of other people just as determined as you to win the war against failure. Those who choose to name the enemies, fight the enemies and engage them until a victory is secured are those who eventually find true success and the ones we should never be afraid to classify as heroes in the highest sense.

Let's take a few moments and break down the three individual parts of this model and determine what possible benefits might come our way should we choose to incorporate them in various areas of our lives, everything from the trivial to the truly important. We'll spend the majority of our time discussing the humility aspect of the model, then you can determine how a similar thought process and corresponding decision could also lead to success via hard work and having a heart for others.

How might humility contribute to your well-being the next time you get pulled over by a police officer? A typical response to the man in blue when he's approaching our vehicle is often one of the following: Either 1) the radar must be wrong because I surely wasn't going that much over the speed limit, 2) his radar was correct but he got the wrong car (mine just looked like the bad guy's car) or 3) he must be short on his quota of tickets for the month and I've been randomly selected to help meet his precinct's selfish goals. Even with the remote chance one of those excuses might actually be correct during your next "Cops" episode, what are the odds of you being spared a ticket if you shared any of them with the policeman? Now, granted, humbly admitting your vehicular no-no may not be all that effective either. But there's a whole lot better chance of you receiving that much-sought-after warning if you remain humble, own up to the offense, answer the officer's questions truthfully and pray like crazy his ultimate authority will grant mercy on your behalf. The likely truth of the matter is you've committed the exact same offense at least a dozen times before and you haven't been caught. So to go the prideful route and stake a claim of innocence isn't going to make a great impression on the one in uniform. But you might be able to momentarily mesmerize him with your quick admission of guilt and totally honest reply, just long enough, perhaps, to cause him to have a small lapse in memory about his philosophy of always making sure disobedient drivers learn their lesson the monetary way.

Next, how might humility be your best friend when you're sitting in a classroom all spaced out with absolutely no earthly idea what the teacher just explained to the class in regard to your upcoming exam? You could convince yourself you understood everything the teacher just said. After all, no other hands went up when she asked if anyone needed further clarification, so it must not be all that difficult to grasp. Or you could wait until the class is dismissed, corral one of your classmates and ask them for greater insight. But can you be sure any of those you'll seek out are any smarter than you, or they were listening better than you? Or you could just wing it on the upcoming essay test, transfer your wonderful gift of gab to the written page and hope your teacher doesn't read through the entire exam and discover your mumbo-jumbo, or reads it when they've had a bit too much to drink. If you're like me, I'm guessing you've probably tried at least one of these methods of madness during your school days, or you're doing so right now. Perhaps you escaped a few times with a passing grade or you found a fellow student kind enough to lend you their brain for a short while. But more than likely, you suffered the consequences of pride and soon thereafter paid the price on your report card. So going the humble route is once again the best possible choice you can make if you want success in the academic environment. Raise that hand when you don't get it. Raise it again! Ask that one question you think is probably the most ridiculous question ever asked in the history of your particular institute of higher learning, the one question you're totally sure everybody else would never need to ask. Endure the laughs and looks you'll get from the guys in the rear of the classroom, or the sigh your teacher might even offer up on occasion. In doing so, you will greatly increase the odds of improving your test results and, ironically, you'll become the student other students look for after class to discover the deeper truths of academia.

Lastly, let's examine how humility can be of great benefit in the area of opposite-sex relationships (or any relationship for that matter!). Suppose you and your spouse (or significant other) are in the middle of a huge argument. You both have valid points, but your unwillingness to see even a small segment of the other side has pulled the two of you farther and farther apart. You love this individual deeply, but it's high time you put your foot down just to make sure they don't get a leg up in the relationship. Here are a few of your options. You could dig your heels in all the way to China if you want. But you'll still be in a pretty big hole if you do, and your partner might not be all that interested in spending time with you in the Orient. You could refuse to apologize first, simply as a matter of fairness and principle because you vividly remember it was you who launched the apology well before they did during your last three altercations. But what has accurate record keeping ever done to promote love and affection in any relationship? Once again, humility is the best available path to take. Not the easiest. And definitely not the most enjoyable! But remember, we're searching for success, not pieces of cake or available parties to attend! Decide to own up to your shortcomings in the matter. Validate what the other person sees in your actions that has temporarily set them off in anger. But don't do it and then take out your stopwatch to see how quickly they humble up in response. You'll finish last in the race to reconciliation and renewed romance if you do that! More than likely, when you apologize, they will as well. If not, you'll need to remain humble for as long as necessary. A good mental exercise I've used in the past to help me in this area (my wife assures me it has been used a number of times on me as well) is to pretend there's a mirror behind each of you in the argument. The more your ego shrinks, the more likely the other person will see their pride in the mirror in due time. However, if you don't remain humble and your pride begins to make you stiffen up and think more highly of yourself than you ought, causing your ego to grow as a result, then they'll no longer see themselves in the mirror, they'll only see you in a familiar position of pride. If you're successful in that mental exercise, you most likely will be the first to apologize. After you've apologized, go the extra mile and send a card or some flowers to confirm your remorse and total commitment to the relationship. Go a third or fourth mile with a nice dinner out, a special gift or offering them relief from one of their unfinished duties. The more miles you log on the road of humility, the more likely you'll discover success in your closest relationships.

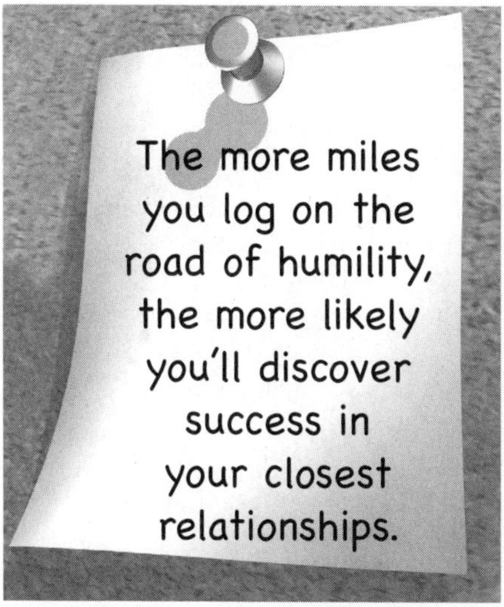

Now take some of these same principles and apply them in other areas of importance in your life. Whether it's at the workplace dealing with co-workers or your boss, on the playing field interacting with coaches, teammates or officials, leading your children at any stage of their lives, figuring out your finances and how to get out of debt or tackling a difficult situation in regard to a neighbor, humility can make the difference.

Shifting our focus onto the importance of hard work in acquiring success, ask yourself the following questions. When has hard work ever hurt your chances of making the team? When has hard work in the weight room ever subtracted muscle from someone destined to get bigger and stronger? When has running consistently ever been the cause of adding weight to someone looking to lose it? When has doing stomach crunches to the point of pain ever brought more flab to a person's midsection?

Moving out of the athletic realm, answer the following questionnaire concerning work-related issues? When has working overtime to prepare for an important presentation ever left a person with less confidence than if they hadn't? When has reading an additional 30-page document on a similar court case ever added to an attorney's doubts about their chances of winning a trial? When has asking five extra questions about a patient's condition ever hurt a doctor's chances of finding a correct diagnosis? The list of questions of this nature is endless, and the answer to each of them will indicate the exact same thing—success often comes a person's way with hard work. A few quotes describing the importance of this principle that each of us would do well to memorize are "the harder I work, the luckier I get" and "the only place where success comes before work is in the dictionary." And heeding the following advice of famous writer and humorist Will Rogers isn't a bad idea either: "Even if you're on the right track, you'll get run over if you just sit there."

Finally, let's consider the advantages of having a heart to help others. Will having that mindset on a consistent basis actually make your life better? Will involvement in other people's lives in order to bring them blessings be a good thing to spend your time doing? Or will it be a waste of time? What positive things might come your way in the neighborhood if you rake and bag some leaves that aren't your own? What negative results would be seen in your life if you were to bring some home-baked chocolate chip cookies to work on occasion for your fellow-employees to enjoy? What are the possible bonuses of helping a co-worker with a project he's a few days late in finishing? Who would be more likely to loan you their pickup some day than the guy you showed up to help move in the middle of the afternoon? What negative feeling could you come away with should you help a struggling classmate prepare for an upcoming exam? What bad emotion would you experience ten years down the road when you ran into the guy you used to spend time with after practice helping to give him a better shot at finding more playing time during the season?

Sacrificing for the sake of others is always a positive thing. It may go unnoticed or unappreciated, but you'll still know what you did! You may not know for sure if that five dollars you gave to the person begging at the busy intersection really went for food or meeting a family member's need as they promised it would, but you gave it and, in doing so, you gave a chance for someone's life to be better than it was before you came along. Perhaps the money went toward the purchase of a bottle of vodka. But maybe it didn't. Had you not given it, that person wouldn't have had the choice of bread or booze, and you should always feel great about providing them with that opportunity!

Now that we've seen some of the benefits of embracing the individual principles in this success model, let me offer you one last piece of advice before moving ahead. These paths to success will be realized most often when they're viewed as a package deal. Let me explain by giving you a few examples, first at the workplace and then in the realm of sports. To display humility during an interview might get you the job you always wanted, and it will probably buy you some time to prove yourself once you're there. But if you refuse to work hard for your company on a consistent basis, no amount of humility is going to keep you on the payroll. If you're humble and hard working, but you have no concern whatsoever for your co-workers, it won't be long before you're forced out of that position as well. If you're a hard worker and really care about others in the office, but your pride won't allow you to be corrected on how you can be even more productive for the company, plan on being let go from your job before too long. However, if you maintain a humble and teachable spirit at your workplace, not looking to toot your own horn or take over your supervisor's position, and if you put in an honest day's work, each day of the week, each week of the year, and if you show a genuine concern for those over you, under you and with you, I think it's pretty safe to say you won't be anywhere near the top of the list when it's time for the corporate execs to discuss the next round of staff cutbacks, and you'll probably be in a fairly good position for advancement within the company.

Any coach will tell you they love working with humble, teachable players. But all the humility in the world won't get you more playing time if you aren't willing to push yourself in the practice sessions or spend time afterward shooting free-throws so your game percentage can climb. A humble and hard-working athlete is a treasure for a coach to have on his team, but if that athlete can't get along with his teammates and has no desire to make them any better, how useful will he be in his coach's long-term plans for success? A player may have the greatest heart imaginable toward his teammates, but if he isn't willing to come to every practice and work hard once he's there, what team will really benefit from his services during the games? A player may work his tail off at practice and during the games, and he may be the greatest encourager his teammates have ever known, but if he isn't willing to humbly listen to his coach tell him how his recent play has really hurt the team, he'll be given a comfortable seat at the end of the bench, probably for the remainder of the season.

For the duration of this book, these three paths to success will be heralded. With every mention of these paths, you'll be faced with some tough questions. First, are you currently walking on these paths? Second, are you willing to walk on these paths? And, third, what practical things will you have to do in order to walk on these paths? Regardless of your answer to the first of these three questions, may this book be a motivating factor for you in answering the second question with a resounding "yes", and may it provide you with many workable solutions to the third and most important question of all.

Chapter Five

Divine Assistance

Some call it coincidence. Others claim it's nothing but good, old-fashioned luck. Most people believe it just happens, in the same way everything else just happens. I'm referring to those times in life when it appears an invisible outside force is at work, either in helping to bring about a remarkable achievement, ushering in a long-awaited or long-overdue accomplishment or rescuing someone from certain failure or fatality. While this phenomenon occurs quite often in all walks of life, it seems to me it happens with great regularity in team and individual sports.

During the last few decades, more and more individuals involved in the world of sports have adopted this intervention-connection. Commentators, coaches and countless players are using terminology that sounds more appropriate for a sermon than a sporting event. In football, a long, desperation pass caught in the end zone by a receiver with seven defenders surrounding him and no time remaining on the clock to win the game is usually referred to as a "Hail Mary" completion. Now, I'm quite certain the Virgin Mary has nothing to do with it whenever quarterbacks and their receivers manage to make those most-remarkable connections. But maybe, just maybe, someone she knows quite well will decide to get involved.

For example, Franco Harris' amazing touchdown grab of a deflected pass from Pittsburgh Steelers' quarterback Terry Bradshaw in a 1972 AFC playoff game against the Oakland Raiders is commonly referred to as *The Immaculate Reception.* Though becoming pregnant without human intervention (*The Immaculate Conception*) ranks high above Harris' reception on the list of "World's Most Amazing Accomplishments", if you've ever seen the replay of that come-out-of-nowhere, shoestring catch, you can't help but think at least a few angels had made their way from heaven to Three Rivers Stadium that frigid December afternoon in order to manipulate a few events on the playing field.

And who can forget the words of ABC sportscaster Al Michaels, asking those glued to their television sets an all-important question as the 1980 USA Olympic hockey team was about to pull off one of the biggest upsets in Olympic history by defeating the mighty Russians?: *"Do you believe in miracles?"* Well, do you? Could God possibly have wanted to make some important point with the eventual outcome of that game? Or, was it just luck and something bound to happen sooner or later? Was God perhaps making a statement to the millions of people around the world watching or listening to the action taking place in Lake Placid, many of them undoubtedly wondering at that very moment if they could overcome a big obstacle they were facing, perhaps a life-threatening illness, a seemingly insurmountable problem at work or a severely strained relationship?

Could Jesse Owens' startling, four gold-medal performance at the 1936 summer Olympics in Berlin (called by many the "Hitler Olympics") simply be summed up by his better training, technique and talent? No doubt Owens was a remarkable athlete, but did God have a message for the dictator attending those Games in regard to his arrogant, Aryan philosophy, making sure Owens not only won each of the sprinting events he entered, but left all of his white competitors looking at his backside as he crossed the finish line?

Disney did their part to promote this idea with their 1994 presentation of *Angels in the Outfield*, a story about a lowly and losing franchise finally winning the World Series, thanks to some otherworld intervention. Sure, it's just a Disney movie, but are you sure strange events like that have never happened before in Major League baseball? Even the biblical record states that angels visited Earth from time to time, but the humans they were hanging out with remained completely unaware of their heavenly identity.

I personally have seen far too many sporting events with unusual activity and unbelievable endings to totally write off the possibility of divine interventions. In November of 2003, Green Bay Packer's quarterback Brett Favre, deep in the throes of grief after the sudden and unexpected death of his father, played one of the greatest games of his career just two days after hearing the sad and shocking news. The three-time NFL Most Valuable Player racked up some remarkable statistics that Monday night before a national television audience, aided by a few completed passes that seemed destined to be intercepted, only to have one of his receivers come out of nowhere and haul in the catch for a touchdown. Now I have no idea where Favre and his family stand on spiritual matters. And despite what many in Wisconsin might say, the Packers are not God's team. But could God have been involved in that game in a greater way than he was in other contests that season? Or was God involved at all in that game, or any other game played throughout the 80-year history of the NFL? Could someone watching that Monday Night Football game have needed to witness Favre's display of pigskin prowess to inspire them to push through something difficult in their own life? And don't you suppose at least some of the people watching the game felt a little tug in their heart, perhaps prompting them to finally tell their fathers just how much they appreciated them before the opportunity was no longer available? And how much do you think the stunning performance did for Favre himself? Is that what he needed to cast out the demons of discouragement hounding and harassing him at the time?

I don't have a definitive answer to any of those questions. Perhaps God enters the sporting arena at times to remove sadness from someone's life, if only for a short while. Maybe, on occasion, he feels it's time to let the little guy with the grit and guts beat the big guy with the brains and bucks so all the little guys in the world won't quit in pursuing their dreams. Maybe he would honor the dying wish of a 10-year-old boy with leukemia—making sure his favorite team won the championship before he departed from this world. Perhaps a serious illness or the death of a teammate causes the heavens to stir with compassion, releasing an angel or two to roam that team's sideline. Could the final season for a coach who's focused more on character than championships become the signal to the master conductor to start orchestrating strange events that will ultimately lead to a much-deserved and long-overdue title for the man with proper priorities? Could a humble coach's death be a launching pad for other-world powers to blast off and begin an intervention to honor the deceased and inspire those remembering him to play in ways they've never played before?

As a minister, I must admit I've told people a number of times God isn't all that interested in sports, at least as far as wins and losses are concerned. Oh, perhaps he will throw his powerful hand into the mix on a rare occasion. But, I'm quick to say, just because an athlete is praying to win, or just because he points to the sky after hauling in a pass for a touchdown or hitting a home run, that doesn't mean he's God's man playing on God's team. More than likely, his opponent said a few prayers for greater athletic ability somewhere along the way, and maybe they had a more private and humble way of honoring God for their remarkable catch or game-winning blast.

While God may not be tremendously concerned about the outcome of the Super Bowl, the gymnastics competition at the Olympic games or an organized game of soccer, I'm quite sure he is concerned with every single person participating in and watching those events. And it makes sense to me that, despite whether or not an athlete is actually on God's roster or is heading to the eternal clubhouse, God might choose to manipulate events in a person's sport of choice just to illustrate some important point. It makes complete sense to me how God's deep interest in people could lead him to becoming more involved in determining who wins and who loses at certain sporting events. Perhaps he would see it as a golden opportunity to preach a different kind of sermon to a large number of people who might not otherwise show up at his house or give him their undivided attention.

From my knowledge of biblical events, whenever God sees someone displaying humility, hard work and a heart to help others, he's quite impressed and keenly interested in becoming a part of their daily regimen. Unfortunately, both in the past and still today, God doesn't get many opportunities to see these *"three h"* qualities lived out by very many people. So when they finally do come into his view, whether in the pew, the private sector, the public arena or on the playing field, chances are he may be very thrilled to work on an individual's or a team's behalf. And since so much of our current culture is centered on people spending large chunks of time playing sports or enjoying them as a spectator, maybe God unleashes his power on the playing field whenever these qualities are being displayed a whole lot more than any of us would ever comprehend or be comfortable to admit.

Three thousand years ago, a king world-renowned for wisdom offered all of us a few reminders about what works and what doesn't in the most important game to ever be played, the game of life. These morsels of truth were proven reliable by people who lived them out in his day, and they will find equal success if applied in the 21st century, whether it's in regard to an entire nation, a group or a single individual, and whether it's manifested in education, business, finance, family matters, relationships or sports. Here are a few of those valuable pieces of advice from King Solomon's best-selling book of success, discussing the importance of humility, hard work and a heart to help others.

Humility:

"When pride comes, then comes disgrace, but with humility comes wisdom."

"For lack of guidance a nation falls, but many advisers make victory sure."

"Pride goes before destruction, a haughty spirit before a fall."

"Before his downfall a man's heart is proud, but humility comes before honor."

Hard work:

"Lazy hands make a man poor, but diligent hands bring wealth."

"He who works his land will have abundant food, but he who chases fantasies lacks judgment."

"All hard work brings a profit, but mere talk leads only to poverty."

"One who is slack in his work is brother to one who destroys."

Heart to help others:

"A generous man will prosper; he who refreshes others will himself be refreshed."

"A kind man benefits himself, but a cruel man brings trouble on himself."

"He who pursues righteousness and love finds life, prosperity and honor."

"A generous man will himself be blessed, for he shares his food with the poor."

With a deep respect for King Solomon and his focus on the most important matters concerning life, allow me to take these eternal truths and bring them to the realm of sports, specifically in regard to coaching basketball. While many people may not consider sports to be an important part of life, I believe the lessons we can learn from this arena are many and, when learned, can successfully spill over into what most of us would consider as areas of greater significance.

Humility:

A humble coach will admit his shortcomings, talk shop with other successful coaches, read numerous books to better his trade, allow his assistants to point out blind spots in his mentoring and even allow his players from time to time to help him plan strategy or address areas of concern.

If a coach is only relying upon his intelligence of the game, his record will be far worse than if he had sought out help from others, those in and out of his profession. A coach who surrounds himself with other people from the past and present, gaining their perspective on his team's performance, will garner victories and championships that otherwise would have eluded his grasp.

An independent coach who relies upon his reputation or past accomplishments, failing to bring others into his decision-making circle, will cause his team to lose games they should never lose.

The outcome of a game or success of a season is often determined well before the actual game or season begins by the attitude a coach carries into it.

Hard work:

The more a coach reads, studies, scouts, stays involved with his players and stays up late thinking of different strategies that could lead to future wins, the more successful he will be.

Any coach can dream of winning a state championship or having their greatest season to date, but the coaches who will actually live to tell about it are the ones willing to pay the price to make it happen.

If a coach is willing to work hard in his role, he may not win the championship every year, but he will see progress in his team on a regular basis. There are many coaches who talk about winning and turning things around, but if there isn't a corresponding effort of dedication to those goals, not much will ever change.

A coach who relies upon talent but doesn't prepare himself and his team for every game is like the student looking to graduate with honors who rarely comes to class.

Heart to help others:

A coach who looks to encourage his players, opens his home to them and is willing to hear their concerns and meet their needs both on and off the court will find good things coming to him somewhere down the road.

A coach who berates his players publicly, focuses more on fear than friendship and is hesitant to offer praise to them on a regular basis for jobs well done is only hurting his chances of success and may be out of work sooner than he realizes.

A coach who cares deeply for his players and looks to model things like sharing and sensitivity more than skills for the court will prosper in his position and will be honored by his players for many years after they graduate.

A coach who works with and encourages his least-talented bench-warmer just as much or more than he does his leading scorer will find success at times when he may least expect it.

Now I'm quite sure God and King Solomon had many other things in mind besides coaching basketball when these words of wisdom were penned. James Naismith and his throw-the-round-ball-in-the-peach-basket idea were still about 3,000 years from becoming reality when Solomon sat down to write what we now know as *The Proverbs*. Yet I believe Solomon would be in full agreement with this—little in life could be more important than having adults setting an appropriate example for our young people and building the correct character into their lives. Wouldn't you want the one leading your child's team to display an overall character they could imitate, one that would greatly increase their chances for success during the later stages of their life? When your children finally find themselves facing issues of greater importance such as morality and maintaining integrity, college and career paths, money and marriage, parenting and persevering through trials, wouldn't it increase their odds of making the wisest decisions on these crucial matters if they had been under a leader with a solid character who regularly modeled these three qualities?

Though this is not a spiritual book by nature, nor a bold attempt to convert anyone, it is designed to grab your attention and encourage you to think more often about walking on these paths, the same paths one of the wisest men to ever live said will definitely lead to success. If you embrace this model for success, I firmly believe you will not only greatly increase your chances of receiving some much-needed divine assistance, but you'll also find great satisfaction and contentment with the way you've chosen to live your life.

Chapter Six

The Small-Town Advantage

From my knowledge of small towns, and from what I personally experienced while living in three of them for the first 20 years of my life, I believe the success model we're focusing on is seen in greater percentages of people living in those locations than it is in those dwelling in larger cities. I also believe this model can be better grasped, developed and refined when someone is living in a small-town setting. Now that's not to say you would rarely, if ever, see this success model lived out by people in our nation's metropolitan areas—you'll see it in people in every size of city! Quite often, one of the main reasons a higher percentage of people from small towns are able to incorporate this model into their lives is due to their slower and less-frantic pace of life and the number of "How will I use my time?" options that exist in their neck of the woods.

To further examine this theory, let's consider some of the unique challenges of living in a larger city. Most of the working population in a bigger city will typically spend an hour or two, Monday through Friday, driving in all the early-morning and late-afternoon traffic jams. While working for many of the nation's largest companies, big-city employees will likely face more intense job pressures and deadlines than those working in smaller towns, and many of these same employees will be expected to travel out of town for important business matters on a fairly consistent basis. Due to the much higher cost of living in the bigger cities, residents there are often faced with the pressure of needing to work additional hours or even finding a second job just to stay current with their mortgage payment and the many other bills that will be substantially higher than for those living in a smaller town. Feeling similar financial pressures, a high percentage of young mothers in the bigger cities are working full time and relying upon day-care workers to watch their kids, in many cases up to 10 hours a day. In addition to the money worries, higher crime rates in the city can cause residents to be skeptical, even suspicious of one another. Being friendly with a stranger or helping them out if they're in need is often deemed risky at best.

Aside from the faster pace, financial pressures and funny feelings about your fellowman often associated with big-city life, here are just a few of the entertainment options for those living in large cities, available 24 hours a day, seven days a week—the live theatre, choosing from a selection of up to 20 recently-released movies, attending sporting events (whether professional, college or amateur), frequenting nightclubs to dance and enjoy live music, eating breakfast, lunch and dinner at the countless restaurants located on nearly every block, going to concerts of various music genres or attending a myriad of multi-cultural activities. Besides the entertainment options, those in larger cities can get involved in a number of political and social causes to consume what little free time they have remaining after work. Those in densely-populated areas also face the challenge of trying to compete with millions of others in a similar environment racing full-speed ahead toward the American Dream. While pursuing this dream, big-city dwellers can easily be tempted to buy into the "really-nice-house-plus-really-nice-car-plus-really-nice-things-equals-really-nice-life" equation that seems, from their point of view, to be working out so well for so many others. In this often hedonistic, hectic and high-strung environment, free time can become so precious to people that any activity not focused entirely on them, their close friends or members of their immediate family is likely rejected. And before they know it, the many challenges, fears and opportunities presented to people in the big city can slowly but surely produce in them a much more selfish and guarded lifestyle than those in a small town.

The bottom line is this—to a large degree, our nation's bigger cities and corresponding suburbs have become places where people live with way too much of an inward focus. This "me-first" mindset has led to some very unfortunate realities in the 21st century. One of the most unfortunate of these realities is how a person can live in the same neighborhood for a lengthy period of time (sometimes 10 years or more), yet still not know anybody else on their same block. It's highly unlikely this un-neighborly scenario would ever be played out in the smaller towns of America. Now if I'm sounding judgmental, I'm pointing the finger at me just as much as anybody else. I must admit I've fallen into this selfish trap on a number of occasions, whether the deadly snare was set in Los Angeles, San Diego, Denver, Portland, Cincinnati, St. Louis or Chicago, where I currently live. You would think, after 26 years of living in the bigger cities of America, I should have conquered this weakness, allowed my small-town roots to burrow into the neighborhoods where I've lived and pulled those closest to me into a similar style of living. But it's a battle I'm still trying to win, and one I'm certain will need to be waged in my heart for as long as I live in the big city.

A prime example of my inability to transfuse the small-town setting into the big-city bloodstream happened recently. Sadly, an eight-year-old boy who lived right across the street from our home died of brain cancer. Unfortunately, my wife and I didn't find out about his death until a few hours after the funeral. We had heard a rumor from someone else in the neighborhood about a child being sick in that house, but nobody knew very many of the details. We had also seen an ambulance come on occasion to their home at odd hours of the day, solidifying in our minds that, indeed, someone across the street had a serious illness. But we still weren't aware of exactly who was sick and the extent of that illness. When we saw a number of cars parked along the sidewalk one afternoon, and people bringing food to the family at different times of the day, we then assumed someone had passed away. Only then did my wife go across the street, talk to the mother, become aware of the young boy's death, express her condolences and offer to take a meal to their family the following day.

This episode reminded me, once again, of the serious danger in developing an "I'm-real-busy-I'm-in-the-big-city" mentality, regardless of how you started out in life or what your core values are at the moment. I must admit I've been an offender on far too many occasions. Sure, I had always smiled and waved to those neighbors when I drove out of our driveway or whenever I saw one of them out in their yard. And my wife and I had definitely thought a few times about going across the street and welcoming them since they were the latest family to move into our neighborhood. But we did none of those things. Was it due to a wicked heart that said, "I could care less about those people?" I hope not! Was it because our family made a firm pact with each other not to get too close to any of our neighbors because, "You just don't know who you can trust these days?" I haven't become that cynical! Could it simply have been because our schedules were packed and we were already completely distracted by our own daily routine and responsibilities? Did we subconsciously feel our circle of friends was already set and its circumference was big enough to satisfy our needs? "And besides," we always told ourselves, "we'll get around to meeting them eventually."

Sadly, my wife and I weren't alone in our failure to meet this family's needs. After talking with a few of our other neighbors, we realized all of them had even less of an idea than we did about the boy's condition. In short, we had failed as a neighborhood to have the type of heart King Solomon encouraged us to have for others. We could have attempted to justify our actions (or lack thereof) by telling ourselves the new neighbors didn't seem too interested in getting to know us since moving in a few months ago. But had we taken the lead in the matter, we quickly would have discovered the biggest reason why!

While I won't say this humanitarian oversight would never happen in a small town, I will say I've never seen it or heard about it, and any occurrence of it would be rare. Yet I believe what I've just described to you about our own neighborhood failure is far too commonplace in many cities in America. But in most of the rural areas of our country, entire towns can be seen coming together in a matter of hours to do whatever they can to counter the negative affects of a tragedy, and they'll typically stay the difficult course with the affected people for as long as they're needed. I can't imagine not knowing about an illness or the death of anyone in our entire town while I was growing up, let alone with someone right across the street.

Not only do small-town folks have a flare for caring for one another, humility seems almost second nature to those often considered strange and unusual just because they've chosen to distance themselves from the hustle and bustle of big-city life. They've accepted their role of runner-up to the bright lights and best action available in the big city, and it doesn't seem to bother too many of them. They know their town's biggest events won't be a topic of discussion outside their city limits, and most are well aware that few, if any, of their fellow-residents will ever "make it big" someday. Most of the children growing up in a small town are taught early on to exercise great humility toward anybody in positions of authority. And should a child decide to test the waters of rebellion, they'll likely be wading into a meeting with a parent and a good amount of pain to their backside, and their lack of staying in line will probably become a matter of public record before long. Many of the adult male residents in small towns are blue-collar workers with no formal education beyond high school, and they're just not put in too many positions where they feel invincible or where they think the world won't be able to survive without them.

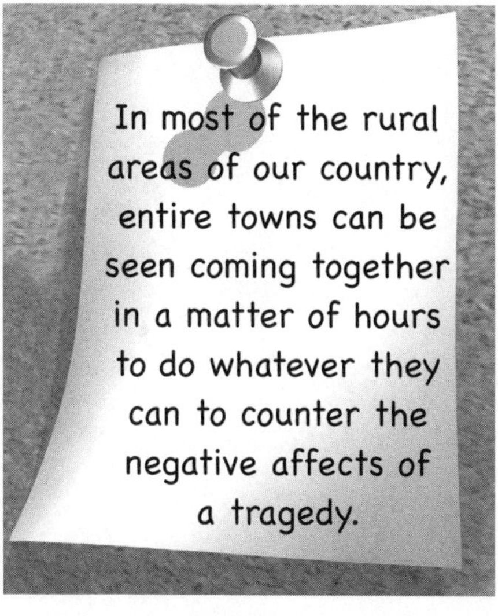

In addition to finding caring and humble people in small towns of America, you'll discover most of the people there know quite a bit about what it means to get a paycheck the old fashioned way—earning it. A hard-work mentality usually gets drilled into most youngsters growing up in a small town, whether it's from cutting a cord of word for the family-room fireplace, bailing hay in the dog days of summer, learning from mom how to bake dinners from scratch, mowing their two-acre lot, walking or riding a bike a couple of miles to pick up a few things at the closest grocery store or running a few extra laps in the summer just to make sure they're ready for football or volleyball practice when school begins. And most of the men working those blue-collar jobs know staying gainfully employed requires plenty of good, old-fashioned elbow grease at the workplace, whether on the farm, at the factory or falling trees.

While it's definitely true not everyone living in a small town displays humility, hard work and a heart to help others, I'm convinced this story is one of those times when these three paths to success were chosen by a few people and good things happened as a result. I've written this story because I believe, in knowing it, you can draw a great amount of inspiration for your life. Then, perhaps, you can begin to taste the small-town flavor, digest it and better your chances of success with the pursuits you hold dear in life.

Chapter Seven

More Small-Town Heroics

While this book highlights the heroic activity of a few people in one small town, it could have been written about other unique individuals cast from the same mold. They live in small towns from California to Connecticut, from Montana to Mississippi, from Nevada to New York, from Alaska to Arkansas, from West Virginia to Washington. They're men and women, young and old, rich and poor, black and white, educated and unschooled, athletic and uncoordinated. So before I begin telling you the story about my father and Jeff Bryson, allow me to point out some other individuals who deserve equal recognition. They, too, are heroes, courageous men and women all of us would do well to imitate. They show a deep respect for life and the lives of those around them, and they're a big part of what makes our nation great. But I won't tell you their names because, in doing so, I would be leaving out thousands of others, at least, who perform similar heroic deeds in their respective towns. I will simply tell you what they do. It's your job to put in the name and the corresponding town. And if you happen to dwell in one of the bigger cities of America (defined by those in most small towns as any city with more than 5,000-10,000 people, though the actual number is greatly debated), while you read this chapter, shrink your city down to a much smaller size and think about the people sharing the same square mile with you on a daily basis.

Maybe your hero is an elderly neighbor, that kindhearted gentleman who acts more like a caring father when your car breaks down or when you're suddenly faced with any kind of crisis. Maybe you're thinking about the hero who walks your school's hallways with humility and without hatred for those who are different. Or maybe he sweeps those hallways with lots of class and little complaining. Maybe it's your mailman who, even on days when he's running behind schedule, never seems to be in a hurry when it comes to carrying on a conversation with you. Maybe she's a member of your church who invited you to come for the first time many years ago. Maybe your hero is your boss who always makes you feel like an equal. Maybe he's your mayor who promptly answers your letters, or maybe she's your state representative who feels it's important to always return your phone calls. Maybe your hero is the college professor who gave you additional time to finish your term paper after hearing of your mother's illness. Maybe she volunteers in the local hospital and takes time to visit the shut-ins throughout town. Maybe it's the owner of the deli down the street who donates her tuna and her time to the shelter for abused women. Maybe your hero is the young man who picks up your smelly garbage every Tuesday morning, then picks up your teenage son every Tuesday night for a time away from the house and a chance to talk with him about how he's really doing since your divorce became final. Maybe he's the permanently disabled man down the street who refuses to harbor bitterness and resentment toward the drunk driver who took away his ability to walk. Yes, all across our nation, heroes are spreading their influence in tremendous ways. Whether you live in a small town or not, hopefully you're well-acquainted with a few of these people and are currently benefiting from their benevolent behavior. But since this is a story specifically about small-town heroes, let's take a quick tour of a typical small town and check in on some of the heroic activities taking place there.

The grocery store owner makes the last of his four perimeter checks in the town's one and only supermarket. After greeting nearly every shopper there that day by their first name, he notices a woman in the checkout line transferring her groceries from the cart to the counter. He's heard a report her husband has been unable to find work after an unexpected layoff at the small manufacturing plant twenty miles north of town, the one he's worked at for the past 13 years. He approaches the checkout stand and informs the checker she can take an unscheduled break from her duties. After engaging in some small-talk with the woman while tallying up her grocery bill and offering his insight on some possible job openings in the area, he hands her the grocery receipt for $125.83 and, along with the receipt, utters four simple, yet sensational words: "This one's on me." With a smile to the shocked woman and a nod to the checker on break to return to her post, he carries the woman's groceries to her car and offers her a pleasant farewell. Not only has he supplied her with free groceries, but another good reason she can be grateful to live in a small town where your heroes know you by your first name.

A frantic father rushes his bleeding son to the town's one and only doctor's office. A middle-aged woman, tripling in her daily duties as nurse, receptionist and accountant, is first to greet the two and hurries them back to a room where supplies are handy to stem the bleeding. No more than thirty seconds elapse before the town's one and only doctor enters a room to attend to the boy's injury—a large gash on top of his head from a nail that scraped across his scalp after he rose too quickly in a crawl space playing hide-and-go-seek with a few friends. A shot to kill the pain, a masterful job of stitching the wound and, best of all for the boy, a baseball cap from the major league ball-club in the big city to wear once his injury totally heals—three expertly used gestures to turn the child from panic and pain to comfort and cure. The hat was taken from the case of hats the doctor purchases every year to give his younger male patients in hope of providing that extra touch of healing. He'll send a bill to the father for the medical services, but it will be substantially less than what he could have charged. But he likes it that way. He recently turned down a lucrative offer from an established practice in the city with a couple of medical school cronies he keeps in touch with regularly. It was tempting for him to accept, but he loves the feeling of knowing everybody in town and knowing just what they need to stay healthy. He's not a doctor for the money, but for the satisfaction that comes from seeing others stay as healthy as possible. He lives in one of the nicer homes in town, but it gets plenty of use by non-family members on the weekends and all the major holidays, and people are regularly told, if necessary, to come on in without knocking. He also doubles as the trainer for all the high school sport's teams and immediately puts all the proceeds from that side-job into the athletic department's fund-raising drive to build a new gymnasium.

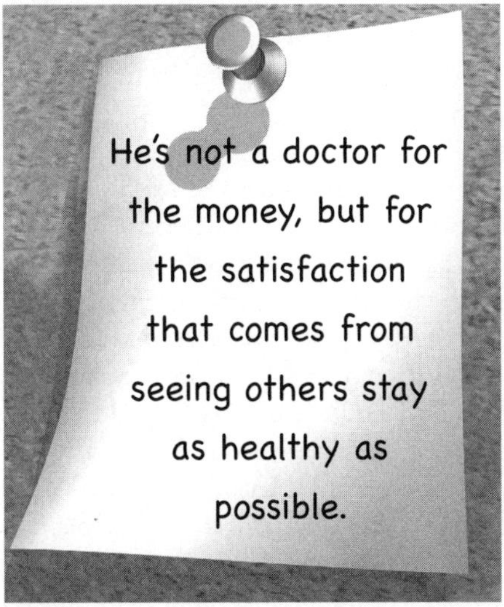

A young married couple has decided to relocate to the area after trying out the city life for a few years, now looking to buy a home and stay there for good. After analyzing the newlywed's financial picture, it becomes apparent to the real estate agent that the only way to get them into the home of their liking is to bypass the commission she's entitled. After considering her previous year's record intake from sales, she draws up a contract for the couple. Stunned by the proposed generosity of the agent, the couple begins to refuse the offer, mostly from embarrassment. But the realtor prevails. To satisfy the couple's desire to do something in return, she draws up a side agreement stating: 1) the husband will mow her yard a few times in the summer months and 2) both of them will pass on the good deed to their neighbors. The couple leaves her office 15 minutes later, ecstatic about the upcoming purchase of their first home.

The 41-year-old second-grade schoolteacher kneels down beside her bed to say her nightly prayers. She's taught at the town's elementary school for 19 years and many of her original students are now married, some raising children of their own. She's been invited to nearly every wedding and special event that has taken place in the lives of her students and their families over the past two decades. Could this untypical inclusion be happening because first on her list of things to pray for every night before bed are the names and specific needs of the children she teaches? She's only missed praying about ten days total in those 19 years, most of those coming six years ago while grieving over the death of her own mother who was killed instantly in a car accident. She's never told anybody she does it, but her heavenly appeals are definitely being felt. She's never been married, though she's not opposed to it. She just hasn't found anybody she's more in love with than the seven-year olds she spends eight hours a day with Monday through Friday from September to June.

The aging barber finishes blow-drying and brushing off hair remnants from the neck and shoulders of his customer. His next scheduled haircut is more than 30 minutes away, so time is sufficient to ask this regular client about how his week has been going before he leaves the barbershop. It's become apparent to the barber something is bothering his client, as the usual free-spirit conversationalist said very little while in the chair. After some unsuccessful probing for a possible explanation of his sudden personality change, the barber feels the need to address the issue point blank. And his gut instincts were right—again! As his customer explained, his neighbor's oldest boy and a few of his friends had been riding their motorcycles the night before and had driven across the newly-planted sod in his front yard, ruining the entire job for all practical purposes. He hadn't spoken a word to the guilty party yet, but he was about to do so. His plan was to settle matters later that night, as this lawn vandalism was the latest in a long line of damage and disappointments coming from across the street. He was angry and wasn't planning to hold back from spewing his innermost feelings to both the father and the son. So, with the wisdom amassed during the thousands of cuts and conversations the barber has participated in the past 27 years, he takes his customer on a journey back to his own teenage recklessness and concludes it with some important inside information about the man's recent discovery of cancer in his youngest son's bones. (Yes, he's a regular there as well.) And another once-active volcano has been declared dormant due to the man in town most skilled with scissors and setting matters in perspective.

The truck driver arrives at home exactly when he told his wife he would be there. It's 6:15 and dinner is just about ready. After kissing his wife and grabbing his two children like a running back carrying the football while plowing through the line, he leaves for the bathroom to clean up after another messy day of loading and unloading wood chips. During the next 45 minutes, dinner will be served, sincere "How-was-your-day?" conversation will be engaged in, laughter will be the predominant sound and dessert will be taken into the living room so the entire family can watch one of their favorite television programs. Not too long after that, it will be bedtime for the kids. He rotates the bedtime storytelling with his wife, and tonight is his turn. Little Red Riding Hood is still the children's favorite, especially the way he tells it, sometimes in full costume acting out the part of the big bad wolf. The kids finally fall asleep, but it's still two or three hours before he and his wife will retire for the night. He'll stay home, perhaps work on the finances, rent a movie to watch with his wife or just be there with her—the exact same way he's done it for the past eight years since their wedding day. Bars and late-night carousing with the boys aren't on his agenda. Neither is time spent wishing he were out of the trap of marriage and parenting. He actually cherishes his role. He's never abused his kids, has always remained faithful to his wife and does all he can to support every one of their activities. His favorite late-night pastime is the Monday bowling league he's been involved in for the past five years. But it's a co-ed league and he and his wife are teammates along with another couple down the street.

The owner of the small lumber mill has another tough decision to make. It's been three years since the company has turned a noticeable profit, and it would be totally appropriate if his employees went without one this year. Every worker there has received a Christmas bonus the past two holiday seasons and deep gratitude is felt for their boss's kindness. But each employee would have little or no problem understanding why this year needs to be different. But when it comes right down to it, the owner doesn't have the heart. He'd rather go without food for a while than go without the hugs he receives when he hands the workers their bright, red and green envelopes at the company Christmas party. And he'd rather sell his house than sell out on the vow he made to give those bonuses to his faithful employees. Sure, the promise was made way back in the beginning of the year when hope sprung eternal, but that's irrelevant according to this man of his word. Each employee then, 15 to be exact, will receive their $500 bonus. He'll be out $7,500, but this man worries much more about his workers' children doubting Santa's ability to bring that much-desired toy than he does a drop in his net worth.

The leader of the local Alcoholics Anonymous chapter prepares some notes for his regular Tuesday night meeting. He's been an active member for more than 20 years since he humbly admitted his addiction at age 24, and he's been completely sober for a little more than 15 years now. Those first five-and-a-half years, though a welcomed member of AA, were spent in and out of sobriety until he finally hit rock bottom just a few days after his 30th birthday. He's hoping for a good crowd tonight. Last week's attendance dipped dramatically as only three showed up for the meeting. He knows from personal observation, as well as from reports given to him by some trusted community spies, many more in town should be scheduling their Tuesday night activities around this gathering. But whether 30 people or three are sitting in the circle, he's always there ready to help someone turn a difficult corner or concede for the first time what they're petrified to admit. He gets paid nothing for his labor of love and usually spends his own money to buy the evening's refreshments.

The captain of the varsity cheerleading squad spends most of her weeknights studying and finishing her homework. Her daily after-school schedule is packed with practices, games and other extra-curricular activities, including her role as Honor Society president. She's beautiful, fun and full of life, but more than anything she's a needed example for her fellow-classmates. And most of them don't even realize it. She lives at home with her mother, but with her mother's many jobs, boyfriends and visits to the local tavern that often last until the early-morning hours, she rarely sees her. Her mom has attended a few games to watch her cheerlead, but she rarely stays until the end. Despite the poor parental role models (her only contact with her father is when he sends a card with some cash on her birthday), she thrives in good behavior. She says "yes" to tutoring struggling students and "no" to the jocks' sexual advances. She welcomes the not-so-pretty girls into her circle of life and corrects the other girls who won't. She talks little of her own accomplishments and absolutely nothing of her mother's failures. Her successes will more than likely lead her out of the small town for good, but for now she's needed to set an example for others who tend to use their beauty and brains for selfish gain.

Just outside of town lives a family of seven in a small and somewhat rundown home—it's mom, dad, their four natural children and a young teenager they've just taken in who can't seem to stay out of trouble. The county judge says it will be the boy's last chance to straighten himself out or juvenile jail will be his next place of residence. So, for at least the next six months, he, along with the six other members of his new family, will do their best to manage life where square footage and surplus funds are at a minimum. Thankfully, selfless living and love are everywhere. They'll do okay because they've had plenty of practice. This will be the fifth troubled and unwanted child to join their family in the past seven years. Two of those kids have seen an amazing turnaround since staying in their home. Sadly, one young man has returned to a juvenile center and they haven't heard anything from the other boy since his departure a year ago. But it's the shot that counts and they simply wanted to be the ones to give it to him.

A wife files a police report chronicling the physical abuse her husband has inflicted upon her and her oldest son. She completely understands, because he brings in most of the money to pay the bills and provide for the nice home they live in, her decision may cause both him and their comfortable lifestyle to be gone for good. But she must protect her dignity and any hope of a peaceful future for her children.

The volunteer firefighter rests at home after spending a few days in the burn unit of the hospital. He suffered second-degree burns on his arms and legs trying to save a family's cherished black lab in the town's most-recent fire.

A farmer donates a large amount of his recently-harvested crops to the local food pantry. Only the head of the local charity knows the generosity comes from him, as he has sworn her to secrecy in the matter. After growing up in a poor environment most of his life, he's very grateful for his personal turnaround and simply wants to make a portion of those blessings available to others in need.

The town sheriff stays busy year-round—not only giving out tickets and making the few arrests that will help to keep his hometown safer, but also playing Santa Claus at the elementary school's Christmas pageant and the Easter Bunny at the VFW's Easter egg hunt. He treats all the temporary inmates with great respect and has been known to go easy, more often than not, on first-time speeding offenders.

A father watches his son play in a basketball game and treats him exactly the same after every contest—win or lose, good game or bad. He doesn't allow his son to talk bad about the coach or any of his decisions, and he refuses to participate in any discussion about how the referees cost them the game. He's there cheering loudly if his son starts, warms the bench the entire game or gets a few minutes of action during garbage time.

The owner and sole mechanic of the auto shop gives out his second car for a customer to use while repairs are being done on his. It will be a little complicated figuring out how he and his working wife will manage to jive their schedules with just one vehicle for the next few days. But, in his mind, it's a whole lot easier than one of his customers determining how to work out his schedule with none.

The waitress works a second shift two nights a week because her preteen daughter really wants to take piano lessons. She's a single mom with a schedule the President couldn't keep, but she never complains and longs to provide her children with a better life.

The retired man rises before the sun and starts shoveling the seven inches of snow that fell overnight on his neighbor's driveway and sidewalk. He will finish long before the young married man even has time to walk out his door to go to work and notice the good deed in progress. When he's finished there, he'll start on the house across the street.

Yes, indeed, there really are good-hearted people like the ones I've just described, and they're doing all they can to uphold the positive reputation long ago established in regard to small-town America. Are there a number of bad-hearted people in small towns doing what they can to counter the positive contributions of these good-deed-doers? Absolutely! Do drugs and alcohol find their way into small towns and into the bloodstreams of the young and the old? No doubt about it! Is sexual promiscuity a way of life for some of the boys and girls in the high schools there? Of course! Do divorce, dysfunction and discipline problems find their way into any of the families there? Certainly! Does gossip get too much air-time in some of the conversations there? For sure! Small towns are not a modern-day Camelot, and none of them exude a total Mayberry feel. But despite the occasional storm caused by some of the problems existing in small towns, I believe the overall climate you'll experience if you live in one or visit one is both fair and mild.

Yes, heroic people like the ones I've just described are in every small town across our great country. Keep searching if you're still skeptical. Ask questions to point you in the direction of a real-life hero. Or visit someone in a small town for more than a minute and get to know them better! Perhaps your brief encounter will be an introduction to the modern-day Superman who strongly prefers the Clark Kent anonymity.

But even better than meeting one of them is to be one of them. Be a hero. You don't have to dart in front of a speeding bullet before it reaches its intended target, and you don't have to flex your muscles to hold back the runaway locomotive before it reaches the ready-to-collapse bridge. All you have to do is care. Or express gratitude. Or offer someone a friendly smile or a sincere "good morning." Or show some humility by being quick to admit your failures. Or do a good deed but don't let anybody else know you're doing it. Or apologize before the other guy apologizes first. Or stay an hour later than you're expected to at work and help your boss finish an important project. Or clean your room the way you know your mother really wants you to clean it. Though heroic activity can be found in many areas outside of humility, hard work and a heart to help others, walking on any of those paths is a pretty good place to start.

Section II

The Story

Chapter Eight

Miniature March Madness

A little more than a third of Darrington's 1,300 residents left town on a Tuesday in early March, embarking on a six-hour road trip through the Cascade Mountains and into eastern Washington to experience big-city living and high school boy's basketball for five thrilling days. They were traveling to attend the highly-popular Washington State "B" Basketball Tournament that would begin early Wednesday morning and run through the championship contest and trophy presentations scheduled to be completed on Saturday evening. Many of the small-business owners from the tiny town nestled at the foot of the Cascades in northwest Washington decided to forego any possible profits for that five-day period, shutting down operations in order to attend the much-anticipated event. Some of the Darrington faithful even decided to borrow from their summer vacation stashes, opting to use the funds on more immediate necessities—gas for the 600 mile round-trip, a 12-meal restaurant plan, four to five night's lodging somewhere near the tournament venue and tickets for the exciting, 16-team tournament in Spokane, the state's second largest city.

Darrington students celebrate their 1955 victory

It was now late Saturday afternoon, about four hours prior to tip-off of the title game. Those from Darrington who had made the trip to the boy's basketball finale a number of times prior to 2003 were taking turns sharing their favorite state tournament memories, events they had personally witnessed or ones their parents passed on to them. They did so with great enthusiasm and unbelievable detail around the tables pulled together at the crowded restaurant near the stadium, the same place many of the team's following had eaten dinner the past three evenings. Thrilling stories were being exchanged of a come-out-of nowhere state championship in 1955 that shocked the Washington basketball community, when Darrington, one of the smallest schools in the tournament that year, stunned the heavily-favored Bainbridge Spartans, one of the largest schools to qualify, to win the coveted state crown. Most of the people there had told the stories or heard them before. But they never grew tired of sharing them or soaking them in one more time. And at the top of their list of most-treasured recollections was the unlikely four-game sweep by the Loggers in 1955 over teams with taller, faster and overall better players; the championship, game-winning shot put in by Roland Mount, an unlikely hero who was encouraged to look for the pass before the shot when he entered the court in those final moments; and the masterful job of coaching by my father, LaVerne Simmons, a 32-year-old mentor, in only his fourth year as a high-school head coach, out-strategizing four other more experienced men positioned at their team's helm.

It was basketball that put the town of Darrington on the map and basketball remained one of the most important subjects on the minds of the townspeople the following 48 years. Like all towns, Darrington had its share of problems, and residents found trouble and daily difficulty in normal rations. But basketball memories often brought smiles to the faces of the folks there, and they served as a welcomed pain-reliever to any resident experiencing a personal setback or sadness. For people in need of some good news in Darrington, talking about basketball was a great escape. It was one of their greatest get-away plans for staying a step ahead of the discouragement that would visit them on occasion. All you had to do to elevate most of the townspeople above some of the cloudy realities of life was to simply mention two years—1955 and 1957. Oh, those were very good years for Darrington folks! Championship years! Each callback to the accomplishments of Darrington basketball in those days could bring the sun out in that part of the world for at least a little while. Even those too young to remember where they were or what they were doing in 1955 and 1957, as well as those who weren't even on the population rolls then, knew the significance of those two years. It was the town's greatest claim to fame—even more than the lumber and logging industry that once employed more than 80% of the town's residents, the gorgeous, evergreen-lined and well-traveled North Cascade Highway built in the late 1970's that weaved its way through town, or Bob Barker, the well-known game-show host of *The Price is Right* who was born in a small house just outside of town. Yes, it was basketball. And for 46 years, the stories told and memories evoked of those two incredible years had an uncanny ability to keep many of the townspeople living on cloud nine, oblivious to the earthly remarks they would hear from time to time from city-dwellers concerning their hick and hillbilly status.

Though Darrington folks love their less-complicated and more-room-to-run lifestyles, and while most of the residents would choose to do it all over again and live in the exact same spot if given a choice, it's still somewhat hard for them to feel important while living in a society that often leaves them feeling judged as goonies-from-the-boonies and real-life rednecks. Many city-dwellers can't understand why residents there don't jump at the first chance to move up to the big leagues and come to the big city. Why, they ask, would anyone choose trees over tinsel and the environment over entertainment? Why would anybody want to go the Green Acres route when vacancies for a penthouse view abounded in the great metropolis? Yes, Darrington folks have endured their share of "it's-your-loss" responses to their "I'm-happy-here" rebuttals, but not always without injury to the self-esteem.

Activity in Darrington rarely gets mentioned in the bigger city newspapers, except for those few times when a raging forest fire on the outskirts of town threatens homeowners, or a homicide occurs. It's a small town like most other small towns in America, just going about its daily grind. But sometimes people in towns like Darrington find it a bit difficult to remove the chip on their shoulder, put there as a result of feeling less important than the high-rollers living in the city, even insignificant at times. Any tool, then, that could help whittle the bothersome chip down to a more-bearable carrying size was highly sought after by those in Darrington. The town's hard court success in 1955 and 1957 was said to be the sharpest in the town shed. But while memories of success from 46 years in the past were helpful, most of the townspeople were hoping for more recent victories to help lighten their load. And many were still planning on basketball being the vehicle they would take to higher self-esteem.

So it's not surprising so many from the town were there in Spokane for the extended weekend. And it's no wonder the high decibels of hope coming from the direction of the Darrington crowd were leaving the other neutral patrons at the restaurant, there for the roast beef and rhubarb pie, wishing they had eaten elsewhere. And a few hours later, the noise was nothing short of deafening in the Darrington rooting section as fans anxiously awaited the opening moments of the final game of the 2003 Washington State 'B' Basketball Championships.

The Loggers, void of championship pride since their 1957 domination over four outmatched opponents, were only minutes from taking the stage and completing a yearlong journey to gather new joy for their fans and a reminder to others in bigger spheres their tiny town was *still* on the map. Forty-six years had been an incredibly long time to wait for another championship moment to arrive. For a few people, a victory that night might just be enough to resurrect hope—hope for an improved economy and a resurgence in the timber industry, hope of a cure for the illness in a relative or good friend recently labeled incurable, hope for a mend in a broken relationship, hope for a better all-around life. Basketball success really could do that in this town. It even had the power in Darrington to turn an erring and empty soul in a better direction, at least for a little while.

You can call that idolatry, small thinking or just plain miserable. You can call it whatever you want. But if you lived there, or if you were at your rope's end and needed some extra twine for survival, cutting down the basketball nets after a championship run and taking a piece of it home with you might be just the material you'd need to hang on to hope a little while longer. Their Loggers just had to win, or else they would be faced with, for another long year, settling for conversations about 1955 and 1957 as their main source for basketball joy. And, thus, the number 47 would become the most hated number in town—47 years since the town's last basketball championship.

Both teams' starting line-ups had been introduced and fans representing both schools were standing on their feet—yelling, stomping and clapping like never before, with absolutely no concern for curbing their enthusiasm or keeping their emotions in check. And on this night, the hopes of many in Darrington were resting on the poise, precise passing and pressure shooting of twelve teenage boys, along with the ability of a coach named Jeff Bryson to rally his troops to play a winning brand of basketball for 32 minutes and bring back the much-desired trophy to their town for the first time in 46 years.

Bryson was confident, but nervous as well, as he felt the weight of the town's hopes pushing down on his shoulders. He knew how important it was to them. But it was important to him as well. And it wasn't just about winning this game and reclaiming the title for Darrington, although he could imagine the pride and wonderful feeling of accomplishment that would come to him and the entire town with a state championship. No, Bryson was also a humble man who believed intensely in the value of tradition and doing whatever he could to uphold it. Bryson knew his recent success had been built upon a winning foundation laid nearly 50 years prior to the events of this night, and he knew one of his greatest responsibilities was to tie the accomplishments of the past with the aspirations of the present. Bryson had felt privileged to meet my father, the successful foundation-builder of the Logger's program, in December of 2000. My father guided his Darrington teams to two state championships, was the man many still say was most responsible for putting the town on the map and the one coach everybody in Darrington knew a little something about.

People there made sure my father wasn't forgotten, just shy of making his legendary achievements a textbook requirement in their public school system. And Bryson certainly wasn't in danger of forgetting my father. He was the one coach Bryson felt most obligated to honor and respect, drawing whatever inspiration he could find from his remarkable accomplishments.

It was a good first visit that morning at breakfast between my father and Bryson, sharing stories from the past, strategies for winning basketball and best wishes for whatever lay ahead. During that breakfast, Bryson invited my father, along with two other former Darrington coaches, to address his team before one of their biggest games of the season to be played later that night. Bryson was moved by my father's pre-game words as he encouraged each player to "take full advantage of this incredible time in your young lives, because it will soon be over." Bryson was grateful, as well, for his post-game admonition that "one loss (this one to state powerhouse, Toutle Lake) did not the season make, and that this is now a perfect opportunity to learn and build toward greater moments to come." Bryson was amazed at my father's zeal for the kids and the game of basketball, commenting it seemed, at 78 years of age, he was ready, willing and able to occupy the bench once again and lead his Loggers to victory. And it was the last time the two ever saw each other.

My father passed away on October 31, 2002, and the sad news of his death spread quickly in Darrington. A town hero had passed. But Bryson was determined to bring this hero of the past into the hearts of his players. So just before the beginning of the 2002-2003 season, he decided to use his conviction about tradition to its fullest advantage. And now, five months later and just before the biggest game of his life, he was hoping the baton of championship moments could be transferred securely into his hands and those of his players.

A few of the players on Bryson's 2003 squad also had the privilege of meeting my father in 2000. But all twelve were familiar with his accomplishments and inspired to lay another brick on the winning foundation he had established nearly five decades earlier. And while excited about the possibility of owning a championship memory for the rest of their lives, they also wanted a championship for Bryson, the new small-town hero-in-the-making and perhaps the one their grandchildren would be talking about someday as the man most responsible for putting Darrington back on the map.

The five starters broke the huddle and came quickly to center court. Farmers and fishermen, machinists and mill workers, small-business owners and secretaries, teachers and truck drivers and welders and widowed grandmothers were in the stands. They, along with hundreds of others from Darrington who came to cheer their boys on to victory, breathed one last sigh, said a quick prayer and sat down to watch perhaps the most important 32 minutes of their recent lives. But this was more than just another game.

This game was also about helping the townspeople find fresh supplies of good-feeling medicine to be on-hand in a troubled moment, with a strong enough storage life to last them for the next 46 years. And, more importantly, it was a game and possible championship season that could provide many valuable life-lessons to be taught for years to come, giving people everywhere a much clearer look at what constitutes success.

In the next number of chapters, you will be reading a story about Darrington basketball. In the last few chapters of the book, we will discuss the implications and applications of this inspiring story for your personal life. This story will highlight my father, LaVerne Simmons, and Jeff Bryson, two men separated by nearly 50 years in their rise to hero status who had before them the same goals—working to build strong character in the boys they coached and winning basketball games.

And it all began in 1955 when residents of Darrington were treated to a most amazing David-and-Goliath replay during a simple game of basketball that changed them and their town forever.

The 1955 Darrington Loggers

Pictured from left to right: Jack Bates, Dick Noble, Ken Estes, Larry Gilbert, Duane Sanford, Daryl Edwards, Gerald Green, Harold Haga, Darryl Smoke, Roland Mount, David Edwards and Bill Green

Chapter Nine

A Hero's Beginning

My father came to Darrington in the summer of 1950 to teach math and history and coach junior varsity basketball, a little more than a decade after his high school graduation in 1940. He served four years in naval military service during World War II, and five years later received his bachelor's degree in secondary education from Western State College in the spring of 1950. The youngest of four boys, he had always been very involved in sports growing up, inspired by the athletic successes of his older brothers, Clyde, Cleo and Cliff. Though not a standout athlete himself, my father knew the game of basketball from studying books on winning strategies and his mindset was to imitate any successful plans he saw unfold from coaches at all levels. And while he thoroughly enjoyed the thought of teaching school, coaching was his first love and greatest passion. So at the age of 29 and still single, my father came to Darrington to assist in revamping a basketball program starving for attention and success. From 1931 to 1950, the Loggers experienced very few winning seasons and qualified only once for state tournament play.

Just one year after his arrival in Darrington, my father was promoted to the position of varsity head coach in the fall of 1951. In his first year, the Loggers were 7-12 and failed to even qualify for district play. In year two, Darrington improved to 15-6 overall but came up just short in their bid to reach the state tournament due to a disappointing, two-point loss in their final game at district play. In the 1953-54 season, the Loggers finished with a 15-8 mark and qualified for the 16-team state tournament. It was the first time my father led his team to the tournament, but the Loggers failed to place in the top eight. Steady progress marked my father's first three years at the Logger helm, and in year number four the town of Darrington was treated to its first helping of championship cuisine—and it had never tasted so good! But it was the most unlikely of stories with a classic fairy-tale ending that helped elevate my father to hero status in the small Washington town and brought him to the forefront of praise within the top coaching circles in the state.

After a somewhat unspectacular regular-season campaign, posting a 15-4 record and finishing second in their own league, the Loggers saved their best basketball for district and state tournament play. After winning three straight games at the always-competitive Northwest League District Tournament, they arrived in Tacoma five days later to begin play at the state finals. Not many attending the tournament from across the state were expecting Darrington to vie for top honors. Opposing coaches, sportswriters and diehard basketball fans wouldn't have been shocked with a Logger's finish somewhere in the top eight, but even the most avid and partial Darrington supporters weren't planning on more grandiose results. And if the Darrington ballplayers had been forced to be brutally honest, they likely would have expressed satisfaction with a respectful showing, simply hoping to keep each of the contests close and a win or two within reach. Leaving the tournament without a trophy that year wouldn't have led to great discouragement in Darrington, especially as fans digested pleasant thoughts of a likely return to the tournament with better results the following years. Perhaps the Loggers would get enough breaks and big baskets during the four days of competition, win at least two games and place somewhere in the top eight. But nobody could imagine them overcoming the giant obstacles of Toutle Lake, with 6-10 center Gary Goble leading the way, perennial powerhouse Dayton or talent-laden Bainbridge—the three favorites to most likely make it into the championship contest and wear the victor's crown. Bainbridge was the odds-on favorite to win, one of the largest schools in the tournament, riding high on a 22-game winning streak and boasting four returning starters from the previous year's squad that finished second in the state.

As far as my father's attitude entering the tournament, nobody could have accused him of being over-confident concerning the Logger's chances of winning it all. He knew he had a strong team, but he was also well aware of the long-shot odds of Darrington walking away with top honors. But with the help he knew he could count on from the spirited fans making the two-hour trek south to Tacoma, my father entered Thursday's first-round contest with one goal in mind—"Win game one and we'll go from there." He was hopeful his undersized, inexperienced and little-known Loggers could do something no other team had done in the school's history—win at least one game at the state tournament. If that happened, they could then focus on coming away with their first trophy ever by winning at least two contests, placing them somewhere among the top eight teams in the state.

Darrington had drawn the first game of the tournament, scheduled for play at 9:30 a.m. on Thursday morning. Battling through eight inches of snow that had fallen the previous night, the Loggers finally arrived to the College of Puget Sound Fieldhouse and began preparing to take their first small step toward a trophy. After some fairly typical pre-game comments offered by my father, the Loggers, with only two players barely above six feet tall, played a slow but steady brand of offense and a tough man-to-man defense to pull out to a 10-point halftime lead against a talented team from Lebam, owners of a 20-2 record coming into the tournament. (Lebam's team name was also the Loggers—strong evidence there really are a whole lot of trees in Washington!) Very little changed in the second half, as Darrington extended their lead to as many as 15 points, allowing my father to rest his starters for most of the fourth quarter and give them a much-needed break before Friday's second-round contest, also scheduled for 9:30 a.m. Darrington defeated Lebam, 50-39, their first-ever win in state tournament competition.

The first hurdle had been cleared, but much higher ones loomed ahead. Chelan was Darrington's next opponent, a strong team from eastern Washington. Most prognosticators were forecasting this game as a toss-up, and my father knew his Loggers would have to play their absolute best to win and reach the semi-final round. After a close battle for two-and-a-half quarters, Darrington pulled away from the veteran team from Chelan, using their quickness and high-percentage shooting to come away with a 58-43 victory, catapulting them into the state semifinals and ensuring them of reaching my father's original goal—two wins at state and a place among the elite eight in Washington high school basketball.

But was it going to be more than that? Was this a classic Cinderella-story-in-the-making? Would one of the biggest upsets in the state's history come to pass in the next 24 hours and push the Loggers into the finals? Or would the Loggers, as most writers and basketball know-it-alls believed, see their run for a title end once the pressure mounted and they finally realized they were drastically undersized and outmanned against the favored Dayton Bulldogs, their next opponent. After all, Dayton was one of the early-season favorites to win it all, and also a team that presented Darrington with its stiffest challenge up to that point in the tournament, led by senior forward and All-State selection Lloyd Bender. Dayton had won their two previous contests by one point each and confidently carried into the game against the Loggers the belief they were the team of destiny in 1955.

But my father had his team prepared and working together—unselfish in their style of play and unfazed by the large crowds or "lucky-to-be-there" comments written by some of the sportswriters in Tacoma covering the tournament. Crisp passing, tough man-to-man-defense, especially on Bender, and a commitment to blocking out the big men of Dayton and securing rebounds on the defensive end all combined to present a challenge to the favored Bulldogs. The Loggers were performing much better than anybody had expected, even beyond my father's expectations, but still found themselves down by three points at the half and five points after three quarters of play.

But with two wins already under their belts and a real shot at claiming a third straight, my father's confidence in his team was growing, as well as in his own ability to take that team places they'd only visited in their dreams. Aided by a few Dayton mistakes and some clutch shooting of their own, the Loggers took a two-point lead with only two minutes remaining. A little more than a minute later, and with Darrington clinging to a 57-56 lead, Dayton committed a huge mental mistake and called a time out, even though they had none remaining. The Loggers sank the technical foul-shot to widen their margin to 58-56 with less than a minute to go in the game. After a tying basket by Dayton, Darrington's Harold Haga was fouled with 23 seconds left on the clock and sank two free-throws to give the Loggers a two-point cushion. A smothering defense in the waning moments forced Dayton to toss up a desperation-shot at the buzzer that was well off the mark, and Darrington, with their 60-58 victory, found itself in the one game everybody said would never be a part of their future.

With their confidence brimming after the narrow win, my father and his players were now beginning to believe in their chances for claiming a state crown. Most of the Darrington fan base, though ecstatic about their team's play in the first three rounds, seemed content just to have made it that far. Sure, they wanted to win, but getting to the championship round was truly a moral victory, something they could take home and be proud of until returning one day with a real shot at winning it all. But by this point in the tournament, my father wasn't all that fired up about claiming a moral victory. Instead, he was making plans to find some way to do what most people there said couldn't be done. "The-clock-will-soon-strike-midnight" remarks shared by fans exiting the Fieldhouse that night typified the crowd's overall prognosis for the Loggers in the title game. They fully expected the Darrington chariot to turn back into a pumpkin, ending their chance of becoming basketball royalty. Though anxious to return the following evening to watch the surprising Loggers face Bainbridge in the championship game of the tournament, most ticket-holders were absolutely certain little old Darrington could never defeat big bad Bainbridge.

Bainbridge was a well-oiled and finely-tuned basketball machine—twenty-five straight wins, the tournament's all-time leading scorer in Dave Beach (who had just scored a tournament-record 40 points in their semi-final contest), three other starters from the 1954 team that nearly came away with the title and a coach, Tom Paski, considered to be one of the best in the state. Most people in Tacoma were picking Bainbridge to win for sure and, more than likely, by double digits. The confidence was so high on the Bainbridge side, a police escort had been arranged to lead their winning caravan to a nearby restaurant where they could celebrate the championship with a steak dinner. And the Sunday sport's section of the

Seattle newspaper was set to contain a large feature story on the Bainbridge Spartans. The decision-makers at the paper were extremely confident Bainbridge would be victorious over Darrington and no doubt certain the article would fit quite nicely in conjunction with the headline and lead story announcing their convincing victory in the state final.

But who could blame either of those groups for their confident and somewhat cocky attitudes? Even the most idealistic Darrington fans were shocked at their team's journey to the title game. Larry Gilbert, one of Darrington's starters in 1955, remembered his father was away in Nevada on important business at the beginning of the tournament, not expecting anything close to a title run by his son's team and, for the most part, feeling justified in his absence.

"After we won the semi-final game, we called my dad," Gilbert said. "When he heard we were in the championship game, he couldn't believe it. He drove straight to Tacoma (about a 14 hour drive) and arrived about three minutes before tip-off."

Gilbert's father wasn't the only surprised spectator there that night. And in most people's minds, it was only a matter of how long Darrington could manage to stay in the game against Bainbridge before encountering the infamous writing on the wall. But by this time, the only writing my father could see in his mind's eye was the message he kept repeating to himself—"We can actually win this thing!" Amazingly, he and his Loggers had come this far and he was no longer interested in a fine showing or fighting hard but coming up short. He wanted Darrington's first state championship and he was 32 minutes away from claiming that honor. But there were no rash predictions being made by either him or his players. No arrogant quotes or "we-deserve-to-be-here" comments were coming from the Logger's side that could have been used as additional motivation for Bainbridge. There was optimism in my father's thinking, but he definitely knew better than to call up a bookie and bet the farm on his Darrington boys. But he also knew he had paved the way for his team to be playing at the top of their game, and he was relying on his November to March mindset to carry them one last time.

Beginning in early November, my father had trained his team for four months with long, tough practices where fundamentals were stressed and extended conditioning drills were a must to put the smallish unit in the best possible shape.

"Coach Simmons' practices were intense but fun," Ken Estes, a Logger player from 1953-56, remembers. "We usually practiced facets of the entire game—shooting, passing, dribbling, defense and foul shooting. We also ran a lot, but we had to because teams were usually bigger and taller than we were and we had to wear them down."

Adding a secret ingredient to his recipe for success, my father had made a commitment of friendship to his players that made them readily submissive to his on-the-court strategies and desirous of playing their absolute best for him. You see, to them, my father wasn't only their coach. Jack (Jackie as he was known in his younger days) Bates, a back-up guard on the 1955 Logger squad, explains.

"Coach Simmons was always very cordial. He would take the time to talk to you. If there was anything he could help you with, he would. He was great with all the kids. And it seemed like he could relate to other people, whatever the situation."

Estes also recalled a humorous situation during his senior year under my father's leadership that typified the kind of heart he had for his players.

"We were playing Oak Harbor and one of the fans had bet me before the game that I couldn't score 20 points. Coach Simmons took me out of the game when I had 16 points. The assistant coach had heard about the bet so he told Coach Simmons. It wasn't long before I was back in the game and I got my 20 points. After scoring the 20 points, he quickly took me out of the game because we already had a big lead."

Assistant coach Bob Patterson remembers similar qualities in my father during his short stay in Darrington from 1954-55.

"His practices were organized but also fun," Patterson said. "During the games he always maintained his cool and was calm and reassuring." Calling my father "unassuming, approachable and down to earth," Patterson believes his greatest strengths were patience and perseverance.

Bill Carroll, another of my father's assistant coaches, said this about the Darrington leader: "He always treated people as equals, deserving of his time and his ear, always straightforward but fair." Carroll served as an assistant to my father for eight years and remembers a "level-headed, relatively quiet, always cool and collected leader both on and off the court."

Gene Boyd, a member of my father's Darrington squads in the early 60s, echoed the sentiments of those assistant coaches.

"Coach Simmons was incredibly calm. He never got real emotional and just seemed to know when to take a timeout," Boyd said.

Boyd also remembers the confidence my father instilled in his players whenever they faced a challenging opponent.

"Coach Simmons was incredibly inspiring," Boyd said. "He taught us all to have a no-fear approach when it came to playing against the bigger schools."

My father not only inspired his players to perform at high levels on the court, he also cared about their performance off the court and was more than willing to stay after a practice to help them with homework or counsel them on the difficulties they were facing at home. Most of all, as many of his players would say, he never came across to them as lord and master, but much more as leader and mentor. In every sense, my father was a hero figure to his players. Now he only needed to win one more game to secure that label in the minds of the Darrington community.

The final-game battle was fierce, watched by an estimated crowd of 6,500 that would have been larger had not the Tacoma Fire Department made a decision to start turning people away due to safety concerns. During the course of the contest, the score was tied eight times and the lead changed hands another 12 times. And with the score knotted at 54-54 with one minute remaining, Darrington had the ball and my father ordered a time out. By now, everybody in the Fieldhouse was standing, most of them totally shocked they were being treated to a classic final-game finish. Thousands of fans from the previous consolation games were still there, many of them now solidly on the side of underdog Darrington.

My father in a casual moment with his 1955 team

"Okay men. We'll play for the last shot. Gerald, I want you to be taking the shot with about five seconds on the clock," my father said, as he made one last attempt to ready his team for a title.

Gerald was Gerald Green, the Logger's sharp-shooting forward who had scored 26 points in Darrington's semi-final victory against Dayton. Green had already scored 22 points in the contest against Bainbridge and my father wanted the ball in the hands of not only his best shooter, but his best player as well. Roland Mount had entered the game only minutes earlier after one of Darrington's starters, Harold Haga, fouled out. Mount was much more regarded for his all-around court skills than his ability to shoot the basketball, and instructions were clear for him and his three other teammates to work to get Green the potential, game-winning shot. But Bainbridge had anticipated those events, and Green was smothered and double-teamed whenever necessary.

Now in virtually every story about a hero-in-the-making, a little magic must be included. Or a light sprinkling of wonder dust must somehow fall from the sky, ushering in the closing drama. Perhaps a packed house in the heavenly gymnasium viewed the situation and called upon their leader to orchestrate a most-memorable finish, one that could motivate all of Washington's unwanted stepchildren to shoot for the stars and find their own happily-ever-after endings. Because with only seven seconds remaining, and wide open from 15 feet away from the basket, Mount put up the shot that still lives in infamy in the city of Darrington—nothing but net! Bainbridge threw up a desperation half-court heave for the tie at the

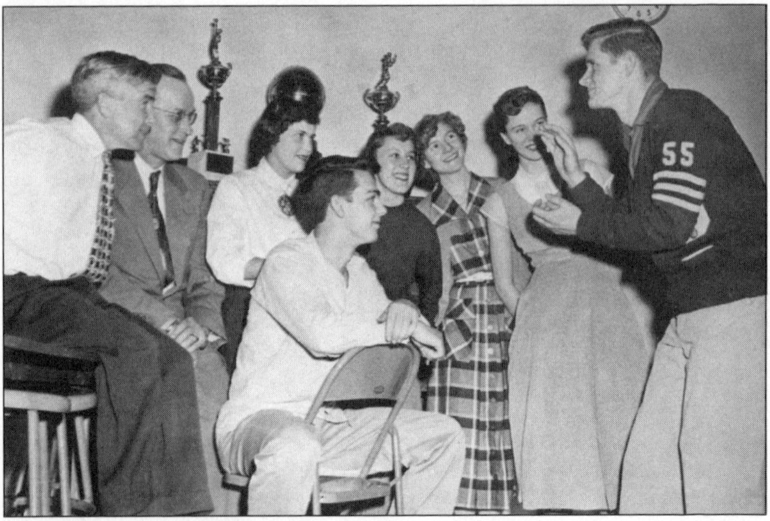

Roland Mount attempts to re-enact his dramatic, game-winning basket for captivated Darrington fans

buzzer, but to no avail. The final score was Darrington 56, Bainbridge 54.

"Goliath is dead!"

"The slipper fits!

"The Giants win the pennant! The Giants win the pennant!"

However those who saw the game or heard the news of Darrington's victory phrased it, the Loggers were state champions. They had defeated this sensational and star-laden team. Three of Bainbridge's starters were so talented they went on to play basketball at Washington State University, and one of them even started for the Cougars as a freshman. Few could imagine how a team with that type of talent could ever lose to such a tiny school with smaller, less-talented players who had never played in such a big game. Though state champions, the Loggers only placed one player on the all-tournament team, Gerald Green, while Bainbridge had three of their five starters selected to the squad.

Many who witnessed the Logger's upset victory credited the win to their unusual defensive strategy. During the game against a squad everyone agreed was a superior opponent, Darrington employed what was called the "straight line defense" and gave Bainbridge fits in trying to figure out how to break it down and effectively score against it. My father had seen the benefits of this defense while attending Western State College. The head basketball coach at Western had found great success by employing that style of defense, and my father learned its many nuances attending the team's practices and games. And consistent with his humble demeanor that prompted him to never be afraid of admitting his lack of expertise in certain areas but to instead simply copy the success of others, my father used that defense in the final game of the '55 tournament. In doing so, the Loggers surprised Bainbridge and had them on their heels for most of the contest.

As word of the monumental upset traveled throughout the state, Darrington would become the prime example of "anything can happen" and "never give up" used in pep talks and important speeches the remainder of the year. At a banquet in Darrington later that year, University of Washington head coach Tippy Dye, who was in attendance at the game, said the 1955 championship contest played by the Loggers was the absolute best basketball game he had seen high school players perform and the best job of coaching he had ever witnessed. The Logger's victory was so impressive, even the Washington House of Representatives, assembled in the state capitol of Olympia, jumped on the upset winner's bandwagon.

My father congratulates All-State selection Gerald Green

Dear Mr. Simmons:

It is my honor and pleasure to transmit herewith a certified copy of Mr. Bernethy's resolution unanimously adopted by the House of Representatives, relating to the recent unexpected feat of your wonderful basketball team.

The resolution expresses how we around the legislature, including members from all parts of the state, feel about your team. We are all proud of you and wish you similar success in the years to come.

With best wishes,

S.R. Holcomb
Chief Clerk

STATE OF WASHINGTON HOUSE OF REPRESENTATIVES

Resolution
By Representative Robert Bernethy

Be it resolved, by the House of Representatives of the State of Washington, in Legislative Session Assembled:

WHEREAS, The basketball team of Darrington High School has won a startling upset victory by capturing the State Class B championship in the tournament just completed at Tacoma, Washington, and

WHEREAS, This little school, with a student body of but 131, has turned out a team of young men, which although rated the underdogs, conquered all in their class, and

WHEREAS, This feat by the Darrington team was accomplished in the traditional American style of overcoming heavy odds, thereby through this display of courage, stamina, determination and spirit, reflecting great credit to the populace of Darrington and to the youth of the entire state of Washington, and

WHEREAS, This victory was so unexpected that the good citizens of Darrington had insufficient time to make proper arrangements to recognize and honor the triumphant homecoming of its young heroes,

NOW, THEREFORE, BE IT RESOLVED, By the House of Representatives of the State of Washington, that it does hereby express its congratulations and commendation to the Darrington High School Basketball Team, to its Coach and Managers for this splendid example of athletic achievement, and

BE IT FURTHER RESOLVED, That we do hereby offer our congratulations to the student body, the mothers and fathers, the school faculty, and the entire population of Darrington for producing this outstanding team of young athletes, and

BE IT STILL FURTHER RESOLVED, That copies of this resolution be sent to each member of the team and to the principal of Darrington High School for presentation to the student body.

I hereby certify this to be a True and correct copy of Resolution
Adopted by the House of Representatives On March 9, 1955

S.R. Holcomb, chief Clerk
House of Representatives

And 48 years later, in March of 2003, Darrington residents still enjoy talking about 1955 and their town's hero in those days, my father, LaVerne Simmons. In stunning fashion, he had taken a bunch of rag-tag players, less skilled, less experienced and less likely to win, all the way to the top of high school basketball in the state of Washington.

The mayor of Darrington spends a few moments honoring my father at a 1955 championship banquet

University of Washington head coach Tippy Dye comments on Darrington's impressive victory in 1955

Chapter Ten

Return to Glory

After a disappointing disappearance from a run at back-to-back championships in 1956, losing by a single point to LaConner in district to end their hopes of a third straight trip to Tacoma, Darrington returned to the title chase in 1957, aiming for a second state crown. The Loggers came into the tournament with a 21-2 record, their only losses coming by two and three points respectively early in the season. Ranked third in the final state polls behind Winthrop and Port Townsend, Darrington, despite having to deal with the affects of a flu epidemic from the week before that shut down the school and touched all but one player in some way, brimmed with confidence about their chances to win it all and secured an easy victory in their opening contest, defeating Kettle Falls, 56-34.

My father had emotionally rebounded from his team's disappointing season in 1956. He had taken personal responsibility for not having his team ready to play in district tournament competition and failing to qualify for the 16-team state tournament that year. But he and his team were now a year older and a year smarter, anxious to bring Darrington another title. My father admitted he had more than likely suffered a championship letdown the previous year and hadn't adequately prepared his squad for opponents taking dead aim at dethroning the Loggers. To have come away with back-to-back titles wouldn't have been an easy task for the Loggers, but those thoughts were now securely in the past and my father had his team primed to play the best basketball of their young lives. Practices had been harder and longer than those in 1956 and my father logged fewer hours of sleep as he mulled over scouting reports of future opponents and analyzed the highs and lows of his team's practice sessions from only hours earlier. Still a bachelor, he had plenty of time to devote himself to one cause—winning basketball games. And his way with the players continued, building friendships that continued to prosper years later.

The Loggers were a vastly different team than the diminutive one of 1955. Playing the role of underdog at almost every turn, and sporting a lineup with their tallest player just over six feet tall, my father had led his '55 squad to a totally unexpected state championship. Now they were highly ranked and favored to make a strong run for the title. In 1955, his Loggers played a scrappy brand of basketball, fast-breaking and trapping the ball on defense whenever possible, and he had his players in the best possible shape in hopes of wearing down opponents who typically towered over his undersized team. But in 1957, my father was primarily focused on teaching his tall and talented team patience. He believed it was a lack of patience in teams they faced in 1955 that proved to be the difference in his team's rise to glory, and he knew the strategies employed by opposing coaches against his squad would likely be similar. He wasn't about to rely on accurate outside shooting to take his team to the top. He expected a constant feeding of the ball into his big men in the middle—6-6 senior, Gary Sweeney, and 6-5 sophomore, Roger Buchanan.

"The best shot is the closest shot," my father was often heard telling his players. And he was adamant about his big men using the oft-ignored backboard to their advantage whenever possible. The Loggers' towering height and strong inside presence were complimented by junior shooting-guard David Edwards, an All-League and All-District selection that year who averaged 15.4 points per contest. Edwards could score from the outside, but was even deadlier when he penetrated the lane due to his quick first step to the basket, often ending in a lay-in for himself or a pass leading to a wide open shot for a teammate. With point-guard Dick Hitchcock averaging eight points per game and about half as many assists, the Loggers were a threat to score at each position on the floor. Yet my father's strategy was simple, and he insisted upon it—work the ball inside for the best possible shot.

The 1957 Darrington Loggers

Pictured from left to right: Daryle Whittal, Dick Hitchcock, Dan Bates, David Edwards, Roger Buchanan, Randall Phillips, Gary Sweeney, John Tanner, Lyle Edlund, David Andrews, Dwayne Whittal and Bob Green: Kneeling are Manager Alyn Rensink and Coach LaVerne Simmons

Patience was the name of my father's game that year and it paralleled his life in many ways. He had learned a tremendous amount of patience growing up as the youngest of four brothers—often finding himself as the one needing to wait the longest to use just about everything around the house and the one receiving the hole-ridden, hand-me-down trousers for the fourth and final time. Throughout his youth, he was often called upon to exercise great patience with those assuming he was of the feminine gender because of his first name. With three energetic boys already roaming the household by 1922, my father's parents had been hoping and praying for a girl. Shortly after getting confirmation of their fourth child's arrival to the womb, they decided upon the name LaVerne, well before the child ever saw the light of day and long before the days of ultrasound that could have eliminated any inappropriate choices for a first name. Needless to say, when my father was finally old enough to realize the difference, he wasn't the least bit thrilled with his parent's choice of names and suffered some persecution because of it, especially in his elementary school years.

On one occasion, upon enrolling at Western State College, he was mistakenly placed in an all-girls dorm. A few days before classes were to begin, my father arrived on campus, went to his assigned dormitory and was about to move in with all of his belongings. It wasn't long before he started hearing the giggles and noticed the strange looks (all from females) being aimed directly at him. He soon realized a persistent and painful blow to his self-esteem had delivered another punch and promptly alerted the housing administration of their mistake. Yet, even with his strong preference to being called Vern rather than LaVerne (which surely would have put a stop to all gender goof-ups), many people still called him LaVerne for the next 57 years, and he never corrected them for it.

My father also understood patience living as a single man into his mid-thirties, waiting on just the right woman to enter his life. All three of his brothers were married and had young children by the time the Loggers raced to the title in 1955, but he would continue to wait. He displayed this patience with his younger, less-experienced players, knowing all too well exactly what it felt like to be the last one in the family to learn how to do just about anything. My father clearly understood mistakes (often many of them in a short period of time) were a necessary part of the learning curve and could be used to gain the needed insight and motivation into learning how to win. And he had learned to be patient even with himself, refusing to allow the problems and disappointments of 1956 to devour the confidence he had in knowing what was needed to coach championship basketball.

My father instilled in his team a satisfaction of simply winning games because of their patient style, even if it meant a low-scoring victory. And a few contests went just that way as teams often sagged their five defensive players into the key, tempting the Loggers to move away from their normal game plan and rely instead on taking and making long-range shots. Most of the teams employing that strategy against the Loggers in 1957 came out on the losing end, albeit garnering a moral victory by keeping the final deficit within single digits. When the Loggers were forced to shoot from longer range a little more frequently than planned, they did it effectively, thanks to Edwards, Hitchcock and Dan Bates, a 5-11 guard who averaged 7.2 points per contest. And about a third of the time their misses were corralled by one of their larger teammates. Buchanan, Sweeney and the other Loggers who played the most minutes underneath for Darrington had been drilled by my father not to rely upon their decisive height-advantage to reach for rebounds over smaller opponents, but to hustle for position, block out and battle hard for every missed shot on both the offensive and defensive end.

Both regular-season losses suffered by Darrington that year were low-scoring affairs, losing 39-36 to Port Townsend and 43-41 to Nooksack Valley, two talented and highly-ranked teams. The competition at the state tournament would pose similar threats to the Loggers and all facets of their game would need to be displayed in top form for them to have a legitimate shot of returning to glory. It was there Darrington would be matched up against veteran and seasoned teams, many of them sporting players of comparable height and similar shooting prowess. After a narrow escape in the opening round of district play via a one-point victory over Granite Falls, a team they had soundly defeated twice in the regular season, the Loggers won their final two games of district by 20 points or more and were poised to recapture the state championship title and regain bragging rights they owned in 1955.

After Darrington's first-round victory against Kettle Falls, the Loggers squared off against Coulee City in the quarterfinals. The locker-room celebration that erupted immediately after their hard-fought, 13-point victory, placing them in the semi-final game, was tempered by the confirmed status of a teammate's late-game injury. With less than a minute remaining in the contest, Logger's playmaker Dick Hitchcock broke his ankle in three places, ending his season and leaving many thinking Darrington was likely destined for runner-up status without the services of one of its key players.

Instead of doubting or using the injury as a good excuse for a possible loss, my father used Hitchcock's absence to inspire his team to once again cherish the role of underdog, just as they had in 1955. For all but one of the 25 games the Loggers played during the season, they had been labeled the favorite, and 23 times they had come out on top. But these final two contests would likely see that role reversed, and the Yelm Tornados would be the first opponent to test the Logger's resolve.

Yelm entered the semi-final contest against Darrington with momentum and the tournament's top player, 6-3 forward Dave Wolf. But my father had his team running on all cylinders, and the powerful engine called size-plus-shooting ran better than ever imagined. Darrington jumped out to an 8-0 lead, built it to 15-1 a few minutes later and never looked back. Leading 39-16 at the half, the Loggers continued their torrid pace and rolled to a 31-point victory, 70-39, moving into the title contest with tremendous confidence. David Edwards led the Loggers with 21 points, while big men Gary Sweeney and Roger Buchanan scored 19 and 10 points respectively. And more than 500 of the Darrington hopeful readied themselves for more championship outbursts. So many people from Darrington had made the trip to Tacoma for the tournament that the man responsible for delivering the Everett Daily Herald to the residents there elected to take the Saturday edition to the Puget Sound Fieldhouse and passed it out in the stands instead.

Moments after the injury to Dick Hitchcock

A surprising result from the other semi-final contest that night put the Loggers right back into the favorite role, as Valley, with only two players reaching six feet in height, squeaked out an unlikely 48-46 victory over number-one-ranked Winthrop. Most of the neutral fans in attendance had fallen in love with what, at first, appeared to be a completely outmanned team from Valley, and nearly 5,000 of them cheered their hustle and unmatched determination against the favored Winthrop squad on every possession. On the positive side for Darrington, they would be the huge favorite in the championship game. Unfortunately, they would discover the vast majority of the crowd, estimated at 6,200 the following night, wanted Valley to walk away with the first-place hardware equally as much as they desired the underdog Loggers to grab title honors in 1955. And though my father accurately warned his players to expect at least 80% of the tournament-attendees to be pulling for Valley, he was confident his team would rise to the occasion, take the partisan crowd out of the game quickly and bring Darrington one more title.

My father searched for files in his mind concerning any strategy he had employed in 1955 against heavily-favored Bainbridge. Knowing Valley would come out like gangbusters from the opening tip, my father had his Loggers ready to match their intensity and they clung clung to a 17-14 first quarter lead. The crowd was silenced in the second quarter as Darrington's relentless defense, sharp shooting from inside and out and enormous rebounding advantage combined to spark a 17-4 second-quarter run and the Loggers went into the halftime break with a 34-17 lead. The Valley squad found themselves in a major hole, forcing them to search harder than ever for any hope of a comeback in the second half. As the heavy underdog in 1955, Darrington had played Bainbridge toe-to-toe from the opening moments of the contest, and they stayed within a few points of the lead the entire first half. In doing so, they had drawn most of the uncommitted spectators solidly into their rooting section, helping them garner momentum and the all-important belief they actually could pull off one of the biggest upsets in state tournament history. For Valley, the 17-point halftime deficit put them in an "I'm-sincerely-satisfied-with-second-place" state of mind.

The Loggers celebrate their second title around Hitchcock

Led by the stellar play and 21 points of first team All-State selection David Edwards and the incredible defensive effort put in by Daryle Whittal (Hitchcock's replacement), who held Valley's top scorer and All-State guard Rod Poppe to only eight points, the Loggers withstood a mild second-half rally by the Vikings before closing out the season with a 56-42 victory. The team and half the town of Darrington found themselves in a familiar place at center court, hugging one another, holding up a beautiful piece of hardware and finding it hard to believe the past three years of basketball prowess and what that success had done for them and their tiny town. Two championships in three years, eight consecutive state tournament victories and an extremely faithful forward look to a 1958 squad many said should be even better than the one currently perched at the top of the 'B' basketball world.

Darrington was a different town thanks to its newfound basketball success. People walked brisker, smiled wider and talked with greater levels of enthusiasm. Small problems seemed smaller to many of the residents there and big problems seemed conquerable. Tough classes seemed a bit easier for students to pass. Teachers once looking for promotional opportunities and a ticket out of Darrington for bigger and better assignments seemed satisfied to stay around a little longer—even proud to tell their big-city friends and colleagues they taught in the town of Darrington.

Championship celebrations continued in the town for the next few weeks, but my father stayed backstage more often than not, choosing to give credit to his team and point the praise in their direction. The Snohomish County Coach of the Year recipient, a candidate for Everett Herald "Man of the Year" honors, interest from a few larger schools looking to lure him away from Darrington and invitations to teach at coaching clinics in the off-season were all in his immediate future, but none of those accolades and accomplishments were going to change my father's humble personality. He had two championships under his belt, his Logger team was favored, by many, to win another title in 1958 and he lived in a town that nearly considered him a Messiah figure, but my father was more interested in securing a soul mate than seeing his name in the paper. Sure, basketball victories and the accompanying awards were sweet, but he was more about people and passing on his loving nature than needing a pat on the back from his many admirers.

My grandmother, Lena Simmons, boasts of her son's win

While visiting his parents in the middle of the 1957 season, my father met a big-city girl, Priscilla Gray, who was living with her mother and father in Kirkland, Washington, a suburb of Seattle. Priscilla and her family lived only a few doors down from where his parents lived, and the two, it seemed, were destined to be together. But at the time, Priscilla was rebounding emotionally from a difficult divorce, and had a three-year-old son named Tommy. My father was hesitant to pursue any kind of serious relationship, not wanting to complicate what he knew was already a very challenging time in her life and also thinking she may have had romantic interests elsewhere. But after a few across-the-fence conversations, he finally asked her out on a date. The two went to the theater where they saw *Friendly Persuasion*, starring Gary Cooper. They both thoroughly enjoyed their initial date, so my father got involved in some of his own friendly persuasion, inviting Priscilla to attend the Logger's district and state tournament games. And it wasn't long before the big-city girl was heating up with the highly contagious small-town basketball fever and the two quickly fell in love.

My father was thrilled with his two titles, but even more so with the budding relationship and the possibility of having a partner for life. The two were engaged shortly after the season concluded and exchanged vows in a beautiful June wedding. He was now a husband, father and championship coach—"in that order" he would always say. The Darrington hero, while basking in victory and the many honors bestowed upon him by his players and peers, found what he had been longing for more than praise or popularity—a woman he could commit his life to, a boy he could raise to appreciate life and hopes for other children in the near future to add to his ever-growing list of life-long companions.

My mother and father at their wedding in June of 1957

My father's marriage to Priscilla Gray in the summer of 1957 accomplished the most important goal in his life. The second goal before him was what Darrington residents were most excited about—back-to-back championship seasons and an unprecedented third state title in four years.

Chapter Eleven

A Wife and a Wrong Ending

It was destined to be his greatest year to date—a new wife, a young son, the anticipation of a new baby's arrival and the most-talented team in his six-year tenure as head coach of the Loggers. From mid-season 1957 to late February of 1958, my father's squad won an incredible 33 straight games. Only an upset loss in their next-to-last game of the regular season marred an otherwise perfect record for the Loggers, and the average margin of victory in their 19 wins was an astounding 18.7 points. District and state tournaments were on the horizon, the exact moments my father had set his sights on since the start of the season in early November. During the regular season, Darrington had secured easy victories against top-ranked teams in higher divisions. So most basketball forecasters were pegging the Loggers to make an easy climb to the top of the mountain where they could proudly plant their third championship flag, something no other school had accomplished in the history of the tournament.

Just prior to the Logger's first game of district play, my mother gave birth to a beautiful baby girl, Susan Marie, and my father had never been prouder. And while much work needed to be done on the home front, he knew most of his immediate focus had to remain on the 12 young men who had dedicated their season to being back-to-back champions. And he did just that. Three consecutive victories in district play by an average margin of 15.1 points catapulted the Loggers into the state tournament as the odds-on favorite and put their record at 37-1 in their last 38 games.

My mother and the two children went to Kirkland to stay with her parents, while my father, his players and nearly half of Darrington's residents loaded up their vehicles and headed for Spokane, a new venue for the finals. My father felt a small amount of guilt from leaving his family behind, but he saw no other viable options. My mother reassured him all would be okay and wished him luck to bring back his first title as a married man. While my father was grateful for her understanding, he couldn't wait until the season was finally completed. Then he could get some much-needed rest, away from the pressures of coaching and focus on more urgent needs in his life—beginning to build and establish a positive family dynamic and learning the needed skills for the following season's juggling act of husband, father, teacher, coach and community hero.

A slow-down strategy was employed by Darrington's first two opponents at the state tournament, no doubt their best-laid plans for staying within reach of the Loggers and avoiding a blowout loss to the reigning champions. The Tenino Beavers, though capably led by Don Ash and his 23.5 points-per-game average coming into the tournament, kept the ball out of the Darrington's hands as much as possible, and their deliberate strategy on the offensive end helped to keep them close for the first quarter-and-a-half. But midway through the second quarter, the Loggers took advantage of a few Tenino turnovers, turning them into easy baskets and turning a close game into a 20-12 lead they never relinquished. The Loggers came away from the low-scoring affair with a 38-24 victory.

In similar style, the Columbia Coyotes came out the following day determined to force the Loggers to panic on offense and move away from their game plan. Once again, patient inside work resulting in easy baskets on offense and a smothering defense that forced numerous Coyote mistakes allowed Darrington to slowly pull away from their upset-minded opponents, highlighted by a 15-0 third-quarter run to put the game out of reach. Despite suffering from intense leg cramps and only playing about half of the contest, David Edwards scored 15 points, while Roger Buchanan added 12, leading Darrington to a 45-30 victory over Columbia and propelling the Loggers into a game of great familiarity for nearly all of its roster players—the State 'B' semifinal.

The opponent for round three was familiar as well—the Yelm Tornados—the same squad the Loggers had annihilated in the 1957 semifinal, 70-39. Yelm was set on revenge, while Darrington was anxious to prove the previous year's lopsided win wasn't a fluke. But Yelm was at the top of its game from the outset. Dave Wolf, who would be voted the top player in the tournament, was at his best, hitting shots from all around the key. Darrington, in my father's opinion, was taking decent shots but firing blanks at a rate unseen in their previous two years of winning basketball. In addition to their shooting woes, Edwards still wasn't able to play at full strength due to ongoing cramping in his legs. Yet the Loggers hung close with strong defensive stands, relentless rebounding, especially on the offensive end, and key time-outs called by my father to stem the tide of discouragement his players were feeling, as shot after shot rolled in and out or was just off the mark.

Remarkably, Yelm only led 25-24 at the half, though Darrington had shot so poorly from the field. Confidence in the Logger's locker room remained high during the halftime break. Each player knew their shooting percentage would improve in the second half and, as was their typical style, the Loggers would slowly pull away from the Tornados and ready themselves to play in the title game for the third time in four years the following night.

The Loggers came out in the second half with the look of champions, and they took a six-point lead midway into the third quarter. And though they had numerous chances to maintain or stretch that lead by making free-throws, Darrington was finding no better luck from the charity stripe, finishing the game connecting on only 17 of 32 attempts for a very poor 53%. And while confident they would see better shooting results in the second half, the Loggers continued having problems connecting from the field and finished the contest shooting a season-low 27%, making only 17 of 63 shots. Meanwhile, Yelm found the range from the field at a much higher clip, shot 23 of 31 from the line for 75% and came away with a stunning 55-51 upset win over the favored Loggers.

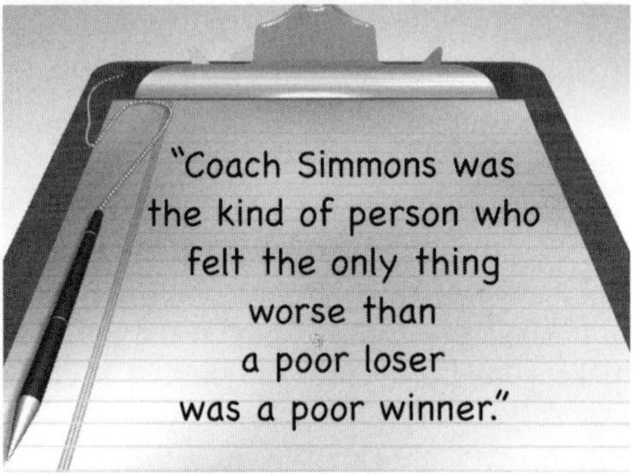

The loss was a big shock to the Darrington contingency and an even bigger disappointment. But my father displayed great class in the loss. He complimented the poise and play of Yelm and wouldn't allow his team to excuse the loss nor lose focus on their next task at hand, the following night's consolation game. Dave Andrews, a member of my father's 1957 and 1958 squads, recalls his coach's conviction about how to properly handle the outcome of any contest.

"Coach Simmons was the kind of person who felt the only thing worse than a poor loser was a poor winner," Andrews said. "He always taught us to be the best sports, win or lose."

Though my father had many more opportunities to prove he adhered to his own philosophy from winning games than losing them, Andrews remembers how much he learned from him during the Logger's remarkable run in the mid-fifties.

"In the fifties, teams didn't score much over 50 points a game," Andrews said. "But, at times, we could have easily scored 80 or more points. I remember Coach Simmons wouldn't let us run up the score on anyone. To keep the scores down, he would make each of us on the floor handle the ball at least twice before a shot could be taken. And if we had an opportunity to make a fast-break bucket, we had to slow it down and set up a play."

Those were the kind of lessons my father wanted his players to take with them beyond the basketball court and out into the real world where they would be facing much tougher situations for the rest of their lives. He firmly believed lessons such as "never rub it in" when you win and "take it on the chin" when you don't were of much greater significance to

The 1958 Darrington Loggers

Pictured from left to right: Cecil Parris, Gerald Howard, David Andrews, Ken Fox, Gordon Hyde, Randall Phillips, Roger Buchanan, John Peterson, David Edwards, Jerry Hayter, Terry Reece and Bill Bethard: Kneeling are Coach LaVerne Simmons and Manager Randall Reece

his players than any winning streak or state title.

In line with my father's style of leadership and the important life-lessons he taught his players, Darrington returned to form the following night in the third place consolation game, defeating a powerful Kalama squad, 56-42. David Edwards led the way with 15 points and Randall Phillips netted 11. But third place was two places below where the Loggers knew they should have been, and it would be the last time my father would reach the semifinal round during the remaining six years he coached there.

Despite the disappointing loss, Darrington was still solidly on the Washington map, and that important point was definitely a pleasant thought to carry for those who called the town home. From 1959 to 1964, my father took his teams to the state tournament two more times but failed to place either year. On the home front, however, he was in championship form, happily married and raising three children who many in Darrngton considered to be just like their own.

All in all, my father amassed an outstanding 208-69 record while leading the Loggers for 13 years. Against the wishes of many, he stood true to his conviction of "people first" and left Darrington in 1964 after feeling one of his good friends and fellow teachers was unfairly fired. And though my father left Darrington that year to the dismay of many, his legacy did not.

My father would coach at two other schools in the next four years before deciding to call it a career in 1968 at the age of 46, still with plenty of active years remaining on his life-clock to lead young men to success

My father surrounded by some of the trophies his teams garnered during his coaching days in Darrington

on the court and garner many more team and individual awards. But once again, I find this another reason why I consider my father a hero and why I'm proud to display his life as one worthy of imitation.

In the middle of the 1968 season, I was a young, fourth grade boy in love with the game of basketball and longing for the day *my* dad could coach *my* team to a state championship. But it never happened. And writing 37 years later about all the reasons why that dream never became a reality brings me great personal satisfaction and a deep level of respect and appreciation for my father.

Chapter Twelve

Life Beyond Basketball

The final four years of coaching high school basketball were quite challenging for my father. During his three-year stint in the town of Rochester, Washington, he experienced losses at a rate he never encountered in Darrington. However, in my limited elementary school recollection, as well as from memories my sister and mother recall, his overall countenance rarely changed during that time. Despite the felt disappointment from a school district that had envisioned immediate success from hiring a legendary coach, and disheartened with his own inability to lead the Warriors to better basketball results, my father established deep and lifetime friendships in Rochester and continued to love his family in championship form. While living in Rochester, challenges also arose with my brother Tom. Some of those difficulties came as a result of him coming to a deeper level of understanding about being adopted, and some with what were simply normal growing pains for a 12-year-old boy. All of these negative forces combined to bring discouragement to my father and he decided to make a change in his coaching career.

So, in the summer of 1967, our family moved to Toutle, Washington, a town deeply rooted in its basketball tradition. The Fighting Ducks of Toutle Lake High School had been to the state tournament a number of times since the early 1950s and finished third in the spring of 1967, aided by the likes of Joe Jones, Jerry Dimbat and Norm Kobberstad, a 6-11 post player many basketball experts believed would likely lead his team to a state title his senior year. And he did just that. Unfortunately, prior to the announcement of my father's hiring, Kobberstad's family moved to Lynden, Washington. And, indeed, Kobberstad did help to lead his new team, the Lynden Lions, to the Washington State 'A' title in the 1967-68 season.

Despite a huge void left in the middle due to Kobberstad's departure, and with a graduating class in 1967 that saw three other starters finish their high school careers, my father led the Fighting Ducks to within one victory of the state tournament, unable to hang on to a halftime lead against a powerful and state-ranked team from Boistfort and a subsequent loss the following week that kept them from qualifying. My father was disappointed in the losses and early end to the season, but excited about the prospects for bigger and better things on the hardwood floors at Toutle Lake in the coming years. But a decision was made later that year to release my father from his responsibilities as head basketball coach. He was surprised with the decision and incredibly disappointed, unsure as to the exact reasons why he was let go from his duties as head coach. Yet he never blamed any person or group of people for the dismissal. And he refused to become bitter about it, always moving away from the subject whenever it became a topic of conversation in the years ahead.

Not wanting to disrupt our family's life any more than it had already been the past four years, my father decided not to pursue another coaching position, but remain in Toutle to teach and raise his family. That following November would be the first November in 18 years that my father didn't bother bringing his whistle and clipboard to school for afternoon practices, and attending games that season was one of the hardest things he ever had to do in his life. Just three months later, in February of 1969, my brother was involved in a horrible motorcycle accident. His resulting injuries put him in a Portland hospital where he remained in a coma for the next three weeks, watched over moment-by-moment by my parents. The typical, fast-paced life my father had lived on the coaching stage was brought to an abrupt halt and his usual joyful spirit was severely dampened by tears and a tearing of his heart.

Tom died in March of 1969, and for my father it was the final episode in a five-year string of unforeseen disappointments. Thankfully, and consistent with the caring spirit found in most small towns, many incredible people in Toutle and nearby Silver Lake rallied around my parents during that difficult time, helping them and the rest of our family to better manage the sadness and subsequent chaos we were experiencing. But the following few months were difficult for my father, and depressing thoughts about his five-year stretch of discouraging situations were staring him down on a daily basis. He had moved from a town he loved deeply where he was a known hero. Then he endured a three-year coaching challenge at Rochester. After that came the unexpected release from his coaching duties at Toutle Lake after only one year, and a fairly decent one at that. And, finally, most devastating of all, came the loss of a son he treasured. But instead of running to a new school for a fairer shot at coaching success and righting his tarnished-of-late reputation, and instead of running to the bottle to drown his sorrows about a son he could no longer raise, my father ran like a hero. He ran to his family in need and spent huge chunks of time just being with us. He ran from coaching altogether, allowing himself more adequate time to be with his hurting family and ultimately allowing me the opportunity to compete in basketball without the pressure of being the coach's son. He ran to fill more humble roles at the school upon request, agreeing to help coach the junior high basketball team. He ran to Toutle Lake varsity basketball games, not to coach, but to take over the responsibilities of operating the game clock. He ran to the practice gym, not to coach me, but to teach me what he knew about the game of basketball. He stayed out of the way completely when I entered the high school ranks, allowing those I called Coach to call the shots in my basketball world. He took his ailing father into our home, a man in his late 70s riddled with Parkinson's disease and wearing a colostomy bag. Due to that illness, my father had to get out of bed two or three times in the middle of each night to help my grandfather deal with his deteriorating physical condition. I never heard him complain. My grandfather remained with us for a few years, and I'm incredibly grateful I had before me, at a very impressionable age, a great example of what it really means to be a servant and putting someone else's needs above your own. He later welcomed his mother-in-law Josephine into our home with open arms, where she remained for the next 16 years until she passed away in 1989. He came to almost every basketball and baseball game I participated in, both home and away, took me to numerous Portland Trailblazers' games to allow basketball to remain a big part of our relationship and put up with my infatuation with professional wrestling by watching the phoniness with me on Saturday nights without bursting my "but-it's-not-fake" bubble. He even was willing to sit at ringside with me on a few occasions when the wrestlers made their way to Longview, Washington, a 30-minute drive from where we lived. And he did many other heroic things to teach our family about what was really important in life and keep us from emotional catastrophe.

Looking back on those years, perhaps the biggest joy I realized with my father came in 1977 during my senior year of high school. Our basketball team had suffered through a disappointing and bitter end to a very promising season when we lost two straight games on two last-second shots by our opponents in district play, one of those coming at the hands of Cathlamet, a team that would go on to place fourth in the state tournament just two weeks later. But baseball would close out my high school athletic career, and my father shared that ending with me in glorious fashion.

Kevin Heimbigner, the head baseball coach at Toutle Lake, and assistant coach Mick Gorton, were very knowledgeable baseball men, and I learned a great deal under their leadership. During my senior year, they helped me tremendously in so many facets of the game and got the absolute most out of my abilities. But I can't begin to tell you how many times my father worked with me that season to hone my baseball skills. Whether it was spending an hour catching my curve balls and sliders in our back yard, pitching batting practice to me on the high school field on an off day or hitting me grounder after grounder to improve my shortstop skills, my father, you might say, was my baseball coach as well. Looking back on it now, those additional practice times were one last opportunity for the two of us to rise to championship form together. And in the spirit of the 1955 state-champion Loggers who were decided underdogs, our team, unknown and unranked, reached the state tournament and needed only three victories to be crowned best in Washington State 'B' Baseball.

Due to an earlier rainout, we played a Saturday, day-night doubleheader, winning both contests against heavily-favored opponents. The state championship game would take place the following Friday afternoon and, as usual, my dad would be there to watch me play. We took a commanding 10-2 lead into the top of the seventh inning and only needed to secure three outs before our opponents from Colton scored eight runs. They scored nine runs and took an 11-10 lead.

With a runner on first and two outs, and trailing by one run in our final at bat, I came to the plate. Two quick strikes put me in a hole, but my father's encouraging voice from the stands behind home plate was the ladder I needed to escape. He had been there in pressure situations, too, and he hadn't melted. Perhaps his winning spirit was transferred to me for the remainder of my at-bat because, after three consecutives balls brought the count to full, I hit a solid single up the middle to move the runner to third. A mental error by the opposing pitcher allowed us to score the tying run and advanced me to second base, 180 feet from a state championship. Lynn Higgins, our best hitter and next in the batting order, walloped a double off the left field wall, allowing me to score the winning run and giving us the state baseball crown.

The celebration was nothing short of euphoric. For the very first time, I knew the feeling that came from being a state champion. And for the first time, my father would enjoy those championship moments through one of his offspring, only now it was on the baseball field. The way I see it, though, he was just as happy with that win as he was with the two state championships he collected as head coach of the Darrington Loggers that would help to one day land him in the Washington State Basketball Coaches Hall of Fame. His excitement in regard to our baseball victory seems perfectly compatible with the heroic character myself and many others had seen him display on many occasions, both on and off the courts and playing fields. For whether he received a statewide coaching honor or faded away into obscurity, whether he was deified by an entire town or fired by a few people possessing the power to do so, whether he was running the game masterfully while on the bench or running the game clock methodically from behind the bench, my father gave his best to every cause he entered and heralded family and treating people right as his top priorities in the game of life.

My father retired from teaching in 1977 when I graduated from high school. He worked as a security guard for Weyerhauser the following 11 years and also as a substitute teacher for two school districts into his late 70s (brave soul!). He spent lots of time with family and friends, was involved in helping others out on a regular basis whatever the need, played golf for as long as his body would allow and watched a lot of ballgames from his living room easy chair as well as live in the stands, rooting on national heroes in the spotlight and local heroes-in-the-making. At age 60, and in response to biblical direction, he began attending church faithfully, was directly involved with many of the congregation's activities outside of their Sunday morning services and developed deep and lasting friendships with many of the men and women there. He cherished his three grandchildren, Tyler, Brad and Brittany, who affectionately called him Papa, treated his wife as royalty and considered his children as better than himself by far.

My mother and father, pictured here in 1986

And on the early morning of Oct. 31, 2002, I stared out the window of the hospital and wept as I anticipated one of my greatest heroes taking his final breath.

Chapter Thirteen

A Hero's Last Days

The phone-call I dreaded receiving finally came. It was 5:45 a.m. on a Friday morning and I answered the phone with great hesitancy. My sister had called a few days prior to that, informing me my father didn't seem to be improving from the pneumonia he had developed in his lungs a few weeks earlier. In the few moments before answering the call, I did my best to prepare myself for the worst, something I always do whenever the phone rings before 6 a.m. or after midnight.

My mother was on the other end and was sounding very concerned. She told me my father had been rushed to the hospital in the middle of the night and was listed in intensive care. After assuring her I would be there as soon as possible, I showered and secured the earliest flight from St. Louis to Portland. About two hours later, I was in the air, not knowing what the up-to-the-minute news would be four hours later when I finally touched down in Portland. Upon arriving at the Portland airport, I rented a car for the 45-minute drive to Longview and arrived about 1 p.m. at the hospital there.

I was overjoyed to discover my father was doing better than I had expected and that I could go in to his room and visit him immediately. Though he was still in intensive care, it was a whole lot better than visiting his body at the morgue, which had been my greatest fear during those seven hours since I spoke with my mother. I had so much wanted to be able to say goodbye to him and let him know how much he meant to me before he finally passed away. He deserved that much and I felt my own heart desperately needed it as well. Not only was I able to fulfill that desire, I was also blessed with overtime with my father, and I think I enjoyed that first bedside conversation with him perhaps more than any other conversation we had ever had. And somewhere in our 20-minute talk, the subject of Darrington basketball became a part of the discussion. Somehow our conversation just ended up there, as so many others had in the past. But that was a good place to be because it brought so much joy to my father's heart to bring those lasting memories of success and personal satisfaction to the surface. And to see him perk up and talk as though he were 50, hanging out at home, sitting back in his easy chair and talking with family and friends—that was about as perfect of a scenario as I could have imagined.

Though he seemed vibrant for an 80-year-old man in the ICU with lingering pneumonia, inside his body lie serious health problems—the most dangerous being heart failure that was contributing to a number of other worsening conditions. My father needed heart surgery to correct the problem, but he needed to regain some strength before doctors could be confident he would survive the dangerous four-hour ordeal. My father wanted the surgery because doctors told him his quality of life would quickly decline without it. And my father wanted nothing to do with that! He had always loved life and lived it to the full, and he definitely wanted nothing to do with those he loved needing to wait on him hand and foot for who knows how long until his final hour.

Initially, the medical staff seemed confident an opportunity for the surgery would become available within a few days, giving all of us who couldn't imagine life without him a lot of hope. For the next two days, my father's condition remained about the same, giving him and I numerous chances to chat. I enjoyed every minute. He could only talk for about 15 minutes at a time before tiring, but an hour later we would be back at it talking shop—Roland Mount's improbable game-winning basket to clinch his first title, and many more of his thoughts about that Cinderella-story in 1955; the 1957 championship and Darrington's march through the winner's bracket with ease; and how his most-talented Logger team ended up on the losing end in 1958. As my father discussed the disappointment of 1958, it seemed as though he was back in Spokane, answering reporters' questions in the loser's locker room just minutes after the loss. Scrunched facial features, a redder face than normal and a slightly elevated tone while recounting his team's shooting woes in the semi-final game seemed to indicate he was gaining energy by traveling back 44 years to that very night.

My father shared as many stories as his energy would allow. I asked a lot of questions I had never asked before, but it still doesn't seem like I asked near enough. My father would fall in and out of sleep on a regular basis, and I needed to be sensitive to other family members and friends wanting to visit him. I would have stayed there every moment of every day with a tape recorder running if I had thought about it then. Knowing what I know now, I would have gone through every year, from 1951-1964, and gotten a dribble-by-dribble, pass-by-pass, shot-by-shot account of his memories coaching the Darrington Loggers.

By Sunday morning, my father's condition had worsened. He was falling in and out of sleep much more regularly and doctors indicated they had discovered signs some of his other vital organs were shutting down. No official length of time was given as to his likely remaining days and, when pressed, the answer was anywhere from two days to two months. And while we were all hoping for the latter amount, I think we knew the clock was running out and my father was too far behind to mount a comeback.

On Monday, I found a 10-minute window of time to talk with him again. I kept asking myself what kind of things I should say to my father. What last thoughts could I communicate to make his final days on earth as pleasant as possible? His breathing was slow and heavy, his skin was pale and his lips were severely cracked. What could bring a smile to his face or a little life to his dying limbs? So I moved our short discussion toward a topic I thought had a good chance of making any or all of that happen—Darrington basketball. We talked once again about his amazing 1955 team and how such an unlikely victory occured. I urged him to view his illness like it was the fourth quarter of that championship game, his Loggers were down by four points and he just had to find a way to win. He smiled briefly and for the next few hours his condition seemed to improve, almost as though our talk that morning was a 1955 repeat performance and he was doing his best to rise to the occasion and claim a title.

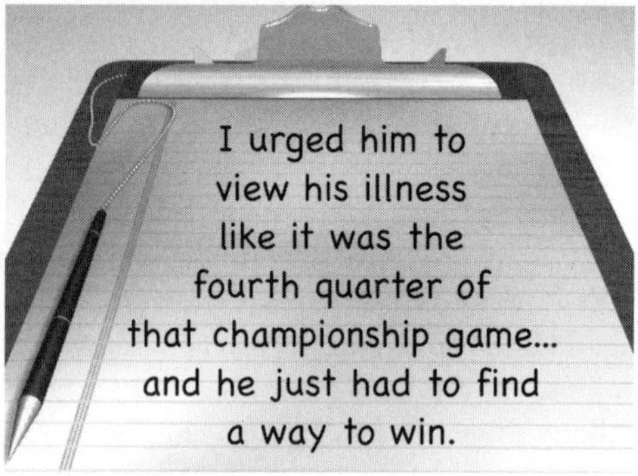

If Monday's small revival in my father's ailing body could be likened to 1955, his condition on Tuesday was similar to his team's performance in 1956—a disappointing decline in positive results. Little or no response was coming from my father whenever we tried to talk to him. He slept through most of the day, almost as though 1956 was being replayed in his body—a title team from the previous season that failed to qualify for the state tournament the following year.

Wednesday morning came and I was ecstatic my father was still alive. Perhaps I should have been hoping for him to fade away into the night, eliminating the possibility of more pain in his life. But when it's your father and you love him deeply, and when his very existence means so much to you, you don't really want him to ever go—especially if there's a chance for a comeback, or at least a few more days of eye contact, or even just some squeezes of the hand or nods of the head.

I slept in his hospital room that night to give my mom a chance to get a good night's sleep at her home just a few blocks away. Throughout the night, my father's health was rapidly declining. His eyes were staying open only occasionally and he gave me slight nods of approval every now and then. I reassured him of my love and appreciation for all he had meant to me and told him I would always love him and remember his heroic role in my life. During the few times he seemed to be slightly awake and somewhat alert, I would talk about Darrington basketball, wiping his brow with a cold washcloth to bring him some slight physical relief and holding his hand to offer some emotional security. The doctors were telling us he could die at any time, but looking back on the events of that day, I see Wednesday as 1957 for my father—one more day and one last championship performance.

Thursday morning came and my mother, my sister and I were there to show our support for the man who so many times had held our family together and made us proud to wear the name Simmons. And at 2: 55 p.m., my father took his last breath. I'm sure he did all he could to stay alive for his family, much like his efforts in 1958 in the state semi-finals. But similar to that contest, my father came up short—it just wasn't meant to be. But as Darrington residents cling to memories of 1955 and 1957 when they discuss the LaVerne Simmons' era, I, too, think only of his victorious life, knowing full well all good things come to an end.

It has been more than three years since my father's death and I would do anything to have one more talk or one more best-of-five cribbage competition with my hero and friend. And if that were possible, I'm sure somewhere in our conversation or during the course of those games, we would discuss the poise and precision shooting of David Edwards, the smooth, inside play of Gary Sweeney, the improbable state title in 1955, his second title run in 1957, defensive strategies, game-winning shots and anything else that lived in his heart regarding Darrington basketball.

Chapter Fourteen

Eulogies

My mother asked me to officiate at the funeral service for my father planned for the following Monday afternoon. I would speak, along with the minister of my parent's church, the one they had attended together the past 20 years. (I can't help but think there's some irony in being asked to officiate at my father's funeral. I guess basketball was destined to remain a part of our relationship even after he passed, and I'm sure he would say I was his favorite "official" of all time.) I was honored to do it for sure, but how does someone so close to the deceased prepare for something like that? What a frightening challenge, but thank God it wasn't because there was little or nothing to say. Oh, there was plenty to say and I was proud to deliver some impressive inside information that afternoon. I brought my father's heroic deeds to the audience, sharing about the great example he had set for me on so many fronts, one that gave me a much clearer picture of the true nature of God and a much clearer understanding of the truly important matters in life. I proudly shared some additional information passed on to me from my wife, my mother, my sister, my brother-in-law, my two children and my nephew, as I read each of their sentiments about what he had meant to them.

Near the end of the memorial service, a few men who knew my father well spent some time expressing their appreciation for his involvement in their lives. One of the first to share was a man by the name of Rob Hippi. Rob's father, Ted Hippi, is another well-known name in the coaching ranks in Washington. Ted Hippi is a member of the Washington State Football Coaches Hall of Fame and his Toledo Indians still hold the state record for most consecutive victories by any team with an astounding 48 straight. Beginning his small-town coaching career in 1949, Hippi garnered an amazing 237-36-2 record before retiring in 1975. Though his and my father's paths didn't cross that often during their coaching days, they ended up being next-door neighbors in a small apartment complex in Longview during the latter stage of Hippi's life. During that time, he and my father developed a tremendous friendship and, as a result, Rob was able to spend time getting to know my father as well. Rob, an outstanding high school and collegiate athlete, and later a pitcher with the New York

Yankee's minor league affiliate in North Carolina, shared about his first encounter with Darrington basketball and a coach by the name of LaVerne Simmons.

"The first state tournament game I ever saw was when I was eight years old," he said. "Darrington was playing Valley in the 1957 state championship game and ended up winning by 14 points. But I got in big trouble from my dad because I was chiming in with all the people from Valley who were booing Darrington. I wanted Valley to win because they were in our district, but my dad wasn't very happy with me and he taught me a huge lesson on sportsmanship that night."

Good sportsmanship was just one of the many positive character qualities Hippi said he learned from his father. And from his many interactions and conversations with my father the last eight years of his life, Hippi said it was quite interesting how the two men, fellow Hall of Fame coaches blessed with so much success in their years on the sidelines, shared so many similar qualities—"They both had a high moral character, they lived by the Golden Rule, they knew the value of hard work and discipline, they never met a stranger and they were incredibly modest in their success."

Like so many of the players' comments concerning how relatable and approachable my father was during his days in Darrington, Hippi also expressed to the memorial crowd just how important my father had been to him after his own father's death in 1995.

"When my dad passed away, Vern took his place for the guy I could talk to," Hippi said. "He was always someone I knew I could get support from as well as getting some good, solid advice. I thoroughly enjoyed coming over to his apartment and just talking about anything."

Though he recently retired from teaching and coaching at the high school level, Hippi is still quite active in the world of sports, following in the footsteps of his father and mine. He's currently helping to shape the athletic ability and overall character of talented young athletes in the Pacific Northwest, working as pitching coach for the highly-respected junior college baseball program at Lower Columbia College in Longview.

After Hippi concluded his remarks, David Edwards stepped forward and addressed the audience. Edwards isn't a household name in most places, but in Darrington, Edwards is known to all. Edwards, now 65 and himself retired from teaching and a successful coaching career at LaConner and Mount Vernon, was there to express his fondest memories of the man he called Coach for four years playing varsity basketball in Darrington from 1955-1958. Most people in Darrington who know anything about Logger's basketball would say Edwards was the best to ever play for my father, and they wouldn't get much of an argument from many others. Even my father, as he answered my question on a few occasions as to who the best player was to ever don a Logger's uniform under his leadership, agreed as well. As a freshman, Edwards played sparingly on the 1955 championship team, then made his biggest impact as an All-State selection in 1957 and 1958, leading the Loggers to their second title in 1957 and a third place finish in 1958. Edwards was also a standout football and baseball player at Darrington, and went on to become a three-sport letterman at the collegiate level.

With tears flowing, and with regular pauses to gather his thoughts and emotions, Edwards shared how much my father had meant to him, not only in his high school years, but also the next 44 years of his life as the two continued a friendship upon his graduation in 1958. (During an incredibly hectic time for Edwards while preparing his LaConner team for state tournament play in 1969, he took time out of his busy schedule to attend my brother's funeral, saying he felt he definitely wanted to be there to support my father in light of all he had done for him through the years.) Calling my father a great coach, as knowledgeable and capable as Marv Harshman and Lenny Wilkens (Harshman was best known for his revival of Husky basketball while coaching for 14 years at the University of Washington and one of Washington state's all-time greatest coaches; Wilkens was a tremendous professional basketball player, began his coaching career in Seattle and currently has the most career wins of any coach in the history of the NBA), Edward's emphasized my father was a much better person than he ever was a coach and how so many of his players, had they been able to attend his funeral, would have said the exact same thing. Here was a man, 62 years of age at the time, and still caught up in the admiration of his high school coach. I never knew my father was that special! I never knew his hero status was so solidly cemented in his player's minds and that it hadn't softened since his departure from Darrington some 38 years earlier.

Sure, my father was one of my heroes, but now I saw just how much I had to share that sentiment with so many others. But what a privilege—the more who claimed my father was one of their heroes, and the more they explained all the reasons why, the more I realized just how lucky I was to have been raised by such a giant of a man.

During the few hours following the funeral, people one by one came to console me and other members of my immediate family, letting us know just how much they appreciated my father. With each compliment I heard, I couldn't help but think how fortunate I was to be who I was, but also how little I knew about how my father had made such a positive impact on so many people. I left the funeral and fellowship time afterward thoroughly exhausted. But deep within me I was energized by the recollection of good deeds my father had delivered to so many people, and greatly determined to be more of an inspiration and hero figure to others.

I went to bed in my mother's apartment later that night, sadder than at any other time in my entire life. Yet I had never been more grateful and content with God's gift of allowing me to occupy a front-row seat to view my father's example for 43 years. And I had never been more determined to find out as much as I could about Darrington basketball and my father's influence on one small town in America.

It was about three weeks later when my mother gave me a huge packet of information containing copies of letters from former players and coaches, all of them written to a committee of men in 1990 in regard to why they believed my father was a worthy candidate for entrance into the Washington State Basketball Coaches Hall of Fame. One of those letters was written by Dan Bates, a member of the Logger's 1957 championship team and the man who took over coaching duties in Darrington when my father left in 1964. In the letter, Bates summarized what so many others felt about my father's accomplishments, both on and off the court:

> To Whom It May Concern:
>
> I am honored to write a letter of recommendation for Vern Simmons to be added to the Washington State Coaches Hall of Fame.
>
> Vern Simmons was my basketball coach at Darrington High School. He was also my math teacher. He served as a model for me and had a direct influence on my decision to enter education and coaching. He was an example of what was good: Demanded your best effort and gave praise when it was appropriate; understood young people; was able to motivate students in the classroom and on the court.
>
> Winning state basketball championships in 1955 and 1957, plus placing several other times are examples of accomplishments for the public; the real accomplishments were the values Coach Simmons taught and stood for behind the scenes, in the classroom, on the practice floor and in every-day life.
>
> Vern Simmons deserves every consideration for the Hall of Fame.
>
> Sincerely,
> Dan Bates

In addition to the expressions of gratitude coming from Bates and so many other men who knew my father during his days of coaching, I would also come to realize even those who weren't there to experience the thrilling 1950s of championship basketball in Darrington were a part of the hero-recognition team. And Jeff Bryson would be one of its greatest spokesman and the man who would do his best to keep my father's name and legacy alive.

Chapter Fifteen

Tradition and Tennis Shoes

It had been 45 years since a Darrington basketball team had hoisted a championship trophy at center court. Would this be year number 46? While confident their Loggers could make a run at the title, most people in Darrington remained somewhat cautious concerning their chances of returning to basketball supremacy. But a hero and holder of traditional values roamed the sidelines for Darrington basketball, and his opinion would count the most. His plans and passion would best determine the odds of a Logger championship. And his faith in his players and belief in their chances of winning it all would go the farthest in bringing about an event not witnessed in the state of Washington in nearly five decades.

November 7, 2002—that was the first day Coach Jeff Bryson could display his level of faith and belief in his team, and it would be the first step in leading the Loggers, now 45 years in championship-basketball bondage, to the Promise Land—a state title in Spokane in March of 2003. November 7th was the first day of practice for Bryson's squad and the official opening of the basketball season. Less than one week later, Bryson ended a very normal practice in a much different way than all the other practices he had conducted in his 12 previous seasons as Logger's head coach. Beyond that, it was a practice session that ended unlike any other in the previous 47 years since basketball success elevated the town of Darrington to celebrity status in 1955. Bryson called his tired and sore players to center court for a wrap-up before dismissing them for showers. Though they were all completely worn out from a demanding pre-season practice, Bryson asked for their attention, then nodded at senior co-captain Jared Grimmer.

Grimmer was one of Bryson's seven returning lettermen from a 2001-2002 team that had qualified for the state tournament. The Loggers won their first game of the tournament that year by a narrow margin, but were eliminated from championship contention in the quarterfinal contest, losing 57-47 to eventual champion, Sunnyside Christian. The Loggers bounced back from the disappointing loss with victories in their final two contests, finishing fourth. Most of Bryson's current players were the same young men he had set his sights on coaching ever since his reign with the Loggers began in 1991, and they were just six years old. In Darrington, basketball scouting begins at an early age and everybody in town gets plenty of chances to see the youngsters in action, from kindergarten all the way through their senior year. Bryson had seen something special in those young boys while they competed in junior leagues, and they often won the championship of the league in which they played. That was the typical storyline for these young men, with the exception of their eighth grade squad that finished a disappointing fourth in their division. (Bryson seized an opportunity later that year at the state tournament, calling those talented eighth-graders together and telling them, very bluntly, he thought they were overrated, hoping to light a fire in them before they entered the high school ranks.) With very few exceptions, each of the teams those boys played on consistently defeated their competition. Now they were seniors, and Bryson knew their basketball abilities and aspirations better than anybody else. Bryson's thoughts were simple and filled with hope: "If any team in my 13 years of coaching has had a chance to go all the way, this team is it."

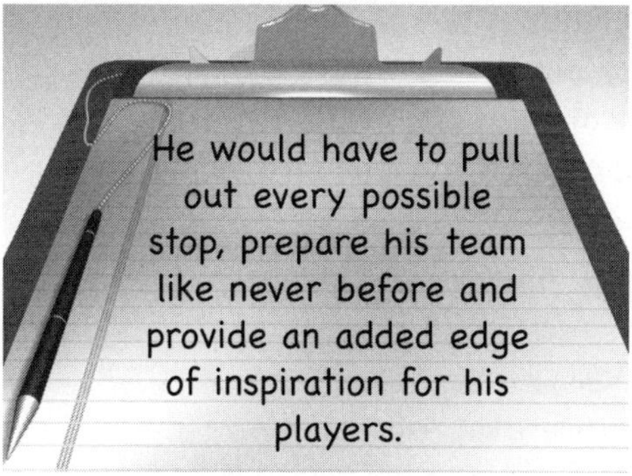

But other Darrington coaches had been saying similar things about their teams for the past 45 years, and all to no avail. So Bryson was confident, but not overly so. He would have to pull out every possible stop, prepare his team like never before and provide an added edge of inspiration for his players that hadn't been available up to that point in time if he were going to take his team to the top of the 'B' basketball world in Washington. With 124 teams vying for the championship, and knowing approximately 100 of the schools competing in that division had never walked away with even a single title in the history of the tournament, Bryson knew there was much work to be done and much good fortune to be had if his Loggers were to claim the crown.

Just a few days after Darrington's first official practice, Bryson received a message from one of his fellow-teachers that my father had died, and news of his death brought him tremendous sadness. Bryson greatly admired my father. He had met him a few times and felt honored to have had those opportunities. He had heard so many "Simmons-stories" over the years and each one caused his mind to stir with thoughts of winning and bringing a championship back to Darrington. Even some of Bryson's successful basketball strategies were copied from what my father had employed in the Logger's amazing run of success from 1955-1958. He knew he was following in my father's footsteps, although two other coaches had preceded him in the 26 years after his departure from Darrington. Many coaches had been compared to my father and what he was able to accomplish, but especially so in Darrington. Not that my father would have wanted it that way, but it was just an inescapable reality and the added pressure coming from following a legendary figure.

But Bryson embraced the pressure. He firmly believed in honoring tradition and wisely concluded if something had worked once, it more than likely should work again. So he imitated my father and drew inspiration from whatever he could find in his life and coaching style. Though my father was dead, Bryson knew heroes and legends never die—their physical presence departs, but their spirit remains. So he decided upon a simple plan to honor my father. He was determined to keep his memory and winning ways alive, firmly embedded in the hearts of the twelve young men now playing for him.

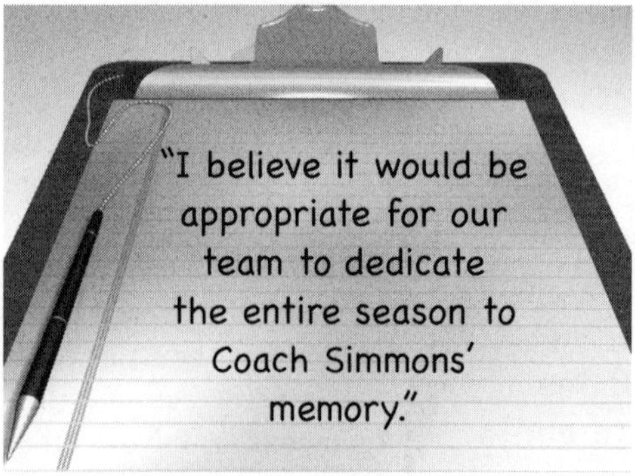

"I'm sure most of you have heard by now," Bryson began, "but, if not, one of Darrington's heroes died last week. LaVerne Simmons was an amazing coach, and he's still the only coach to ever bring home a title for Darrington basketball."

Bryson proceeded to read my father's obituary then addressed his players.

"I believe it would be appropriate for our team to dedicate the entire season to Coach Simmons' memory," Bryson said. "I've talked with Jared and he feels great about the idea. I'm going to let him tell you of the plan."

Grimmer addressed his teammates. "Guys, what we would like to do is keep Coach Simmons' name and memory alive all season long."

Bryson handed his co-captain a green felt marker from his pocket. "What we're going to do," Grimmer said, "is write Coach Simmons' initials on our tennis shoes and use them as a reminder of what this season is all about."

After Grimmer had finished sharing his thoughts about the plan, each player, one by one, passed around the permanent marker, pausing to write the initials 'L' and 'S' on their tennis shoes. What would be the end-result of Bryson's and his team's actions? Their promotion of tradition and their heart to honor a past hero were now in visible form. Were these some of the missing ingredients in the long-lost recipe of basketball success for the Darrington Loggers? Was this the beginning of some divine intervention on behalf of Darrington and, if so, would it be enough to help them return to championship form?

The 2003 Darrington Loggers

Back row, left to right: Assitant Coach Les Hagen, Head Coach Jeff Bryson, Jason Ashe, Sean O'Connell, Bryce Boyd, Ryan Frable, Evan Smith and Assistant Coach Ric Cook; Seated: Matt Koch, Kris Reece, Billy McMillen, Jared Grimmer, Matt Reece, Lance Chambers and Jake Wicken; On the floor: Managers Greg Rosselli, Travis LeMance and Garrett Gladsjo

Chapter Sixteen

Local Boy Comes Home

For the first 18 years of his life, Darrington was home to Jeff Bryson. His grandparents were some of the earliest settlers in the community, arriving there in 1935 from North Carolina with a number of others from the South, seeking greater employment opportunities and relief from the difficult and impoverished lifestyle they faced in the East Appalachians. Bryson's father, Bill, also grew up in Darrington, and later met his wife, Bettie, while working in Alaska. The two married in the summer of 1948 then returned to Darrington in 1949 where they raised six children, four girls and two boys. Bryson was born in December of 1964, just a few months after my father made the decision to end his teaching and coaching tenure at the high school there. As the youngest of six children, Bryson enjoyed his small-town upbringing and, like all the other young boys living there, was very familiar with logging and Darrington basketball.

Bryson played his first official game of basketball in the seventh grade, but it was an unscheduled event a year earlier that brought the love of the game into his heart.

"Actually, growing up, for some reason basketball was my least favorite sport," Bryson said. "I didn't think I was all that good. But then I just happened to get asked to play in a pick-up game at the school with some of the older kids. I made a couple of shots over the varsity center and I guess I impressed the others."

In awe of his basketball prowess, other participants in the game that day asked Bryson his age and were astonished to learn of his pre-junior high status.

"I guess I started to realize I was a pretty good player," Bryson said. "And basketball became my favorite sport."

Bryson's talent and love for the game increased during his days in junior high. Entering high school in 1979, Bryson's goal as a freshman was simply to start on the junior varsity team. Instead, Bryson landed a position on the varsity squad and started in a number of the games. In one contest near the end of the year, Bryson hit a game-winning shot and was carried off the court by all of his teammates. He was now on his way to becoming a Darrington celebrity and his remarkable freshman showing on the court brought the town renewed hopes for things to come in his final three years.

Bryson helped his team reach the state tournament his junior year and, in his senior year, led the Loggers to the semi-final round before they lost their last two games to finish sixth. In the quarterfinal contest, Bryson scored 32 points for Darrington, shooting 15 of 19 from the field, still a school record. He earned All-League honors in basketball from 1981-1983, and was the Logger's starting shortstop on their 1981 state championship baseball team.

Bryson possessed plenty of basketball skills but, due to his size of just over six feet and having played at a small school, he knew his chances of playing college ball somewhere were limited. Bryson decided to attend Western Washington University (WWU) in Bellingham, Washington, located about 90 minutes northwest of Darrington near the Canadian border. He tried out for the basketball team and made the top 15, but received very little playing time.

"It was tough," Bryson said. "I practiced real hard every day, but I just wasn't good enough to find any playing time. But I think that experience helped me because now I can relate to the kids who have to sit at the end of my bench."

After his first year at WWU, Bryson transferred to Skagit Community College in nearby Mount Vernon, where he played for one year as a reserve, the fourth guard, he said, in a three-guard offense. Near the end of that season, Bryson met his future wife, Tracy, and decided not to return to the team the following year. But Bryson's love for the game remained evident and he played for a few years in a highly-competitive city league after his time at Skagit. And while he knew his playing days were officially over, the basketball fires were still burning in his heart. Bryson returned to WWU in 1988 where he completed his degree in secondary education, hoping an opportunity would arise in the near future to coach basketball at the high school level.

Bryson had his heart set on coaching, but he also knew he had huge amounts to learn about the game he loved. He applied for a position at the Lakewood School District, a larger school district than Darrington located about an hour west of there, where he would teach junior high, coach seventh grade boy's basketball and, in the spring, coach baseball at the high school level. Bryson was excited about the possibility. He would learn the ropes of teaching and coaching, then hopefully land a position as a varsity basketball coach within a few years. Shortly after he sent in his application to Lakewood, Bryson was invited to interview for the position and was thrilled with the chance of getting his career started.

Meanwhile, back in Darrington, an enormous void was being felt. Tim Cousins, a former standout player at Seattle University and teammate there of NBA legend Elgin Baylor, had been the Logger's head coach for the previous 19 years. He had decided to end his tenure as varsity coach, and Darrington was in need of a man who could uphold their strong basketball tradition, someone who could revive a program that had, over time, fallen from its lofty position of state powerhouse.

"I got a call from the elementary principal in Darrington the same day I was to interview at Lakewood," Bryson remembers. "He said he wanted me to come and interview. There was an opening for a sixth grade teacher and the head basketball coach at the high school."

Staying consistent with his humble demeanor, Bryson declined the interview.

"There was no way I was ready to be a head coach at that time," Bryson remarked. "I thought Darrington had too good of a basketball tradition for someone green to walk in there and take the job."

Bryson's initial thoughts of declining the offer were bolstered by the state of Darrington basketball at the time.

"The talent pool had greatly diminished and the excitement in town about winning basketball had slipped a lot," Bryson said. "I felt the job needed to go to someone who could turn the team around right away."

Bryson accepted the position at Lakewood, but one year later the offer from Darrington was back on the table. And this time, he said, he couldn't resist the urge and accepted the challenge.

"I really thought I was done there," Bryson said about the idea of coming back to his hometown. "But I'm so glad I came back."

Bryson absolutely loves being back in the small town—"So much so," he said, "that if I stopped coaching basketball, I would still stay in Darrington and teach."

In his first year of coaching at the varsity level, Bryson was thrust into a situation that could only be described as challenging. He had one returning senior from a team that finished 5-15 the year before, and he was a reserve. But Bryson chose to look at the entire situation in a positive vain, seeing the set-up as an advantage to him.

"There really were low expectations from the administration and the community," Bryson said. "I felt I could grow with the team."

Though Bryson felt some relief from the basketball bar being set so low for him and his team, he had his own set of standards and was looking to accomplish one thing—bring back Logger Ball.

"I read everything I could get my hands on," Bryson said, referring to his thirst for basketball knowledge that led to many late nights and early mornings in his office, mulling over pages of material written by some of the greatest coaches of all time.

Between studying a book written by legendary UCLA coach John Wooden, called *Coaching Basketball*, (his favorite of the dozens of books he was able to get his hands on), and attending as many coaching clinics as possible, Bryson immersed himself in learning the secrets of successful coaching. He had been successful as a player, but this was an entirely different game. Along with that, he felt the pressure of following in a short line of coaches who, for the most part, had been successful in keeping Darrington pride at fairly high levels. Bryson was following Cousins, who had coached the Loggers from 1972-1991. Before Cousins, Dan Bates led Darrington from 1965-1971. And the biggest name of all he knew he would be compared to was my father, the coach of the Loggers from 1951-1964. Up to that point in time, my father was still the only one in the town's history who could boast of being a championship basketball coach.

Bryson would be tested immediately with his dedication to the Darrington basketball program and what it was going to take to bring back a winning tradition to the school and community.

"We started out the season my first year going 1-13," Bryson said. "I immediately started to think—would people be patient with me?"

Bryson did his best to put those concerns of job security behind him and do what he could to focus on the positives. But there weren't many.

"During that first year, we would be so outmatched," he remembered. "But we made it our goal that first year in some games to lose by less than 30 points. It was just a way of trying to keep the kids focused."

The positive focus seemed to spark the outmanned Loggers in the latter part of the season. Bryson's squad went from 1-13 to finish at 5-14, winning four of their last five games in league play to qualify for district competition.

It was merely a baby step according to Bryson, but a step nevertheless. Year two for Bryson at the helm looked promising. With experience under his belt, a renewed attitude and commitment to excellence from his players and a town re-energized with the possibility of a trip to the state tournament in Spokane, Bryson laid out one goal for his team—going to state. He would return his entire starting five and his team would finish with a much-improved 15-10 mark, missing out on an opportunity to go to the state tournament when a last second-shot was put in to defeat them during district play.

"I thought my life was over," Bryson said of his feeling after the loss. "I think that was the most bummed out I've been in my entire life."

While Bryson may have been reeling from the loss, the school's administration and townspeople couldn't have been happier. The stands were being filled once again for home games, young boys in town were eager to enter the high school ranks and play for the Loggers and Bryson was now calling the shots—a coach committed to winning and a local boy who knew all about the great tradition of Darrington basketball.

In Bryson's third year of coaching, the Loggers placed eighth in the state. But just as things were looking up for Darrington, Bryson's 1995 team suffered through a 3-17 season. Once again, Bryson decided to focus on the positive. He remained strong in his commitment to hard work and stayed humble in regard to learning from others and from his own mistakes. He wasn't about to give in to believing he had made a big mistake by returning to coach at his high school alma mater.

The Loggers bounced back strong the following year, finishing second in their league and falling just one victory shy of reaching the state tournament. Then, in 1997, the Loggers, according to Bryson, came out of nowhere to finish third in the state. But it was a loss in the semi-final game that sent Bryson to another low level of discouragement.

"About 17 things had to happen in two minutes for us to lose that game, and they all did," Bryson said, remembering the painful loss to eventual champion, Republic. "But it brought our program to a new level."

That new level was one of Bryson's main objectives when he accepted the position in 1991. Darrington basketball was officially back, but still looking for their first title since 1957. But from that point on, the Loggers were a power to be reckoned with, qualifying for the state tournament each of the next four years. From 1997 to 2002, the Loggers failed to reach state tournament play only once, in 2001, and they placed somewhere in the top eight each of those years. In 2002, Bryson had one of his strongest teams to date, a talented squad picked by many to make a run at the state title. And they did just that before losing a quarterfinal contest to Sunnyside Christian.

But the following year was the one Bryson had been aiming for since his return. Those talented and focused first-graders, who everyone in town had been talking about for years, were now seniors, and Bryson knew he also had been in strict training for 11 long years for a shot at the title. So he set his sights on doing what hadn't been done in 46 years in the town of Darrington—winning a state championship.

To aid him in that effort, Bryson relied heavily upon his two assistant coaches. Ric Cook, who also teaches math at the high school, has been an assistant for Bryson since 1995. Cook was born in Bremerton, Washington, and graduated from college at Northwest Nazarene College in Nampa, Idaho. He began his coaching career at Bellingham High School in 1994 before moving to become the Logger's assistant a year later. Les

Hagen has been a volunteer assistant coach for the Loggers for 22 years while also working as a minister for one of the town's churches. Hagen is a native of Washington, graduating from Marysville High School, and he received his college degree from Northwest University in Kirkland. Hagen began volunteering with the Loggers in 1982, which was also Bryson's junior year. Bryson said Hagen was an integral part of his team's success, as he would volunteer to take many of the kids to basketball camp in Spokane during the summer months. These three men used their combined wisdom and experience to plot strategies for success, doing what they could to put their team on the path to Spokane and an appointment at center court to receive the victor's crown.

While Bryson is quick to give tons of credit to his assistant coaches for his success, nobody deserves more credit, he says, than his wife Tracy.

"She mostly just keeps me calm and incredibly positive about everything," Bryson said. "She's great about helping me find perspective and to remember what's really important."

Though Bryson is eager to share the credit for his success, his wife is just as eager to point out the strengths in her husband she believes have greatly contributed to his winning ways.

"Truly, Jeff leads by example," she said. "Jeff's strength as a coach and as a leader is his relationship with each one of his players. He takes an interest in them as individuals and as players, and he does whatever is needed to take care of them."

But perhaps the greatest compliment Tracy could pay to her husband's coaching style is heard in her words about what each player has meant to him.

"I feel like he treats them like they were his sons," she said.

Proving those sentiments are indeed accurate, Bryson stays in contact with many of his former players and loves spending time with them long after their high school days are done. No doubt many of those young men have felt the father-son bond while under his leadership, and many of them stay in contact with Bryson on a regular basis as well.

The Brysons have been married 16 years and have three boys—Marcus, who is 12, Kaleb, 10, and Drew, seven. Nothing brings more enjoyment to the busy coach, he says, than simply being with his family and spending as much time as possible with them. Knowing he misses a great deal of time just being with his family during a typical season, Bryson limits his outside-the-home activities, saying he looks for whatever needs to be done around the house to fill up his free time, any excuse to stay home with the family he adores.

The Bryson family currently live in Arlington, a town of about 11,000 people located 30 miles west of Darrington, but just outside the Darrington School District's official zoning parameters. In light of those strict boundaries, Bryson said he anticipates a move to the small town in the next few years.

"I want my boys to play for the Loggers," he said. "They totally look up to the players and I would also love for my boys to play ball for me."

If Bryson's sons get that chance, like all the other players under his direction the past 15 years, they will discover a humble and hard working coach with a big heart to help others, three heroic qualities that often translate into wins for Darrington basketball. And while Bryson freely acknowledges he has his share of weaknesses as a man and a mentor of young men, it is my belief his overall character is one any town, big or small, would be fortunate to find in anyone designated to teach and train the next generation.

Chapter Seventeen

Introducing: The Loggers

For more than 70 years, teenage boys playing varsity basketball for Darrington High School have been some of the most popular residents in town. "Great game," "good luck" and "go get 'em Friday night" are three phrases the easily-recognized athletes hear from townspeople wherever they go. Players through the years have admitted receiving an occasional free haircut or hamburger in town, bestowed upon them by local business owners as a simple way of saying thanks for how they hustled on the court the previous night. Many of the entrepreneurs there feel justified engaging in that type of generosity, saying business is usually a bit better during a winning season.

Since 1935, approximately 500 young men have enjoyed this kind of privilege and popularity, having the honor of playing varsity basketball for the Loggers and doing everything within their power to lead Darrington to a winning season and a shot at a state championship to close the season. Many players from decades past remain popular years later and are treated with great honor whenever they return as spectators. And most of the boys in elementary school will tell you they can't wait to get their chance to enjoy the benefits of that local stardom one day, hoping to make the high school team and contribute another page in the book of Logger lore.

Beginning in 1991, seven of those boys were being touted by basketball know-it-alls as a group of kids who could finally have a legitimate shot at securing a championship. They showed early signs of a team that could one day lead the Loggers to a title and, once and for all, bring an end to the painful conversations about a championship drought. For eleven years, these seven boys had played the game of basketball together, and for eleven years, with very few exceptions, they had been winners against all levels of competition. As juniors, they finished fourth in the state. Now, as seniors, the championship stage was set. With the addition of one very talented junior athlete who played with the seniors since the fifth grade due to his advanced court skills, the Loggers seemed on the brink of their best basketball results in 46 years.

Before sharing some of the specifics on those eight players and four of their younger teammates, I need to mention an individual many

Darrington residents would say played a huge role in developing the skills of these players, the man who coached them from the time they were in first grade until they entered high school and were under the direct influence of Bryson. Kevin Ashe, a former standout player for the Loggers who graduated from Darrington in 1971, accepted the challenge of taking this talented group of youngsters and molding them into a championship-caliber team. Ashe, along with the tremendous help and support of his older brother Randy, coached this group of players (including his son Jason) for eight consecutive years. He's a firm believer that establishing a successful high school basketball program doesn't just happen, but instilling a commitment to excellence in children at an early age is key in bringing about future success. As an example of his dedication to this principle, Ashe gave the following charge to his fifth grade team during one of their mid-season practices.

"Tonight, at this very moment," Ashe told them, "a hundred other teams are practicing. But we want to be the hardest working fifth grade class in the entire state."

Along with instilling a hard-work ethic into his players, Ashe also gave the boys a vision and specific goal of winning a state title once they finally entered high school. Ashe remained committed to his goal each year, knowing the talent those kids possessed was more than enough to put them in the upper echelons of competition in their division of play, but not enough to ensure a title. And to help keep his team focused on what would hopefully be achieved at some point in their high school careers, Ashe decided to keep "Loggers" as the name for his team each and every year.

Ashe also realized, if these players were to have any real shot at a state championship someday, he would need to get them playing against the toughest competition in the state. So he entered his Darrington squads in tournaments where they faced teams from much larger school districts, and initially the results weren't pretty.

"At first we were losing by 30 points or more to those larger schools," Ashe remembers. "But it wasn't long before it was 15 points or less. And eventually we started playing every team close."

Getting to play in those highly-competitive tournaments, as well as in various leagues where every opponent would put up a stiff challenge, wasn't easy logistically. Darrington is located about 35-40 minutes from the closest interstate highway, and Ashe said he and his wife Sheila, his brother and all the other parents (whom he described as amazingly supportive for so many years) would often drive two hours or more just so their boys could play in the best tournaments. But he also knew it wasn't enough just to show up for those games. He had to get his teams prepared to face some of the most talented young ballplayers in the state. And for Ashe, that meant practice! And more practice! But he knew without the hard work and extra practice sessions, his players wouldn't be able to compete at a higher level, something he wasn't about to surrender.

While Ashe was a stickler for excellence and hard work, he also instilled a conviction in his players to model good sportsmanship, something they carried with them throughout their high school playing days.

"I didn't allow any trash-talking from my players," Ashe said. "My team was expected to shake hands with their opponents before and after every game. And win or lose, I always wanted each player on my team to be able to go home after the game and say, 'I did my best.'"

Kevin, Jason and Randy Ashe, pictured here in 2003

Though Ashe and his brother had been largely responsible for their team's seven-year string of success, they knew when those young men entered the high school ranks they would have to step back and allow Bryson to do his work. It was no longer their team, but Bryson's, which worked fine for them since they had been two of the town's biggest supporters in regard to his hiring.

Though not responsible for coaching duties anymore, Ashe, with the help of many others in the community, did what he could to continue his contributions to basketball success in Darrington. Along with many other supportive residents, he helped to raise money to send Bryson to various coaching clinics and was there to offer him advice whenever it was solicited. But Ashe said that wasn't a real problem since Bryson was more than open to getting help from him and others in the community.

"Jeff is very humble," Ashe said. "He doesn't have a Lone Ranger mentality. People can come and watch practices and he allows others to get involved. And, more than anything, I feel he respects me and my input because of the time I spent with these kids."

Ashe is another strong connection to my father's coaching days in Darrington. He played high school ball for Dan Bates, who played for my father from 1956-58. Ashe remembers listening to games on the radio during their championship run in the 50s and, in addition to that, remembers how much Bates passed on to him about the game of basketball he had learned from my father. And while the 2002-2003 Loggers were no doubt Bryson's team, most of his players had been privileged to learn many of their skills and secrets to basketball success from Ashe. And Ashe will be quick to remind you he owes much of his knowledge of the game to Dan Bates. And should you get a chance to have a chat with Bates, it won't take long for my father's name to be mentioned in any conversation dedicated to how he acquired his basketball knowledge. With the Simmons-to-Bates-to-Ashe connection solidly established in Darrington basketball, and with Bryson's willingness to learn from that particular trio's run of success while also trusting in his own convictions about how to best prepare his team for a title, twelve young men began the season with great eagerness and even greater anticipation of a return to basketball glory.

Matt Reece started at shooting-guard for the Loggers. Though he averaged 13 points per contest, Reece's strength was on the defensive end, aided by his long arms, quickness and "you're-not-going-to-beat-me" attitude. Reece was typically assigned to match up defensively with the opponent's number-one guard, and usually held that player to well under his scoring average. According to Bryson, Reece had an overwhelming desire to go get the ball, often with a reckless abandon and a complete disregard for a floor burn in his future. Reece was a fair shooter, but at 6-1 and incredibly quick, his greatest offensive strength was in driving to the basket.

Jared Grimmer was Darrington's starting point-guard, a master, Bryson said, in ball-handling skills. Bryson said of Grimmer that in his last several years of coaching the Loggers and watching their opponents, he hadn't seen a point-guard with skills like Grimmer's. Though not a great outside shooter, Grimmer more than made up for it with his ability to drive and score or pass off to a teammate for an easy basket. Possessing greater quickness than straight ahead speed, Grimmer also excelled on the defensive end and led the Loggers in steals. As a testament to his team-play mentality, Grimmer's teammates voted him as Logger's co-captain. Bryson said Grimmer would make his share of mistakes but atone for them instantly with relentless hustle. Impressed with his overall mindset about the game, Bryson said he plans to challenge future Loggers to look back on Grimmer's attitude as a prime example of what should characterize a Darrington ballplayer.

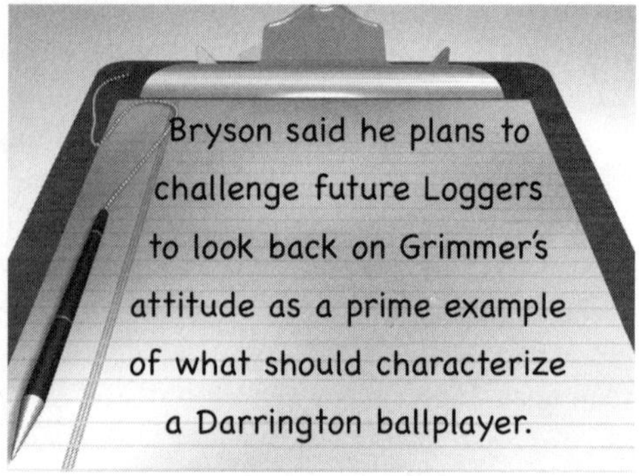

One of the Logger's starting forwards was Jason Ashe. Ashe was a solid scorer and rebounder, an above-average ball handler and a tremendous assist man. Throughout the season, his motto in regard to his role was simple—"Do whatever it takes to help my team win." Bryson called Ashe, "a second coach on the floor." An extremely unselfish player who looked for the pass before the shot more often than not, Ashe could drain the three-pointer when called upon in key situations.

Bryce Boyd was Darrington's big man in the middle and the Logger's other co-captain. At 6-4 and 205 pounds, Boyd posed big problems for opponents. Bryson's offense was designed to first look inside to Boyd. If a shot or move to the basket wasn't an option due to a double-team, Boyd had great court vision and often would push the ball back to the perimeter for a wide-open shot. Though not a flashy player, Boyd was a solid center with good abilities in all phases of the game. His strength on the inside was a 10 to15-foot jumper and he was most deadly with a short jump-hook. Boyd was usually the target of a double-team and opponents would typically design their defensive strategy around preventing him from scoring. A quiet, easy-going individual, Boyd turned it up on the court and always stepped up even more in the bigger games. Not only was Boyd physically strong, his emotional make-up was proven to be tough as well. Midway through the regular season and throughout the remainder of the year, Boyd was faced with the daunting challenge of maintaining focus on the court after his uncle Troy Dawn was killed in a snowmobiling accident.

Evan Smith, a 6-1 forward, was the lone junior on the Logger's starting five. On a few occasions, Smith was so well thought of and mature he was mistakenly introduced as a senior at away games. Smith was the top athlete on the squad, perhaps the best athlete to ever put on a Darrington uniform according to Bryson. Loaded with natural ability, Smith had an incredible vertical leap. Smith could be seen jamming home a missed shot by one of his teammates or leaping high to take a rebound away from someone six inches taller. Smith often electrified the crowds with his thunderous dunks and sensational drives to the basket. According to Bryson, he was the Logger's most intense player and struggled throughout his high school career with being able to control his anger and frustration, but learned to channel those emotions into a never-quit attitude. Proving the desire to bring a championship to the town of Darrington had been on his heart for years, Smith recalled a time when he was 11 years old, right after listening on the radio to the Logger's semi-final game at the state tournament in 1997.

"We lost that game," Smith said. "I was so disappointed. But I was so determined to get better as a player that I immediately went outside into the rain and just starting shooting baskets."

Like every great team at all levels, the Loggers had a few players who could come off the bench and contribute immediately. Ryan Frable was the Logger's sixth man. At 6-4 and 190 pounds, Frable usually spotted Boyd or one of the two starting forwards. He often found court time along with Boyd, putting a presence in the middle few schools of their size could effectively counter. Frable never started during his three years as a member of the varsity unit, but looked for ways to contribute on the court and on the bench. Bryson said from what he saw in most of the teams they played against, Frable would have started on each of those squads. His hard work, perseverance and determination more than compensated for his lack of natural ability and, as Bryson says, he was a huge part of the team's success.

As a freshman, Frable was weak, chubby and, as Bryson remembers, unable to do even one pull-up. He was placed on the 'C' team that year, but committed himself to an intense weight program and worked hard for the next four years to make his body stronger.

Jake Wicken was the second man off the Logger's bench. He was the player with the best build, a physique "to die for" Bryson said, and would substitute at both guard and forward positions. Wicken was a consummate team player, short on star quality but huge on desire. Bryson said he knew Wicken felt he deserved more playing time, but put his disappointments to the side and didn't cause any trouble for the team. Prior to the start of the season, Wicken informed his teammates he was thinking about not playing his final season, and even missed the first few practices. A few Darrington alumni heard the rumor of Wicken's plans, then took it upon themselves to have a little chat with him to emphasize how much the team needed him in their quest for a title.

Lance Chambers was the senior who logged the fewest minutes on the court. But Bryson was impressed with his supportive attitude, as Chambers knew all season he would likely spend most of his time on the bench. (Chambers grandfather, Bob Green, was a member of Darrington's 1957 championship squad.)

Sophomores Billy McMillen, Sean O'Connell and Kris Reece played primarily on the junior varsity squad during the year, but found some playing time with the varsity as well. (Reece's grandfather, Jim, was a member of the first Darrington team to qualify for the state tournament in 1950.) Junior Matt Koch was also a member of the varsity, but played sparingly.

In each of these player's minds, it would be inappropriate not to include Travis LaMance as a member of the 2002-2003 Loggers. LaMance transferred to Darrington High School in 2001 and was extremely shy, introverted and set apart from the mainstream of school life. Bryce Boyd was the first player to befriend him, and he encouraged LaMance to think about becoming the manager for the team. After taking some time to consider the offer, LaMance accepted. And, says Boyd, he was an important part of the team from that day forward. Boyd and Ashe, speaking on behalf of the entire team, said they saw LaMance come out of his shell during the season and added many players on the team had built a great friendship with him.

It was a team of small-town heroes. A healthy mix of humility, hard work and hearts to help each other best described this team. Personal egos were cast aside and replaced with the motto of "Everyone Matters." Making the team better was more important than minutes played. Hustle on any given night was heralded more than how many points someone scored. Team chemistry and camaraderie were the main focus rather than individual pursuits or the possibility of personal accolades at season's end. And with high hopes and a commitment to excellence before them, the 2003 Darrington Loggers began their pursuit of winning a state championship.

The young Loggers in 1998 during their final year under the leadership of Kevin and Randy Ashe

Chapter Eighteen

One For The Ages

In a story that focuses on the important topic of being successful and how success, in this particular case, was achieved on the basketball court, it normally wouldn't make much sense to take time to tell you about something that seems so trivial—the gymnasium where the Loggers play their home games. After all, aren't all gymnasiums pretty much alike? But if you've ever been inside Darrington's gymnasium, or if you get a chance to see it someday, you would likely agree not mentioning it would be a horrible oversight.

The Loggers play their home games in what is called "The Pit" by those in Darrington. Opposing players and coaches probably have renamed it "The Pits" because that's where they typically find themselves after facing the Loggers on a road trip to Darrington. Built with a combined community effort in 1954, the gymnasium (also called the Darrington Community Center) still has its original fir floor and is the only arena in the state of Washington where high school basketball players shoot at baskets attached to non-square backboards. The baselines are only seven to eight feet away from the east/west walls, just enough room for players to stand for inbound passes, but daringly close for any athlete contemplating a dive for a loose ball headed in that direction. Elevated bleachers on both sides of the court hang eight feet above the sunken floor, offering young Loggers-to-be a chance to slap their favorite players a high-five on their way in and out of the locker room. A mountain mural decorates the wall at the east end of the court and large windows on the opposite end allow natural light to illuminate the glistening floor, a perfect setting for folks who love the outdoors and live at the base of majestic White Horse Mountain.

The gymnasium is another strong connector for the past and present in Darrington basketball, as players from six different decades have displayed their skills on its hardwood floor. And most of the teams they represented found success a lot more often than not whenever opponents came to town.

"We definitely feel like we have a huge home-court advantage," Bryson said. "All of our players absolutely love this gym and our opponents hate it. I'm sure that a lot of the aura and mystique is purely a mental thing."

And Bryson doesn't think "The Pit" is on its last legs either.

"I can see teams playing here for at least the next 25 years," he said without hesitation.

If it happens to survive that long, that would be a total of 75 years of exciting games, standing-room-only crowds and pretty good odds on a Logger win. In the gymnasium's second year of existence, the Loggers went on to win the state title in March of 1955, a little more than a year after the townspeople put their brains and brawn together to construct the all-wood facility. In a recent Seattle Times article highlighting the older, classic gyms in Washington, the Logger's home palace was voted second best, quite an honor, you might think, for most Darrington folks. But most of the people there believe they and their one-of-a-kind gymnasium were slighted with the runner-up honor.

On game nights, the atmosphere is nothing short of electric, and the noise level is unlike anything the Loggers experience on the road. On an average night, anywhere from 500 to 750 of the Darrington faithful enter the Community Center, confident of a win. They'll do their part in making sure their Loggers emerge victorious—stomping, yelling, clapping and doing their best to intimidate the opponent from the beginning of warm-ups to the final buzzer.

For those of you familiar with college basketball and some of the venues that create the most havoc for visiting teams, Darrington Community Center could be likened to Cameron Indoor Stadium, site of Duke University's home games where the "Cameron Crazies" occupy the first number of rows from baseline to baseline, standing the entire game, screaming, bobbing and weaving to make basketball life as miserable as possible for teams visiting Durham, North Carolina. Not many of Duke's opponents have anything good to say about the atmosphere there, and a loss usually accompanies their lousy attitudes. A Darrington game against an archrival on a cold Friday night in January would be a scaled-down version to what is witnessed at Cameron Indoor Stadium when the Blue Devils play a late-season conference game against the likes of North Carolina, Maryland or Wake Forest.

Two other arenas in the collegiate ranks that create a similar sensation for visiting teams are also called "The Pit." One is located in Eugene, Oregon, on the campus of University of Oregon, and the other is in Albuquerque, New Mexico, on the campus of University of New Mexico. If a visiting team is fortunate enough to come away with a win when they play in either of those arenas, it's usually by the skin of their teeth or because the home team is experiencing an off year. The same could be said for visiting teams that have managed to eek out victories through the years at the Community Center.

At this moment, very few people in Darrington are interested in discussing plans for a more modern, state-of-the-art arena, one more in line with other high school gymnasiums in the state. In these parts, those thoughts would probably be considered blasphemous. And 20 years from now, when the topic will likely be revisited by some daring soul, plan on a lot of people showing up at a heated town hall meeting to debate the subject, and most of the folks will be willing to go to war to protect their basketball relic.

Despite the age of the Community Center, there's little or no concern from even the harshest of critics about the appearance of the place. The floor always shines, the paint is fairly new, the cracks are filled in whenever they're noticed and the parking lot is well-marked and lit. No light bulb, on or off the court, is missing, all the colored lights in the scoreboard are operational, the locker rooms are squeaky clean and the chairs for the coaches and players are cushioned and comfortable. It's home, sweet home to the Loggers and has been for more than 50 years. They take great pride in their gymnasium and its appearance, and many in Darrington think Bryson's estimation of 25 more years of viable service is too conservative. Many who were there to help in its construction or who witnessed the two championships in the 50s probably won't be around to see who's right, but you can bet their children and grandchildren will do all they can to keep "The Pit" as presentable as possible and the place where Darrington basketball dreams keep coming true.

One of these days, square backboards might hang in the gymnasium, but don't count on it. Those fan-shaped backboards are just one of the many nuances in "The Pit" that make it nothing short of perfect for players and fans in this small town and nothing short of a pain for those teams scheduled to face the Loggers on their humble home court.

An inside look at the gymnasium in the Community Center, called "The Pit" by those in Darrington

Chapter Nineteen

Let The Games Begin

The Loggers entered the 2002-2003 season with high hopes. Coming off a 16-4 regular season mark during their 2001-2002 season, and coupled with a fourth place finish at the 16-team state championship tournament that brought their overall record to 22-5, Bryson and his seven returning lettermen were confident they would improve upon their previous year's performance. The statewide pollsters responsible for compiling a Top-10 had apparently been impressed with the Logger's showing in the 2002 state tournament, and they were certainly aware of the talent pool that would don the green and gold, picking Darrington as the team to win it all in their pre-season rankings.

But Bryson was concerned with only one thing—taking the season one game at a time. He knew his team possessed the talent to go far in the state tournament, and he was pretty confident he had the type of squad needed to win it all. He knew his returning lettermen were hungry to show their fourth place finish in the tournament the year before was merely a warm-up for better things to come. And, in bringing my father's memory to the forefront, Bryson knew he had traveled the extra mile to locate the motivation around which his players could rally.

Bryson's players were sold out to the championship cause. Upon conclusion of their very first day of practice, each player (joined by their coaches) met in the coach's room adjacent to the home team's locker room. The lights were off and the room had been lit with candles. It was an opportunity for each player and coach to commit to the upcoming season. Few words were uttered at the time, but a promise was made by each player called "The Pact", a simple commitment to abstain from alcohol for the entire season and, just as important, not to attend even a single party, just so the temptation to drink would be totally eliminated and any hint about any of them having a lukewarm attitude in regard to the season would be impossible to locate. They agreed upon their goal of a state championship then agreed it would be the last time the goal was mentioned for the rest of the year. After all, they all knew what they wanted. There was no great reason to bring up old news along the way. There was only time to work harder than ever and do what each knew was required of them if a title was a real possibility. Each player and coach then signed their name on a 20 x 20-inch board that had been sanded down for the occasion, indicating their promise to keep the two promises they had just made to themselves and to each other.

Over the next few weeks of practice, the Loggers became sharper in all facets of the game. While Bryson and the town felt great about what they were seeing in the Logger's pre-season regimen, it all meant very little until it showed up in the win column during the regular season. And, for Darrington fans, it went well beyond that. This brand of basketball had to last well into February and early March, when the games really counted.

The first opportunity to strut their state-championship-stuff came on December 3, 2002. It was Friday night and the Community Center gymnasium was jam-packed with enthusiastic fans itching for a first chance to see the Loggers begin their quest for basketball supremacy in the small towns of Washington, as they hosted a four-team tournament to begin the regular season. Stealing a tradition from Notre Dame football, Bryson, as he had done with his teams since 1997, directed each of his players to touch the sign reading, "Play Like A Champion Today," located near the locker room exit, just prior to heading onto the court for pre-game warm-ups.

The Loggers were playing against the King's West Knights, a team from a rival conference that was also returning a number of starters to a squad many said should be considered a state contender. Bryson welcomed the early-season challenge, knowing his team would benefit from logging some valuable minutes against stiff competition early in the year.

Playing against talented and experienced teams in the regular season, both in and out of their league, was a positive in Bryson's mind, even though he realized his Loggers might stub their toe a time or two along the way. He knew those kind of games would prepare his team for the toughest competition to come later in March against the best teams in the state. Undoubtedly, every one of those teams would come to the tournament refined by their own wins and losses against stiff competition in their regular-season campaigns. But Bryson wasn't expecting to begin the year with his team learning the hard way. He still expected a victory, one filled with the very things he taught his players to embrace—a tough man-to-man defense, an attitude to never give up an easy shot and a willingness to block out, hit the outlet man and run like crazy on the offensive end. Bryson believed strongly in this style of play, especially the man-to-man defense, but also remembers how often he was reminded about the importance of this strategy by Darrington fans.

"I can't tell you how many times I heard something like this: 'You need to teach the man-to-man defense like Dan Bates taught us, who learned it from LaVerne Simmons,'" Bryson said. "Those may not have been their exact words, but the message was loud and clear."

And the Logger's defensive effort was firing on all cylinders opening night. After a few first-game jitters that led to three Darrington turnovers and a few missed shots from close range, the Loggers displayed their adherence to Bryson's expectations by employing a smothering man-to-man defense. Hustle and determination on the defensive end resulted in numerous steals and subsequent lay-ups for the Loggers and a 16-8 first-quarter lead. Evan Smith and Bryce Boyd led the way with six points each, while Jason Ashe had four steals and five assists in the first eight minutes of play.

Bryson rested all but one of his starters to open the second quarter. But no drop off in intensity was evident and the Loggers extended their lead to 14 points midway through the second period. Bryson knew his second unit would need to gain confidence from valuable in-game experience if his Loggers were going to win the state title. Surely, he believed, some of his best players would have an off night somewhere on the road to a title. Perhaps the entire starting five would play poorly on a few occasions. Bryson, then, would need a Roland Mount copycat, someone who could be there to sink a clutch shot at the buzzer and propel his team to an important victory. Or, perhaps a top player would suffer a season-ending injury and the unfortunate turn of events couldn't be used as an acceptable excuse for losing down the stretch. After all, my father hadn't allowed a key injury to slow his 1957 Loggers when starting point-guard Dick Hitchcock broke his ankle in the quarterfinal game of the state tournament. So Bryson would push his second string players just as hard as the starters in every practice. He would expect them to give the starting five all they could handle whenever they scrimmaged. And he wasn't afraid to put a backup player into a tough situation in close games. And, especially in games when the outcome wasn't in doubt, Bryson provided ample opportunities for his younger and less-skilled players to find plenty of playing time. While the bench players learned to trust themselves in key situations, Bryson was determining how much he could trust them in similar moments.

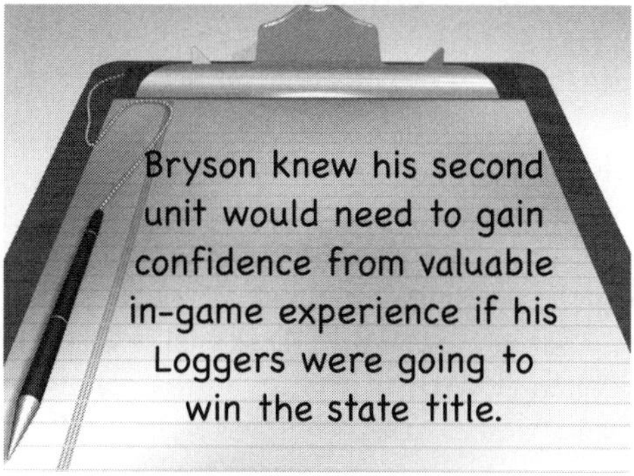

Darrington seemed reenergized for the final 16 minutes of play against King's West. A quick 5-0 spurt from the opening tip put the Loggers on top 37-18 and they never looked back. Darrington fans were delighted with the opening presentation as the Loggers achieved their first goal with a convincing 57-43 victory. Starting guard Matt Reece led the

Loggers with 17 points. Two other players scored in double figures and Boyd collected a game-high 17 rebounds.

It was a team victory in every way—just the way Bryson liked it! That was my father's winning style more often than not and Bryson was determined to imitate it throughout the season. Perhaps Darrington teams of the past 45 years had better individual players than those on this squad. But Bryson was determined, just like the 1955 Loggers who won the state title with only one player being named to the All-State squad, his 2003 Loggers would win because of a well-choreographed team effort, not one player's amazing display of talent night after night.

The second goal of the Logger's season was accomplished with a thrilling 51-48 victory over Cedar Park Christian, a team that had defeated them in the 2002 district championship game. Trailing by two at the half, the Loggers bounced back in the second half and took a lead midway through the third period they never relinquished, aided by four three-pointers put in by Jason Ashe.

With two wins under their belt, Bryson and his players could already feel a sense of destiny. Goals three and four were all met the following week, a thumping of league rival, Concrete, 88-48, and a hard-fought victory against Friday Harbor, 58-48, overcoming a six-point halftime deficit.

A game-five loss proved to be the first real test of resolve for the Loggers, as they fell 65-55 to the LaConner Braves, a talented team from a larger school classification. With the loss, Darrington relinquished their number-one ranking in the Seattle Times poll, falling one notch to second. Bryson was disappointed with the loss, but moved ahead with a focus on the team's sixth goal and some fine-tuning in areas he felt cost them during the game with LaConner. His players had visions of an undefeated championship season, and they seemed discouraged with the loss. Bryson would have loved a perfect record accompanying a title as well, something no Darrington team had ever accomplished. But my father's championship teams lost four games in 1955 and two in 1957, and he was certain nobody really cared about those losses.

The Loggers bounced back the following week with two victories over tough opponents, defeating a talented Coupeville squad 68-61 after trailing by eight points at the half, and gaining an easy victory over Orcas Island, 61-39. Darrington was now a solid 6-1 heading into the holiday season, but dropped a few more spots in the latest state rankings. Bryson had scheduled a game during the holiday season, knowing his team couldn't afford a letdown or a two-week hiatus without an enemy to face. The opponent would be Wanneroo, an all-star traveling team from Australia, known to give each of its American opponents a formidable challenge. This, too, was part of Bryson's championship strategy, as he knew his Loggers would face teams more talented than Wanneroo in the state finals.

And this game, he believed, would be excellent preparation for the games that mattered most. Darrington played well, but the young Aussies' size was too much to overcome and the Loggers fell, 70-61.

Bryson gave his players a few days off to celebrate the holidays then it was back to work preparing for the toughest stretch of the season. The Loggers returned from the holiday break with a renewed resolve and zeal, rattling off six consecutive wins to raise their record to 12-2, the biggest win coming at home against defending league champions and archrival, Shoreline Christian. In their most lopsided win, Darrington downed Snohomish County Christian, 81-29, led by the season-high 28 points of Bryce Boyd on 14 of 19 shooting from the field. Another big win came against LaConner, avenging an earlier loss, as they beat the Braves 54-45. The average margin of victory for the Loggers during their six-game winning streak was an astounding 27 points, and pollsters took notice. Darrington vaulted back to second place in the Seattle Times poll, impressing the contributing coaches and sportswriters the most with their convincing 65-51 victory over state powerhouse, Shoreline Christian.

Whether it was cockiness, crummy play or a combination of both, the Loggers followed up their six-game mastery of opponents with a three-game stretch inconsistent for a team expected to make a run for the state title. A standing-room-only crowd was on hand at the Community Center as the Loggers played their Homecoming contest against a tough team from Mount Vernon Christian. The Loggers, as Bryson put it, played lethargic and plain old lousy, coming out on the short end of a 45-43 contest. Squandering a seven-point halftime lead, the Loggers scored a season-low three points in the third quarter. Darrington fell behind by 11 points early in the fourth period but closed the margin to within two with a little less than two minutes remaining. The Loggers had a chance to win the contest in the closing seconds, but missed three consecutive shots to seal the loss, dropping them out of the league-lead for the first time all season.

No longer the state's second-ranked team, Darrington played their next two games as part of a four-team tournament, hosted by Shoreline Christian. In the first contest, the Loggers played a sloppy game against Grace Academy, a team lurking near the bottom of the league standings. The Loggers led by 19 points at the half, yet Bryson felt his team's intensity and passion had plummeted to a season low. Though the Loggers defeated Grace Academy, 63-36, Bryson and the Darrington fans in attendance at the weekend tournament knew this wasn't the type of team they envisioned at the beginning of the year, nor the team they watched play those first 14 games of the season. And looming ahead was another showdown with Shoreline Christian, a team that hadn't lost since falling to the Loggers in early January.

Unfortunately, Darrington continued their downward slide, losing the game to Shoreline Christian, 59-47. But the game wasn't the only thing the Loggers lost that night. They lost some statewide respect as well and sunk to eighth in the state rankings, the lowest spot of the season for the team picked to be champions at the beginning of the year. But would they lose their confidence as well? Player's heads were hanging low as they sat stunned and discouraged in the visitor's locker room, and Bryson knew something had to be done to turn his Logger ship away from the impending iceberg of indifference ready to sink their hopes for a championship season.

The first portion of the bus ride home that night was unlike anything they had experienced the entire season. To say the mood was somber would be an understatement. And no player was about to bust out a deck of playing cards, organize a poker game on the journey home and pretend they weren't concerned. It was soul-searching time for players and coaches alike. And in the 90-minute drive back to Darrington, plans and possible proposals for pulling themselves out of their present pit were entering their minds. After 30 minutes of feeling intensely disgusted with what he could remember about his team's play against Shoreline Christian, Jared Grimmer broke the silence. Grimmer asked each of his senior teammates to make their way to the back of the bus for a meeting. What happened in the next few minutes was just the beginning of a late-evening, round-ball revival.

Bryson was extremely discouraged with the loss to Shoreline Christian, but even more determined to learn from it. He knew he had to get his team mentally ready for their three remaining regular-season games and those to follow in the district and state tournaments. Longer practices weren't the answer in Bryson's opinion, and a good, old-fashioned scolding or a "you-blew-it-big-time" speech didn't seem to fit the need for his team's personality. Just exactly how he would rally his team was escaping him for the moment.

While Bryson searched for the right response to his team's poor play, he still remained confident. Though the Logger's four regular-season losses were nowhere to be found on Bryson's beginning-of-the-year map to success, regular-season setbacks hadn't been a major concern of Bryson's at the onset of Darrington's quest for glory. It was a state championship he had in mind as his ultimate goal. And reaching that goal, he believed, continued to be a very real possibility.

Chapter Twenty

Basketball Burnt Offerings

The loss to Shoreline Christian was a big blow to Darrington pride and a wake-up call to a team looking anything but invincible. The Loggers had suffered two losses in their last three games, their only victory coming in a contest against league cellar-dweller, Grace Academy. Bryson knew it was a critical time for his team. He felt the next few days of practice and the next few games his team played would be a tell-tale sign of things to come—either his Loggers would rise to the occasion and play like champions, or they would allow discouragement and a big bump in the road to be the end of the road in their drive for a title.

Bryson spent most of his waking hours on Saturday night, and all day Sunday, trying to determine how to get his team refocused for the final three games of the regular season and believing, once again, in a championship cause. What symbolic act could he employ to bring the early-season fire back into their bones? What slogan could he come up with to help his players understand that now, not later, was the time for action? How could he keep the dream of a first championship in 46 years alive and well in their hearts?

Bryson struggled to find the appropriate act or motto to help his talented team turn a tough corner, one that wasn't too corny or too critical of their efforts. He would soon come to realize his players had been walking a full step ahead of him in coming to some conviction about their recent play on the court, and they were closing in on a renewed resolve to do whatever needed to be done to return to championship form.

Although the Loggers suffered the disappointing loss to Shoreline Christian during the weekend tournament, Jared Grimmer was voted the sportsmanship awarded and given a lettered t-shirt after the loss representing his accomplishment. While Bryson was a stickler for his players displaying positive attitudes before, during and after each game, win or lose, none of these young men were finding contentment in a teammate receiving an award for kindness on the court. They were determined to make sure the award presentation at the state tournament a few weeks down the road had a whole lot more to do with basketball prowess than being polite.

After a long period of silence on the initial leg of the bus ride home, Grimmer and his senior teammates made their way to the back of the bus for a short meeting. He had with him the t-shirt representing his display of sportsmanship that weekend, but he wasn't about to wear it or present it to the next nicest guy on the team. He was irritated, and he held in his hand a black marker.

"Guys, we have got to turn our season around," he said. All heads nodded in agreement. "Right now we stink," he continued to say, "and we're going to write down everything wrong about how we're playing right now on this shirt."

Selfishness. Turnovers. Not playing as a team. Not running the court. Passive. Timid. Not playing Logger Ball. Those were just a few of the words and phrases that littered his all-cotton trophy. And near the bottom of the marked shirt were seven signatures—seven seniors determined to own their admitted weaknesses, work on every one of them for the remainder of the season and eliminate them from their basketball future.

When the team bus finally returned to Darrington, the seven seniors and five underclassmen hopped into a few trucks, drove to a remote area about 10 miles from the school called Clear Creek and finished doing the very thing Bryson had been wracking his brain to figure out. To symbolically represent their disgust for how they were currently playing, and to show their disdain for good-guys-make-good-effort-but-fall-short awards, the sportsmanship shirt presented to Grimmer, now covered in black marker representing the black marks of their recent play, was ceremonially burned.

"Jake Wicken got his gasoline can out of the back of his pickup and we torched that thing on a stick," Grimmer said. "We were dancing and hooting and hollering," he said proudly. "And we took pictures just so none of us would ever forget."

As the twelve players observed the t-shirt inferno, every heart and soul represented there was feverishly stirring with emotion and a call to greater commitment. Without a specific plea from any individual, each player had called themselves to a renewed and radical commitment to finish the season strong, and to doing whatever the team needed to make the difference in wins and losses the remainder of the year.

Upon leaving the ashen altar of better basketball to come, the players headed back to the high school. As they were exiting the Clear Creek area, a teacher from the high school happened to be driving by. She immediately wondered if they had been to some kind of party, thinking they were no doubt discouraged with their recent losses, or perhaps carefree in their attitudes toward the remainder of the season. When she returned home, she made a call to Coach Bryson, telling him she thought some of his players might have been out partying after the game. But had she been in attendance at the pre-season meeting of coaches and players where "The Pact" was signed, she would have been hesitant to come to such a conclusion.

"We had signed an agreement at the beginning of the year that there would be no parties during the season," Jason Ashe said. "There was no way we were going to break that agreement."

Though quite confident his players hadn't given up on the season or given in to the temptation to drink, Bryson gathered his team before practice on Monday afternoon and told them he had heard a rumor they might have been out partying after the loss to Shoreline Christian. Bryce Boyd was the first to set the record straight, sharing the details of the Friday night frying of the sportsmanship shirt.

"Nothing further needed to be said or done," Bryson remarked. "The boys knew the significance of the moment and they were already thinking what I was thinking, and beyond."

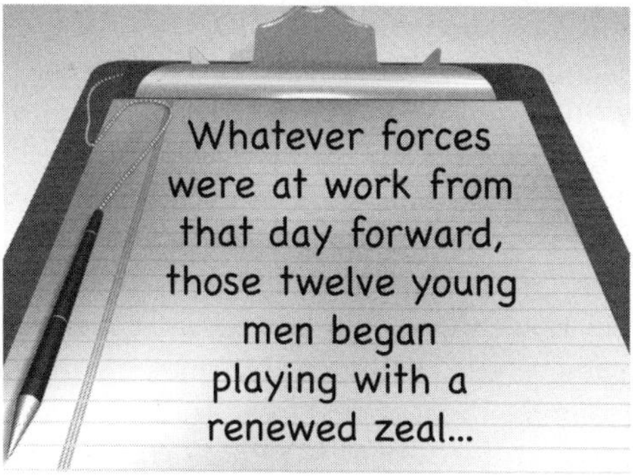

The burning of the sportsmanship shirt was a significant benchmark in the Logger's season. Perhaps the smoke that night ascended to the heavens, providing a rarely smelled but most-pleasant aroma, and setting in motion a final call to orchestrate events during the final lap of the Logger's run for a championship. After all, humility could be clearly seen with the specific naming of their weaknesses. And a greater hard-work ethic, one to be displayed for the remainder of the season, was agreed upon by each player. And, lastly, a renewed pledge to honor the pre-season promises they had made to each other not to drink alcohol and to turn down every party invitation had been solidified.

Whatever forces were at work from that day forward, those twelve young men began playing with a renewed zeal, their eyes focused intently on the goal they had set for themselves at the dawn of the season—the first championship in 46 years.

Chapter Twenty-One

Finishing With A Flourish

Ten games remained for the Loggers. Only five were on the official schedule—three to close out the regular season and at least two in the double-elimination district tournament they had already qualified for, slated for the end of February. But 10 was the only number the Logger players had in mind—three to wrap up the regular-season campaign, three in district play and four hard-fought contests to close out the year in Spokane at the state championships.

While sportsmanship remained a strong suit for the Loggers in their final three games of regular-season play, championship caliber basketball made a comeback and Darrington demolished their next three opponents. In their first game after the Shoreline Christian loss and the subsequent "Clear Creek Cremation", the Loggers defeated Snohomish Christian, 86-41. Scoring the game's first 12 points, the Darrington starting five signaled to Coach Bryson and their rejuvenated fans that Logger Ball was back. The Loggers followed up that win with a 92-18 victory over Lopez Island, the most-lopsided victory ever for a Bryson-coached team. Darrington's seven seniors combined to score 80 points in the contest, the last home game of their high school careers.

One final game remained against Mt. Vernon Christian, a team that had defeated the Loggers by two points only three weeks earlier. But this was a different Darrington team playing now, the one Bryson and Logger fans had been familiar with watching during the early part of the season. Led by Matt Reece's 26 points and four steals, the Loggers came away with a convincing 60-37 road win and headed into district play the following week with a 16-4 record. But, more importantly, they were now playing with confidence and had recaptured their champion's swagger. Despite the fact their three season-ending wins came in convincing fashion, the Loggers actually dropped one notch in the state polls, moving down to ninth, and finished a disappointing second place in their league, runners-up to Shoreline Christian.

Though quite surprised with their decline in the state rankings, Bryson said he wasn't shocked at all by his team's end-of-the-year display of winning basketball.

"These guys have always had a quiet resolve about them," he said. "When things don't go well, of course you would always question, 'Gee, are they under pressure?' You're always questioning things. You always ask yourself, are these guys going to be able to step up? And, once again, they did just that!"

While the district competition was a double-elimination tournament, the Loggers weren't making any plans to earn a trip to Spokane through any loser's bracket. Three teams from their tri-district tournament would qualify for state championship play, but Darrington had its sights set on securing the top seed, knowing the honor meant getting placed in a much better bracket to begin their quest for a title the following week.

Bryson knew he had to keep his team from overlooking their next three opponents. They had been playing so well the past few weeks, but could they keep up that type of intensity for the remainder of the season? Evergreen Lutheran would be the Logger's first opponent. They had finished fourth in their league but had won seven of their past eight contests coming into the tournament. But Darrington jumped out to an 11-point lead at the end of the first quarter and never looked back, defeating the Eagles, 67-52.

King's West, a team Darrington had defeated by 14 points in their opening game of the season, would play the Loggers in the semi-final round of the district tournament. The winner would gain an automatic spot in the state tournament, while the loser would need to win two more games the following week to qualify. Darrington came in focused, knowing a victory would land them at their pre-season destination. King's West, sensing a need to simmer a high-spirited and talented Logger squad, employed a slow-down offensive strategy and led the low-scoring affair, 22-18, at the midway mark. But neither Bryson nor his players panicked. The Loggers outscored the talented team from Bremerton 31-16 the rest of the contest, even without the services of Jared Grimmer, who left the game in the second quarter with an ankle injury. Darrington defeated King's West, 49-38, earning a trip to Spokane and a spot in the 16-team state tournament.

The win brought a smile to Bryson's face and a relief to many in town who had already mapped out their itineraries for Spokane. It was official. The Loggers had qualified for state tournament play once again. The players felt a sense of pride and satisfaction about securing a spot in the tournament, yet they knew full well they still had plenty of work left to do. But Spokane was the one location they had to reach. If not, the season would have been considered a complete failure in their minds. With a trip to the eastern half of the state now a done deal, the Loggers could focus on the next task at hand—a district crown.

Clallam Bay would battle Darrington in the district championship game. With Spokane in their back pocket and a state championship in the back of their minds, the Loggers faced their most-challenging opponent of the year. Clallam Bay entered the contest with a 19-0 record, were ranked ranked fourth in the state and overflowed with confidence after their win over Shoreline Christian in the district semi-finals. At the onset of district play, the Loggers were hoping to face Shoreline Christian in the title game, and they seemed disappointed not to have an opportunity to win the district championship against the Crusaders, in what would have been the deciding game of their season's best-of-three series.

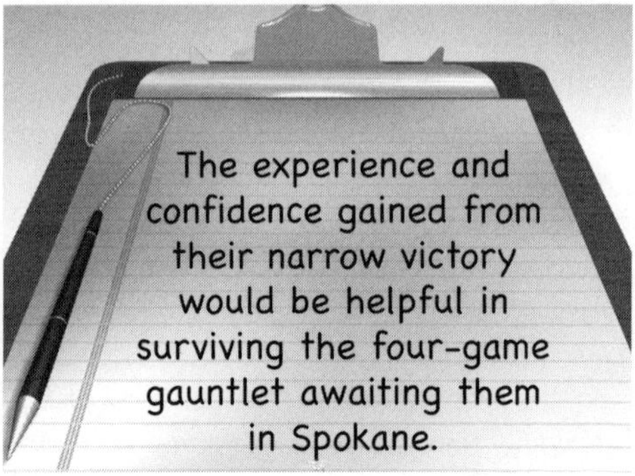

While Bryson found it somewhat difficult to rouse his team for the title contest, once the game began the Loggers found themselves in a dogfight and played their Logger-Ball best. The game was tied 12-12 after one period and Darrington took a 31-30 lead into the locker room at the half. The lead changed hands five times in the third quarter, but Clallam Bay jumped out to a five-point lead early in the fourth quarter before Darrington mounted a final comeback. With 20 seconds remaining and the score knotted at 65-65, Jared Grimmer sank one of his two free-throw attempts. (Grimmer was listed as doubtful for the contest and hadn't practiced since the Logger's victory over King's West three days earlier. Limited by his injury, Grimmer used the practice sessions to focus on his free-throw shooting.) The Bruins had two inside scoring opportunities in the final seconds but couldn't convert, giving the Loggers a 66-65 win, a district championship and a number-one seed in the upcoming state tournament.

Bryson was happy with the win, even a bit excited about the close call with Clallam Bay. He assumed it was a high probability each of the Logger's remaining contests at state would be close and could come down to his team needing to sink a final shot with little time remaining or playing tough defense to hang on to a slim lead. The experience and confidence gained from their narrow victory over Clallam Bay would be helpful in surviving the four-game gauntlet awaiting them in Spokane.

Sixteen teams qualified that weekend for the state tournament. Sunnyside Christian, champions in 2002 and ranked first in the latest state poll, was the favorite. Shoreline Christian, rebounding from their upset loss to Clallam Bay in the semi-finals of district play, came back with two wins to secure the third and final spot from the Northwest District. Garfield-

Palouse came to Spokane riding a 12-game winning streak and were picked just behind Sunnyside Christian as the team to beat. Darrington was ranked sixth in the latest state poll, and that was just about where most basketball experts were expecting them to finish. None of those experts lived in Darrington, however, and they certainly didn't play on the team or man the Logger's bench. Bryson and his veteran team were confident this was their year. But they weren't overly cocky. They were all well aware of the possible struggles looming ahead and what they hoped would be a showdown, at some point in the four-day tournament, with Sunnyside Christian and the opportunity to avenge their only loss in the tournament the previous year.

Chapter Twenty-Two

Tournament Time

Coming to Spokane with a 19-4 record, runners-up in their own league during the regular season and nary a title trophy in 46 years, most basketball fans around the state of Washington had written off Darrington as the team to beat in 2003. And the town of Darrington, though quite hopeful, remained humble in regard to those same three statistics that put the odds of a basketball title run in nearly the same category as a Chicago Cubs' World Series championship or a dramatic presentation by The Three Stooges. Even Bryson felt tempted to succumb to some pre-tournament doubts, mostly due to the overall health of his team.

"Jared Grimmer had sprained his ankle and wasn't playing at 100%," Bryson remembered. "Matt Reece had a severely inflamed big toe, Jake Wicken had a bad back and Evan Smith had been complaining of chest pains during our district contests. And Evan was a tough kid. He hadn't missed a practice in four years. I couldn't help but think, 'Maybe this wasn't meant to be.'"

Adding to Bryson's doubts was the harsh reality that teams from the western side of the state had won very few titles since the tournament's inception in 1931. Some attributed the poor performance to the wear-and-tear coming from the long cross-state journey to Spokane. Some chalked it up to better coaches at the helm on the east side, others to the hard-work mentality found in players representing teams from the east, many of them from farming families raised with an emphasis on discipline and hard work. Others said it simply was a mental thing, that teams and players from both sides of the state were usually of equal ability. But due to rumors of a Westside curse, and knowledge of an Eastside domination ringing in the minds of the athletes west of the Cascades, many of the close games between squads representing both sides of the state went to teams from the east. And eastern power Sunnyside Christian was eager to show the 2003 tournament would be one more piece of evidence the east reigned supreme, poised to win back-to-back titles.

Bryson, his assistant coaches and 12 varsity players left for Spokane on Tuesday morning. Their first-round game would take place

Wednesday evening, and the Loggers would be pitted against Valley Christian, an unranked opponent. Bryson's goal was to arrive in the Spokane area sometime in the late afternoon, or a little more than 24 hours before tip-off of game one. This would give his players ample time to relax, stretch their sore muscles from the six-hour bus ride, get in a short practice session at a nearby gym and get to bed at a decent hour in order to be well-rested for their initial contest.

Most of the player's families left on Tuesday morning as well, while the largest percentage of Darrington fans would leave later that afternoon, hoping to check in to their hotel before the midnight hour. A few who weren't able to talk their bosses into giving them an additional day off planned to hightail it to Spokane on Wednesday morning. They would leave before sunrise and, barring flat tires or failed radiators, arrive at the Spokane Arena around noon and catch a few of the games prior to Darrington's first-round contest. About 450 hopeful humans beings would wind up in Spokane to root on Darrington, causing their home quarters to once again turn into an essential ghost town for a few days. Making the cross-state and over-the-Cascades trip is a yearly tradition for many of the townspeople. Chances are pretty good they'll see their Loggers play in the tournament every year, but some make the trip even when the Loggers don't qualify.

Most of the Darrington fans made accommodations at the Red Lion River Inn, a hotel located about one-half mile from the Arena. A few made plans to stay with relatives or close friends who lived in Spokane or one of the nearby suburbs. Large clusters of Darrington fans could be seen together at most hours of the day—eating, watching the other games, spending a few hours at one of the nearby casinos, swimming or just relaxing by the indoor pool and reading pre-game and post-game reports about the tournament in the Spokesman-Review, Spokane's daily newspaper.

Bryson was well aware too much time spent with grandparents, girlfriends and good-hearted fans would be a distraction for his players, and he did what he could to eliminate the temptation for both sides. And parents were in complete agreement with Bryson's desires. They, too, had a meeting before tournament play began, stressing to each other the need to leave the players and coaches alone so they could focus on their main task at hand.

Bryson wanted his team thinking about one thing—the next game. He wanted his players nearby should he feel the need for an impromptu team meeting, and he wanted to monitor their daily regimen to have them physically and mentally prepared for upcoming games. He wasn't a coaching dictator, but his players were never prone to think of him in those terms. They, in many ways, were harder on themselves and their need for rest and relaxation than he was. They had no desire to break curfew or be with the girl of their choice. They remembered how they had felt after finishing fourth the previous year, and anything short of a title would be considered a major disappointment. And if anybody on the team felt the desire to go out-of-bounds with the proposed schedule, a teammate, not Bryson, would be the first to reel him in.

Since the Loggers first two games on Wednesday and Thursday were slated for the evening hours, Bryson allowed his players to eat breakfast on their own and watch some of the morning contests at the Arena. At noon on Wednesday, each player was to be on the bus for a trip to a local grade school to participate in an assembly where sportsmanship and a good work ethic were to be promoted. After their time at the school, Bryson took his team to Spokane Community College for a shoot-around and short practice session. About four hours prior to tip-off of game one, the Loggers gathered at Cyrus O'Leary's Restaurant for a pre-game meal, a tradition Bryson has followed since 1997. After dinner, it was time to go back to the hotel and relax for an hour or so, then head over to the Arena for their pre-game ritual.

On the evening before tournament play began, room lights were turned out and basketball fellowship ended for most of the Logger players before midnight. Though many of the young men couldn't get to sleep until well after the midnight hour due to butterfly activity in their midsections, they all abided by their coach's proposed schedule. Those quiet moments in bed were crucial for each player. It was the time to picture the game-winning shot they would put up with one second remaining—and make! It was the time to mull over their specific role for the upcoming game, the player they would be responsible for guarding in the man-to-man defense the Loggers had played all year, what their opponent's weaknesses were and how they would capitalize on them and, best of all, how they would ultimately feel once the contest was over and a victory was in hand. Those were the thoughts Bryson wanted the boys to possess, the thoughts and wide-awake dreams that might very well spell the difference between the delightful thrill of victory and the dreaded agony of defeat. Those were the waking dreams to finally usher in dreams of the sleeping kind, providing an eight-hour break from the pressures they would face throughout the four-day affair.

The Logger's first-round opponents weren't expected to be a formidable foe, or so said most of the sportswriters there in Spokane covering the tournament. But Bryson knew any team qualifying for state had talent, momentum or both. With about four minutes left in the third quarter of the game prior to theirs between Pe Ell and Brewster, Bryson and his team headed for the locker room to get dressed and focus on their upcoming opponent. By now the Darrington rooting section was almost full, and fans rose to their feet to acknowledge support for their team as they departed the stands.

After getting dressed, some of the players were standing and chatting about the earlier games, others were reclined and listening to music and a few were off by themselves, praying or putting things in order.

After some pre-game instructions from Bryson, each player touched the "Play Like A Champion Today" sign that had been carefully transported to Spokane and the Loggers entered the court for warm-ups. About 3,500 basketball junkies were in attendance for the evening contests, and PeEll fans, excited about their opening victory, were staying put to watch the activity of their possible second-round opponent.

Bryson was very familiar with the Arena setting, coaching now for the eighth time in the same tournament he had played in for two years during his high school career. And this season he was confident he had brought what was perhaps his best team ever to try and bid farewell, once and for all, to a 46-year absence from championship play. His players had incredibly high expectations of themselves as well. They, too, believed in the talent and chemistry of their team. But, even more, they believed in each other. They knew their roles and, especially in their last six games, had lived them out, almost to perfection.

Valley Christian entered the tournament with a 15-8 record and Bryson had reminded his team again and again not to take them lightly or look beyond any first-round opponent. The Loggers heeded his words and came out playing a smothering defense. Both teams were shooting poorly, likely due to big-gym and big-game jitters, but Darrington forced numerous Valley Christian turnovers and took a 22-11 lead into the locker room at the half.

Darrington kept up the defensive pressure in the early minutes of the third quarter, and their lead grew to 17 points. But Valley Christian stayed determined to get back into the contest. On the strength of three straight three-point field goals, they closed the gap to within four points with three minutes remaining.

Bryson called a timeout and directed his players to stall, forcing their opponents to foul and put his team at the foul line. He was confident in the strategy, as his Loggers were better than average when it came to protecting the ball and a solid free-throw shooting team. Darrington was already in the bonus and made four key free-throws in the waning moments to come away with a hard-fought, 55-49 victory and a date to meet Pe Ell (21-5) in the state quarterfinals. Bryce Boyd tallied 16 second-half points to finish with a game-high 22, while Matt Reece scored 13 points, gathered seven rebounds and dished out three assists in the first-round victory.

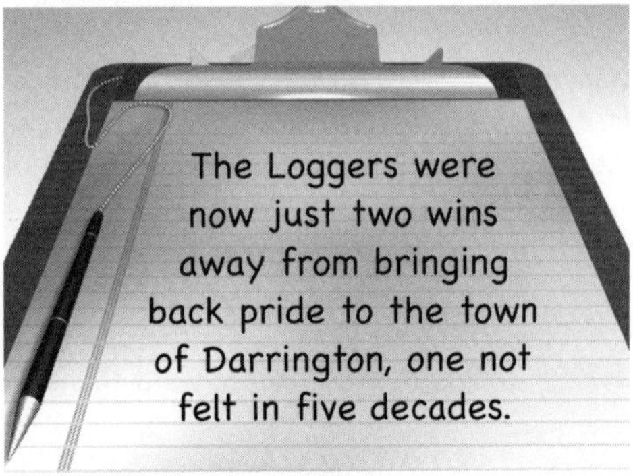

The PeEll Trojans were Darrington's second round opponent, a strong team from southwest Washington. The Loggers continued their assault on the title with a stellar second-half shooting performance. Leading 32-24 at the break, Darrington shot a torrid 69% in the final half. After outscoring the Trojans 15-5 in the third quarter, the Loggers eased to a 66-50 win and a spot in the state semifinals. Once again, Reece and Boyd led the way for Darrington. Reece scored 21 points while Boyd netted 14 to go along with 13 rebounds. Evan Smith finished with 13 points and seven rebounds.

The Loggers were now just two wins away from bringing back pride to the town of Darrington, one that hadn't been felt in nearly five decades. Bryson's team would face the winner of the Garfield-Palouse/Sunnyside Christian contest to be played later that evening. Defending champion Sunnyside Christian would look to stake their claim as the team to beat once they reached the final four, and were favored to meet the Loggers in a rematch of the previous year's quarterfinal round. But Garfield-Palouse pulled off the big upset. Using a slow-down offense and a last-minute surge, the Vikings overtook Sunnyside Christian in the final minute to come away with a 41-39 win. West would meet east in the semi-final game, and the Loggers had to wait an incredibly long 25 hours after their victory over Pe Ell before play would begin.

Friday would be a difficult day of waiting. The Loggers would again play a late-evening game and time moved by in turtle-like fashion throughout the day. After an early dinner, they headed to the Arena to ready themselves for action. This was the first chance this group of players had to participate in a game of such significance. Never before had they reached the final four of the tournament, and they felt honored to be there and represent Darrington. The Loggers would face their most formidable opponent of the year in Garfield-Palouse, a team ranked fifth in the state, owners of a 20-6 record and coming off their emotional, upset win over top-ranked Sunnyside Christian.

The semifinal round was a familiar spot for Garfield-Palouse. The Vikings had three state titles in their school's history, the first coming in 1990, then back-to-back championships in 2000 and 2001. They were also riding a 10-game, state-tournament winning streak. The Loggers knew they would need to play their best game of the year to land them in the one game they had dreamed about playing in for twelve years.

If the Loggers were nervous about the semi-final game, or if they felt intimidated by the Viking's history of tournament domination, it didn't manifest itself on the court. Darrington jumped out to a 10-0 lead and maintained a comfortable 30-22 halftime margin. The Loggers kept the pressure on the Vikings in the second half and owned a 50-38 lead with three minutes remaining. But on the strength of three consecutive three-pointers by the Vikings, the Darrington lead was cut to 50-47 with only 1: 47 to play. Bryson ordered a time-out to give his squad a needed rest and a final charge to focus first on protecting the ball and sinking foul-shots, and after that to be ready to play their typical, pressure-style defense. Bryson knew Garfield-Palouse would do their best to pressure the ball, hoping to create a turnover but fouling if necessary, forcing the Loggers to win the game at the free-throw line. He was confident his team could withstand the pressure and maintain their lead, making clutch free-throws when called upon to do so.

Darrington did just that, making four consecutive free-throws to take a 54-51 with only 20 seconds remaining. The Loggers had possession of the ball and simply needed to secure it, draw a foul and sink one or two foul-shots to create a two-possession game and make it nearly impossible for the Vikings to mount a comeback. Garfield-Palouse made two attempts to steal the ball but came up empty, then fouled Logger's point-guard Jared Grimmer with 11 seconds to go. Grimmer came to the line, knowing the incredibly crucial nature of his upcoming free-throw attempts. After a time-out by Garfield-Palouse in an attempt to ice Grimmer, the senior stepped to the line with 4,000 basketball fans on their feet. Grimmer dribbled three times, took a deep breath and fired his first shot. The ball, in Grimmer's opinion, looked to be long and heading off the back of the rim. Instead, the ball hit the back of the iron, took a soft bounce straight up and fell back down through the hoop. Appearing a bit calmer on his second attempt, Grimmer drained it, giving Darrington a 56-51 lead. Garfield-Palouse called their final timeout but, trailing by five points with only 11 seconds remaining, there was little real hope for the Vikings. Garfield-Palouse starting guard and All-State selection John Smith put up a final three-pointer with seven seconds to go, bouncing it off the back of the rim. Boyd corralled the rebound and the Loggers ran out the remaining five seconds of the clock to gain a 56-51 victory and a much-coveted trip to the final game of the state tournament—their first in 46 years.

Jason Ashe was the key player in the Logger's semi-final victory, scoring 15 points, 12 of those on four of eight shooting from beyond the three-point line. He also had six rebounds, two assists and two steals. Prior to the game, however, it was questionable whether or not Ashe would even play, as he was throwing up and experiencing intense stomach pains. But inspired by his recollection of what Bryson had shared with him and his teammates in regard to former Darrington standout Ned Miller and his play-through-pain, never-give-up mentality (that, along with a visit Miller had made a year earlier to address the team at a practice), and knowing Miller would be in attendance at the game, Ashe not only played, but played what his coaches called the best game of his life. Boyd was also a big key in the Logger's victory, continuing his outstanding tournament play with 17 points and six rebounds.

Darrington was in the championship round, but which team would they face? Would it be Waterville or the more familiar opponent, Shoreline Christian? Prior to tournament play, most of the players had been hoping for a final-round match against top-ranked Sunnyside Christian. But now it really didn't matter. They had already beaten Shoreline Christian earlier in the year, but had been soundly defeated by the Crusaders in a road contest a few weeks later. A title game would be a big boost for Westside pride, as it would pit two teams from the west side of the Cascades against each other in the final game for the first time since 1983. Waterville, on the other hand, would be an unfamiliar opponent. But the Loggers knew enough about the Warriors to gain instant respect for them. They were ranked second in the state and owned a 24-2 record, the best mark of any tournament team. Shoreline Christian came away with a convincing win, defeating Waterville 65-50, joining Darrington as the only team with a final shot at glory in 2003 and their first opportunity for a state title in the school's history.

Coach Bryson and his players left the Arena around 10:30 p.m. that night and headed back to the hotel for one last night of rest before the biggest game of their lives, a championship contest against arch-rival Shoreline Christian set for 9:00 p.m. on Saturday. Most of the Darrington fans didn't sleep well that night. After all, in less than 24 hours they would get their long-awaited shot at redemption, and they had never been more anxious or antsy. For many years (for some it had been all 46 years), Darrington fans had to continually answer the question of when—when will the Loggers ever get back to the top? And it was the same question they had been asking themselves for quite some time: "When will we get back to the top?" It had been 46 years to this point, and their doubts remained. But at least, for now, there was hope.

Many of the most anxious fans rolled over continuously in their beds on Friday night, and Bryson was wide awake as well, thinking about so many things, one of which was what it must have been like in 1955 and 1957 for my father the night before his two championship games. In 1955, the Loggers were the heavy underdog. In 1957, they were the huge favorite. But Bryson was neither in 2003 as the game was predicted to be a toss-up. Each team had defeated the other in the regular season. Each had a similar won-loss record. And each had looked impressive in their three wins that put them in the title game.

While Bryson couldn't draw upon any strategy my father may have employed in either of his title games, he couldn't stop thinking about him. He had started the year with a humble act of dedicating the season to my father, calling his team to write his initials on their shoes. He had worked as hard as he ever had while coaching the Loggers, even though this was the one team he believed had the best chance of any to win it all. And, along the way, he had displayed a heart to help his players at crucial points of the season. He had trusted his players. He hadn't given in to personal discouragement during a highly disappointing three-game stretch in the latter stage of the season. He had allowed his team the opportunity to help him create strategies for upcoming games and his players felt a great sense of appreciation for how he had led them. And he had remained a gentleman throughout the season, not becoming agitated or frustrated with his players when their performance wasn't up to par. So was this the year the Darrington drought would come to an end? Would a coach already successful in more important matters of life find first-place success for the first time in his coaching career? In less than 24 hours, those two questions would be answered.

Darrington fans cheer on their Loggers during the 2003 State 'B' Tournament in the Spokane Arena

Chapter Twenty-Three

The Final

Darrington fans finished their own pre-game meals and made their way to the Arena. Most of them arrived early, around 6:45 p.m., to stake a claim on the best seats possible in the Darrington rooting section and watch the consolation game that pitted Garfield-Palouse against Waterville for third place. Watching that contest seemed to make the time pass quicker and it was a welcomed break from the nervousness of knowing their Loggers would soon be playing for a state title. But the final game couldn't come soon enough. Fingernails were getting substantially shorter, the sweet taste of long-lasting gum was disappearing more rapidly than a stick of Juicy Fruit and feet were tapping the floor at a much higher rate than a fiddler in a bluegrass band. Oh sure, fans were confident, but who could blame them for their borderline neurosis during the consolation game. Most people aren't very comfortable when they travel in uncharted territory. And that's what this game was to most of those from Darrington. Married couples in town hadn't encountered this type of stress before, even on their wedding day. Players' fathers felt the agonizing wait for the final game to be a bit more challenging than the one 17 or 18 years prior to that night anticipating their baby boy's emergence from the womb. And those with a good memory of their college years would say their first 20-minute speech in front of more than 50 fellow-freshmen was a walk in the park compared to this run for a championship.

On this night, the Loggers would face league champion and archrival Shoreline Christian in the final game of the Washington State 'B' Basketball Championships. Not many had expected either team to advance to this point. Darrington's final ranking in the polls just before the state tournament games began had dropped from sixth to ninth, and Shoreline was a few notches below that. Besides that, Shoreline Christian had never appeared in a state-final game, and this was the first time in 46 long years for the Loggers.

More than 4,000 people were in attendance at the Spokane Arena and thousands more would be watching the game across the state on live television. Most of the 450 in attendance from Darrington were well beyond nervous, finding it nearly impossible to erase the subtle doubts in

The Loggers are introduced moments before their championship game against Shoreline Christian

their minds about their team's chances to win. Sure, they believed their Loggers could defeat Shoreline Christian. After all, they had done so in impressive fashion earlier in the year. But the most recent meeting between the two teams hadn't produced similar results, as the Loggers lost by 12 points on the Crusader's home court. The Loggers, however, had rebounded incredibly since that loss, and Darrington hadn't felt the sting of defeat for nine straight games. A win on this night would culminate a 10-0 run to the finish line, give the Loggers an impressive 23-4 overall record and, most importantly, allow players and fans alike the right to call themselves state champions.

Garfield-Palouse defeated Waterville in the third-place contest, and it would be approximately 25 minutes before the Loggers would tip off against Shoreline Christian. Those 25 minutes seemed a lot like 25 hours to the Darrington faithful. They wanted action. As soon as possible, they wanted to know what set of emotions they'd be experiencing. Would they be feeling ecstasy and euphoria basking in the pride champions are allotted? Or would they suffer from depression-like symptoms after another discouraging loss? Could they plan the championship celebration parade on their ride home to Darrington? Or would they have to endure a long and silent journey home, day one of another difficult, yearlong battle to manage life in the 47th consecutive year of a drought-ridden basketball climate.

Between games, fans reloaded on hot dogs, nachos, candy bars and Cokes. They would need all the manufactured energy from a sugar and salt high just to make it through the next 90 minutes. Somewhere around 10:15 p.m. the jury would return with its final verdict. Until then, it would be a wait-and-watch proposition. But waiting was something these folks were very familiar with! They had waited 46 years, so another 90 minutes, though hectic and heart-wrenching, could be survived. A few of the people in the Darrington stands had attended the title games in 1955 and 1957, and each of them appeared a bit calmer than those who had never witnessed such an event.

For the final time in the season, twelve young men and their coaches touched the "Play Like A Champion Today" sign and jogged to the entrance of the Arena court. A few of the most in-tune fans caught sight of their team's upcoming entrance and nudged their neighbors for the night, letting them know it was time to make some noise. Loud clapping began and soon, in unison, all 450 were screaming, "Loggers, Loggers, Loggers . . ."

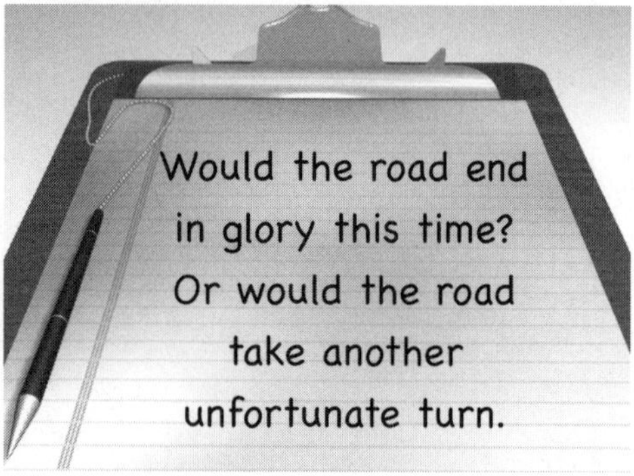

For the following 25 minutes, twelve young men stood at the brink of a dream becoming reality, doing lay-up drills, a three-man weave, going over game situations and practicing free-throws. With about seven minutes left on the clock before game-time, Bryson and his Loggers returned to the locker room. Not much was said in the next few minutes. It was more of a final opportunity to relax, laugh off some nervousness and do a little last-minute focusing on the opponent. Nothing more needed to be said. After all, the Loggers were very familiar with their foe and each player knew his role and responsibility. And more than anything else, they all agreed they had what was needed to win.

Darrington players returned to the court with about two minutes remaining before game time. After some final preparations, the buzzer sounded, signaling the end of warm-ups and the beginning of player introductions. Upon his team's return to the bench, Bryson huddled his players one final time before sending them out on their title quest. This was it. This was the beginning of the end of a long road, one paved with practices, plenty of wins and a few tough losses, hard work, recommitments and high hopes. Would the road end in glory this time? Or would the road take another unfortunate turn, indicating Darrington still had a ways to go before reaching their final destination? Would divine intervention enter into play this night? Were the heavens stirring? Did an angel or two seek permission to sit on Bryson's bench? And could any heavenly help for Darrington be possible playing against a team from Shoreline Christian? Was a humble, hard-working man with a huge heart to help others going to be the center of heaven's attention for the next 90 minutes? Was a godly king's promise made thousands of years prior to this night about to be fulfilled, the promise that blessings would come to individuals if they displayed certain heroic qualities? Was this the moment twelve players and their coaches would be rewarded for following the king's advice? Was this the year for the Loggers to win it all? Was a championship cigar destined to find its way into Bryson's mouth? Or would it just be Darrington's championship dreams going up in smoke?

Darrington players, coaches and fans in a relaxing moment between tournament games

Darrington came into the contest riding a nine-game winning streak, their last loss coming against the team they would face for the title. The Crusaders had won 13 of their last 14 games, including three close victories in the tournament by a combined 11 points. It was destined to be a barnburner from the very beginning. Apparently, someone forgot to tell the Loggers to bring their matches! When your only shot for glory comes around once every half-century or so, you better take full advantage of the opportunity. And Darrington did just that! On the strength of play from Evan Smith and Bryce Boyd, the Loggers scored the game's first six points and followed that up with a 9-0 run to post a 20-6 lead midway through the second quarter. They extended their lead to 29-12 with another 7-0 burst and ended the half with a 29-16 cushion. All of Darrington's first-half scoring came from three players. Smith and Boyd led the way with 11 each and Matt Reece chipped in the other seven. The trio was a combined 13 for 21 from the field in the first half.

Family members show their support for the Loggers

A 13-point lead was nice, and the margin seemed to lower the anxiety level in the Darrington stands. But fans knew all too well of the Crusaders' comeback abilities and could only hope their team wouldn't come out flat for the final half. Shoreline Christian had scored the final four points of the first half and many Darrington fans seemed concerned the momentum going into the break didn't belong to their team. Bryson was also familiar with his opponent's ability to mount a comeback and he kept his players on high alert during his halftime talk. He did all he could to make sure his team remained focused on the fundamentals and kept the same intensity for the second half. But Bryson knew the championship trophy was very much in sight for Darrington, and that a heavy, 46-year-old monkey was about to be tossed off the town's aching back.

Everything appeared to be going the Logger's way that night, even during the halftime festivities. Darrington High principal Ken Schutz had been pre-selected to attempt a shot from half-court. If the shot were made, his school would win $100. And much like the Logger's shooting touch in the first half, Schutz was right on target. He made the improbable shot, a sign to many in the Darrington stands this was definitely their year. Bryson commented afterward how the entire night, including the principal's shot, had to have been a bit magical because, as he put it, "Schutz can't shoot a lick!"

Darrington picked up where they left off to end the half. Smith began the second half just as he had in the first, connecting on his first four field-goal attempts, propelling his team to a 50-34 lead at the end of three quarters. Only eight minutes remained, and now it was just a matter of poise and playing smart. The title was theirs and they knew it. The fans knew it. The media knew it. The Crusader crowd, though holding out slight hope for a comeback, knew it. Bryson knew it, too, and he wasn't about to have anything interrupt his plans for a championship.

The Loggers maintained their double-digit lead during the first four minutes of the period, then extended it to 20 points with only a few minutes remaining. Bryson had the opportunity to play all of his players as Shoreline Christian waved the surrender flag midway in the final quarter. Smith, Boyd and Reece continued their torrid shooting, and the Loggers came away with a 64-43 victory. It was their tenth straight win, giving

Darrington coach Jeff Bryson instructs his team during a time-out in the championship game

them a 23-4 season record. But those two statistics meant little or nothing to Darrington folks. Only one thing mattered! It was the one statistic they had desired for nearly a half-century. Not since Dwight Eisenhower was in the White House and Disneyland was making its entrance into the American culture had Darrington been able to rock-around-the-clock like they did that night. Not since a stamp was three cents and Leave it to Beaver was televised in prime-time had the Loggers been king of the hill in high school basketball in the small towns of Washington. The win moved Darrington into a fourth place tie for most state titles since the tournament's inception in 1931 with three. Among the 124 schools that compete in the 'B' division, only Brewster (5), Reardan (6) and St. John (7) have claimed more.

Darrington players celebrate the championship

"It's the perfect way to go out," Boyd said. "I would have been disappointed if we had come out of it with anything but the championship."

"We wanted this for years," Smith said. "We've played together since we were little kids. I just love these guys and I can't believe our dreams have come true."

But perhaps nobody wanted it more and would have been more devastated with a loss than Bryson.

"This is something we worked on for 12 years," he said. "I definitely appreciate it much more now."

Remaining his humble self, Bryson reiterated his recipe for success.

"You've got to have talent, you've got to have good athletes and you've got to have kids who work hard. And we had all of that," he said.

Bryson remembered how folks around Darrington had been predicting a possible state title for that year's group of seniors when they were still in grade school.

"They're just a special group," Bryson said of his team. "Their quiet resolve is what stands out to me. They don't say a lot. They just play hard, play good defense and move the ball around. They respect themselves as players, and as people."

No doubt his sentiments are true. It's hard not to be that way when it's modeled for you for so many years by the one in charge.

In keeping with his team-first strategy for life and winning basketball, Bryson was quick to point out the Logger's success was a shared effort. He went to great lengths to praise everyone involved in his team's triumph, including former players, past coaches and the hundreds of Darrington fans who followed the team to Spokane. Bryson even set up a post-game meeting between his current and former players, reminding his seniors of just how important it was for them to understand their success had been built upon those who came before them. And he reminded his underclassmen that any future success would be bridged by the past and a deep sense of gratitude for what had come before them. Bryson also gave special thanks to three members of Darrington's previous state championship teams who made the trip to Spokane—Roland Mount, the hero of the 1955 championship contest with his game-winning shot in the closing seconds, Ken Estes, also a member of the '55 squad, and David Andrews, a back-up guard on the 1957 title team. But Bryson reserved his biggest praise for an individual who wasn't even there, yet still the one he considers most responsible for his championship run.

"Coach Simmons was the author of Logger Ball," Bryson said. "Our basketball program is what it is because of who he was and what he started more than 50 years ago. We played this season in his memory and his championship spirit was a key to our season's success."

Nobody in Darrington disagreed, especially Bryson's players.

"Coach Simmons was the one who started it all."

"He was a role model for all the other coaches to live up to."

"He had a presence throughout the year."

"We all had a lot of respect for the man."

Those were just a few of the sentiments about my father being shared by the most-recent state champions. Those aren't typical statements made by teenagers in regard to their personal success, but Bryson had instilled in each of his players the importance of tradition and bridging the success of the present with that of the past. Though my father became a small-town hero in the 50s and 60s, his elevated status hadn't been marred in Darrington the following 50 years. Only now, he shared that honor with another man who believed in the very things he believed in that led to his success both on and off the court—humility, hard work and a heart to help others.

As long as Bryson leads the way for the Loggers, these three qualities are what his teams and the townspeople cheering them on will no doubt notice. Whether it leads to more basketball titles in Darrington or not isn't really important. What's important is his leadership will most definitely lead to many more young men entering the adult world with a huge shot at real success and a good chance of being crowned champions in life.

Chapter Twenty-Four

A Hero's Welcome

Back at the Logger's hotel, classmates, relatives and friends gathered with the team in the grand ballroom for a championship celebration. Each party-participant was thrilled with the outcome of the evening's events and unbelievably relieved they could thoroughly enjoy the six-hour trip home the following day where conversations would be void of "what if?" and "what do you feel about our chances next year?"

After the celebrations waned, fans headed for their rooms and a rest that would no doubt be better than any they had experienced in quite some time. Most of them managed to get to sleep around two or three in the morning, but a few decided to shun the mattress option entirely and stayed up until sunrise. They could sleep some on the ride home, they said, taking turns on driving duties with a family member or friend.

The team bus headed back for Darrington on Sunday morning a little later than expected, as Bryson and his players took full advantage of an offer made by a Spokane businessman earlier in the week. Before the tournament began, the entire team and coaching staff ate dinner together at the International House of Pancakes, located near their hotel in Spokane. After learning of their identity, the owner/manager of the restaurant promised each of them a free meal should they come away with the title, and the Loggers weren't about to bypass the breakfast of champions. They contacted the owner, told him of their exploits from the night before then enjoyed as many pancakes and pieces of bacon as possible.

Most of the Darrington fan base would leave for home around noon on Sunday. The loyal supporters would arrive in Darrington sometime around six or seven in the evening if all went according to plan. The approximate agenda was reported to a point-person back home, and on Sunday afternoon the communication tree began spreading its branches in regard to the latest update on the champion's estimated time of arrival. In the next few hours, about 300 residents made their way to the high school and waited in a cold and wet parking lot to meet the newly-crowned champions. A number of them were children, many of them tightly clutching a pen and piece of paper, hoping to get an autograph or two from their favorite players. But there were a number of Darrington residents who didn't feel a welcome-home from the school's parking lot was suitable for state champions. So about 150 people piled into their cars and headed west to Arlington, the closest town of some size where the returning entourage would pass through on their way back to Darrington. Joining those automobiles were the town's two fire trucks, driven by volunteer firemen who planned to sound their sirens most of the way home and serve as an escort for the team and its many supporters. Kevin Ashe said the escort provided by the many fans was bigger and better than ever, but not a shock to him.

"Most every year that we've come back from state we've gotten an escort into town," he said.

Ashe also remembers hearing stories of Darrington's basketball domination in the 50s and 60s and a town caught up in their team's success.

"When I was a kid, because of the '55 and '57 teams, we thought the players and the coaches were like gods," Ashe said.

It was about 6:30 p.m. when the Darrington team bus finally made its way into Arlington carrying the newest icons in town. As the bus made its last turn eastward to head for home, a line of cars, estimated to be more than a mile long, was waiting to lead the way. It was a moment similar to the scene in *Hoosiers* when fans of the small-town Indiana basketball team followed the team's bus to away games. Drivers honked their horns for most of the 30-minute trip. People were standing on the side of the main road heading into town, as well as the one going south toward the high school, waving and holding up champion-worthy signs. About a mile outside of Darrington, Bryson's emotions reached their height as he passed by the cemetery where his father had been buried about eight years prior to that day. It was one of the biggest days of Bryson's life, and he was thinking just how special it would have been had his father been able to be there and experience it all.

But the sadness he felt would soon be overshadowed by the celebration that would take place about a mile down the road, as about 750 people were there to party and proudly proclaim the Logger's victory, relishing every moment of their championship reality. There were strong feelings of pride and satisfaction, but, more than anything, relief ruled the day. Darrington needed that title. There were plenty of reasons why and perhaps as many reasons as there were residents. And Bryson recalls feeling the townspeople's relief in the comments he heard that night and in the days and weeks to follow.

"I was real surprised how many people said "thank-you" as opposed to "congratulations"," he remembered.

Those comments helped Bryson understand how much the title meant to the town, and he felt a deep sense of satisfaction knowing he had made a significant contribution.

Some of the players remained at the school throughout the night and into the early-morning hours, enjoying the moment and engaging in numerous conversations about their latest Spokane experience. Most of the people who came to celebrate with them were long gone before then, off to their homes and off to bed to get a few hours of sleep before beginning another week of work on Monday morning. But they would go to work with a bigger smile, a better attitude and a bottle full of pride that bubbled over during the day.

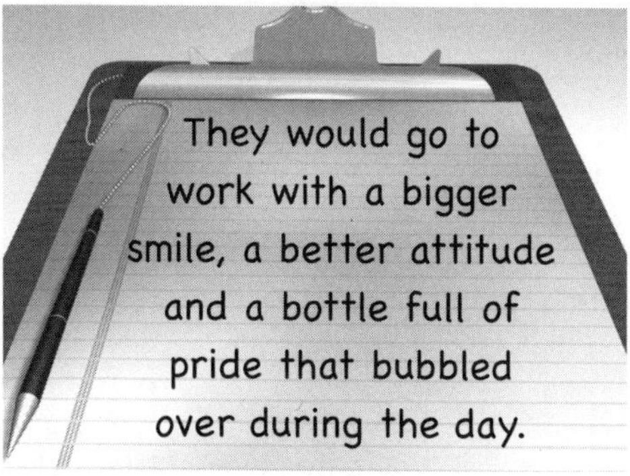

Young children woke up the following morning and headed off to school with a backpack full of books and, more importantly to them at that moment, autographs from All-State center Bryce Boyd and some of the other players.

Business owners came in an hour or two later than store hours indicated on their signs. But who in their right mind, they reasoned, would come for early-morning business after all the late-night celebrations? Almost 100% of the conversations on Monday were about—what else—Darrington basketball. A few outsiders passing through town unaware of the greatest news to hit Darrington since 1957 got an earful how the rain had started falling late Saturday night, bringing a sudden end to the 46-year drought.

Kevin and Randy Ashe, the two men most instrumental in preparing the oldest players for basketball prowess before entering the high school ranks, also own and operate the IGA grocery market in town. On Monday morning, a hand-written sign appeared over the meat-cutting department, symbolizing the town's euphoric state:

"Please forgive us if you don't see what you need. Basketball is being spoken today! Everything will be back to normal tomorrow."

After returning from a hard day's work that Monday afternoon, fathers took their young sons outside to shoot baskets, despite the inclement weather. They focused on helping the future Darrington stars keep their elbows in and their eyes on the front of the rim while shooting, important instructions to perhaps put them in a better position to help the Loggers win another title when it came their time to shine. Players and their classmates returned to school and to the classes they'd been excused from the previous week. Teachers decided to make Monday as low-key and lesson-free as possible, a special assembly honored the Logger's on-the-court achievements and Principal Schutz was deciding where to spend the $100, thanks to his on-target, half-court heave.

Bryson returned Monday morning to teach math and geography to seventh through tenth-graders. He, too, was exhausted, but came to do what he enjoys doing just as much as coaching basketball. He provided more important insights for his students in the scholastic sense, but on this day he took a few breaks from the regular routine to talk about his Logger's amazing win and answer questions from those who weren't able to attend the tournament games.

Jeff Bryson and his family pose for a photograph around the 2003 championship trophy

For the next number of weeks, Darrington residents had to pinch themselves (and each other) on a regular basis just to make sure they weren't dreaming. With every pinch they were reminded the news was indeed true—the Loggers were champions once again. For many of the people there, this title will be enough good-news medication for the next 46 years. They'll be reminded their town is still on the map and they'll have something significant on which to hang their humble hats. And though they all hope for an earlier return to championship form than 2049, or another 46 years, most of these small-town folks have the character needed to ride the good feeling of this latest victory for a long, long time.

Chapter Twenty-Five

A Banner Night

I received a call from my mother in early November of 2003, informing me of some sort of championship banner ceremony coming up in Darrington to honor my father's teams and his contributions to the town. I must admit I had no idea the Loggers won the championship eight months earlier, and I assumed the townspeople simply wanted to get some championship banners representing his teams from 1955 and 1957 and hang them in the Darrington Community Center.

About two weeks later, I learned of the exciting events that took place in Spokane in March of 2003 after receiving an official invitation from Kevin Ashe to attend the ceremony. Initially, I felt a bit melancholy about the news. I guess a part of me wanted my father's accomplishments to remain unparalleled, and I knew, up until 2002, no Darrington basketball team had ever won a title except the two my he had coached. I had just passed the first anniversary of my father's death, so anything to keep his heroics unequaled in the small town was probably something my heart wanted to cling to for as long as possible. But after I put aside my initial thoughts about my father no longer being Darrington's only championship coach, I began to think how incredible their recent victory was and how interesting the timing was as well—that a Darrington team won the championship for the first time in 46 years, the very first season after his death.

The invitation was for our family to come to Darrington in mid-December to help honor the three title teams and witness an unveiling of the championship banners. The ceremony would take place at halftime of the boys' varsity game and Kevin asked me if I would be willing to come and share a few words on my father's behalf. Every player, coach and manager from those teams had been invited to come for a evening designed to tie the glory days of the past with the Logger's latest run of success in 2003.

My first thought was to respond to Kevin's invitation with a simple "thank-you, but no," mostly because I was pretty sure my schedule wouldn't allow me to come. I had just flown to Washington to spend time with my mother prior to receiving Kevin's invitation, and making another trip so soon after that didn't seem feasible. I'm so glad my first thoughts weren't my final thoughts! After a few days of point/counterpoint on whether or not I should make the trip to Darrington, I decided it was the right thing to go and take my mother to the evening's events. I could sense she really wanted to attend, even though she assured me it wasn't a big deal whether we ended up going or not.

It wasn't long before I concluded the event was a great shot at redemption for me, as I had lived for 12 years with a deep regret for not attending my father's Hall of Fame induction ceremony in 1991. I had just moved from Lincoln, Nebraska to Cincinnati when I heard the news of his upcoming induction and, unfortunately, I made a decision not to travel to Washington and participate in that special gathering. Though my father and I talked at length on the day of the ceremony, and though I wrote him what he said was an incredible card of congratulations, to this day I can't believe I let a few minor things stand in the way of a major opportunity to show my father the honor and respect he so richly deserved. Though I had apologized a number of times to my father for not being there, and though each time he assured me of his complete understanding, I couldn't seem to get over my incredibly selfish decision about not attending a once-in-a-lifetime event for the most important man in my life.

So I wasn't about to make another bad choice when it came to honoring my father's accomplishments. This, I thought, would be a great chance to not only honor him, but to see many of the players I had heard so many stories about through the years. Kevin had informed me in his letter and subsequent e-mails that nearly all of my father's players and assistant coaches from the 1955 and 1957 teams were planning to be in attendance. Some players were coming from as far away as Nevada and many had told Kevin they welcomed the opportunity to honor their former coach. Even a family representative for one of the deceased players would be there for the celebration.

Once I made the decision to go, I became more and more excited about getting there. I didn't have an exact idea as to what would transpire that night, but I knew I had a chance to speak for a few minutes to what I thought would be an overflowing crowd at the Community Center. I rehearsed a number of options as to what I should share, and in the next few weeks settled on the words I would relay to his players and the many Darrington fans.

I arrived in Portland on a Thursday afternoon and rented a car to travel to Longview. As soon as I saw my mother, I could sense the same nervousness in her that I was feeling. Some of it was probably from wanting to make sure we would do our best to represent my father in the most appropriate way the following evening and the rest was from unknown expectations. We left Longview on Friday morning and arrived in Darrington about four hours later. We checked into the Stagecoach Inn, Darrington's one and only resting place for outsiders, and had about a three-hour wait before leaving for the game and banner ceremony. The banner ceremony was to take place at halftime of the men's varsity game, but all the invitees were encouraged to come early, meet each other and take in the girl's varsity game that began at 6:00 p.m. I used those three hours to relax and go over my thoughts about what I was going to say. My mother was curious as to my specific plans, and I'm sure much of it was to help prepare her heart for what both of us knew would be a very emotional night. I gave her a brief sketch of my speech and, as she always remarks about any of my sermons she's had a chance to hear, said it sounded perfect and was confident I would do a wonderful job.

We left the motel around 5:00 p.m. and had dinner at the Backwoods Cafe, one of the few eating establishments in town. On the walls and tables throughout the restaurant were fliers announcing the banner ceremony and the special honoring of Coach LaVerne Simmons that was to be a significant part of the evening. I grew more and more nervous as the time grew closer for us to finally set foot in the gymnasium my father helped build and the one he had worked his coaching magic in so many times. I was going to meet Randall Phillips, Gary Sweeny, Gerald Greene, Roland Mount, Dick Hitchcock and many other Darrington greats for the very first time. I could anticipate many of them would be letting me know how they felt about my father, and I was just hoping to hold it all together emotionally for the next few hours. My mother was anticipating similar conversations with many of the men and women she thought would be there, those she knew in Darrington from 1957-1964 and others she had kept in touch with the next 40 years.

We arrived at the Community Center around 6:15 p.m. and walked into the hallway just outside the gymnasium doors. Within a few seconds, my mother and I received a very warm greeting from Kevin, though he wasn't completely certain of our identity. To say he was friendly and welcoming would be a major understatement. After discovering who we were, it was as if his entire world no longer mattered and we became the only people who did. He presented us with a program chronicling the evening's event, placed a yellow boutonniere on our jackets and began introducing us to former Loggers who had returned for the ceremony. A few minutes later, I had the pleasure of meeting Jeff Bryson for the very first time. Both he and Kevin told me they were extremely grateful I had made the trip from Chicago, then shared a few stories about my father their parents had relayed to them. Honestly, I felt I was king for a day and they were my willing subjects. In all my years of speaking in front of hundreds of people and being associated with big churches in the big city, I had never been treated so royally.

After some pleasant exchanges and awkward moments of meeting players from my father's teams, we went to the Darrington side of the gym and climbed the stairs leading to the stands overlooking the court. We didn't get to watch very much of the girl's game, as my mother was recognized by so many people in the Darrington stands and I was immediately welcomed into her ensuing conversations.

All the championship participants were told to gather in the multi-purpose area of the Community Center after the first quarter of the men's game. We talked with many people in the next hour or so, and it was a good distraction from thinking about what I was going to say and being overly concerned I might end up saying something stupid and embarrassing myself.

At the appropriate time, I escorted my mother down the steps then down the hall to the multi-purpose room where Kevin walked all of us through the plan for the ceremony. The 1955 Loggers would be introduced first, then the 1957 team and finally the members of the 2003 squad. My mother and I were to walk out with the 1957 team and, after each player from that team had been introduced, I would be asked to speak on my father's behalf and on behalf of his two championship teams.

The second quarter had just ended, and it was time to begin the team introductions. The gym was packed and everybody there, even the visiting crowd from Concrete, was standing. They, too, knew the Darrington legacy well (they had contributed to it many times you might say) and appreciated the town's effort to connect the past with the present. As each player and the lone assistant coach on the 1955 team was introduced, thunderous applause came from the crowd when they stepped forward to acknowledge their identity. The names were all familiar to those in the Darrington stands, but some of the players hadn't been seen in more than 45 years. But it didn't matter. They were still considered champions and heroes and they weren't about to be forgotten by the townspeople.

Then it was our turn. My mother and I walked out to center court along with the members of the 1957 team and my father's assistant coach that year, Bill Carroll. After each player had been introduced, assistant coach, Les Hagen, spoke for a few moments about the death of my father. He introduced my mother to the crowd and then presented her with a beautiful bouquet of roses, bringing tears to her eyes. Tears began welling up in my eyes as well, but I knew I had to stay under control if those in the audience were to understand what I was about to say. I knew my track record the past year of finding it difficult to hold back tears sharing about my father's death in a sermon, or even in a casual setting. Les then introduced me and told the crowd I had been asked to share a few words on behalf of my father.

There I was, on the small-town stage, addressing more than 1,000 Darrington residents. What would I tell these people? What did they need to hear from me? I decided early on I wasn't going to ad-lib anything. I knew the more I stuck with my original plan, the more likely it would come out correct. With a lump in my throat and a legend in my mind, I spoke of how much joy my father's teams and the town of Darrington had brought to him. I shared about his last few days in the hospital and how it was his memories of basketball that brought the biggest smiles to his face and greatest bursts of energy to his dying body. I thanked them for making my father's life a blessing and for treating him the way they had, like a hero. I thanked his players for the joy they had provided him while he coached them and the amazing amount of encouragement he felt the past 40 years whenever he remembered his days on the bench coaching Darrington basketball.

When I finished, I, too, received an amazing ovation. I was so incredibly blown away by the way the townspeople made me feel, and so grateful I had come to Darrington to participate in this special, once-in-a-lifetime occasion. I couldn't help but think how much I wished my father had been able to join in the ceremony and how he would have enjoyed seeing his former players, talking with all the old-timers still reminiscing of championships and being back in the town that still called him a hero.

Now it was time for the latest champions to take the court. Members of the 2003 Loggers made their way to center court, four of them in uniform as member of the 2003-2004 team. (Travis LeMance, the Logger's team manager in 2002-2003, also attended the celebration. Every player said they wanted to make sure Travis would be there because they truly considered him another member of the team. It was consistent with the other kind gestures the players had made to show their appreciation for all he meant to the team, allowing him to help cut down the nets after the win against Shoreline Christian and presenting him a championship ring later that year.) After each player had been introduced, Jeff Bryson shared some of his thoughts about the championship team, as well as his feelings in regard to the entire ceremony. It wasn't anything fancy or fiery, eloquent or elaborate, but it was thoroughly real and meaningful, focused a whole lot more on his players than on himself.

When Bryson finished, our attention was directed to the east wall of the gymnasium where three banners would be unveiled, one at a time, representing the championships of Darrington basketball. It was long overdue, many people said. Though no banners hung for 46 years acknowledging the feats of the 1955 and 1957 Loggers, few in town had forgotten their accomplishments. But now, they said, the banners seemed to make it official.

At the conclusion of the ceremony, all the champions huddled at center court around the 2003 championship trophy the Loggers had claimed earlier that year in Spokane. I started to wonder what it must have been like in 1955 and 1957 when my dad and his players were the only ones privileged to experience such a moment. And I couldn't help but think about all the additional questions I could have and should have asked him about Darrington basketball. And, once again, I felt a deep sense of disappointment from missing out on the Hall of Fame moment my father was granted by his coaching peers in 1991. Though a few of those disconcerting thoughts raced through my mind, most of my thoughts were positive, another golden opportunity to realize how blessed I was to have had a father like him.

We finished the evening by watching the latest Darrington team secure a 55-45 victory over Concrete. It was an evening one visitor, quite familiar with high school sports in the state of Washington, described in this way: "This was the most remarkable evening I have ever witnessed in a high school gymnasium. It was just amazing!"

My mother and I were both pretty tired after the game was over, and we were debating whether or not to attend the final event of the evening, a cookies-and-punch reception in the high school's music room adjacent to the Community Center. After going back and forth on the issue, we decided to stay, but just for a few minutes, we said, and then go back to the motel and get some needed rest before heading back to Longview the next morning.

After spending about 45 minutes mingling, munching on some refreshments and making our acquaintance with others who had decided to stay, we watched a short video of the Logger's championship season and then got up to leave. Before leaving, however, we made a special effort to once again thank Kevin for making the night possible, and I was also able to spend a brief moment with Coach Bryson as we were walking toward the parking lot. He thanked me for coming, complimented my father for his role in their championship then asked me if Kevin had shared what he and his players had done to begin their season. I'm pretty sure he thought I already knew the story, but I told him I wasn't aware of anything. It was then Bryson shared the story with me about how he brought my father into his team's goal for a championship season and how they dedicated the entire season to his memory. Needless to say, I was blown away! I began to cry and thanked him for such a kind gesture and especially for letting me know about the honor. The night would have been terrific without that revelation, but hearing the story how tradition and tennis shoes helped to bring about a Darrington championship was a most unbelievable ending to one of the best days of my life.

My mother and I returned to the motel shortly thereafter, but my mind didn't stop resting for days. I couldn't wait to tell all my friends about what I was calling a small-town miracle and the events of that incredible evening. And every time I told the story, I couldn't help but think how it all made perfect sense. No wonder the Loggers won the title. Why did they win it in 2003 but no other year since 1957? To me, the answer was quite obvious. Now, no doubt the Darrington ballplayers were highly skilled in 2003. No doubt they were, on ability alone, a strong contender to win the championship. But how many other Darrington teams could have said the exact same thing the previous 46 years? And how many teams around the world in all types of sports have more than enough talent but still can't find a way to win it all. I'm convinced, and always will be, Jeff Bryson was the biggest reason the Loggers were state champions in 2003. His humility to include my father in his season's goals and his march to success was just the beginning. His hard-work ethic since arriving in Darrington in 1991 had finally paid off as well. Sure, he realized his team's talent pool, but he refused to slack off in his "hard-work-not-talent" mentality for winning games. And his heart to treat current players right, former players right and Darrington fans right, as much as he knew how, was a final rallying call to the invisible forces looking to bless individuals possessing those attributes. It was a signal that anything short of a Darrington title would be a crime and considerable blown opportunity to teach interested observers in other places the really important matters in life. Whether these powers were simply on-call all year to make sure the Loggers won it all, whether they found no need to intervene due to the team's stellar performance or whether a few errant shots were put back on course or a few referees were moved to make a critical call go in the Logger's favor, we'll never know. Would the title have come to Darrington if Bryson hadn't remembered my father and encouraged his team to put his initials on their shoes? We'll never know that either. Yet it all happened exactly this way and now you're hearing about it. And maybe that's the biggest reason why these events took place. Because the more people who know about the Simmons-Bryson winning combination, the better off Darrington will be and the better off the rest of the world will be, whether it's small-town Sally or big-city Bob. And the more people who choose to imitate either man's plan for success, the more likely a war will be avoided, a marriage will be saved, a prison cell will stay empty or a life will be lived out for the better. And even if you end up being the only person who chooses to walk on these paths to success because of what you've read in this book, my decision to share this story was well worth the time and effort.

I've also come to realize other banner unveilings have taken place in my life as a result of these events. I believe three championship performances were orchestrated to rock my world, and each one was clearly played out for me in the 18 months following my father's death.

First, for some reason I was moved in my heart to come to Darrington for the championship celebration, even though my initial plan was to decline the invitation. So why did I end up going? Did God know I needed to be there? I believe my presence was primarily to remove the guilt I had been feeling for so many years for not attending my father's greatest moment as a coach in 1991, his induction into the Washington State Basketball Coaches Hall of Fame. I'm convinced God had no desire for me to continue living in guilt about that poor decision and he offered me this opportunity to move beyond the pain of a past failure. I believe coming to Darrington to participate in the banner ceremony was my chance to make things right.

Champions separated by nearly 50 years come together at center court in the Community Center

Secondly, Jeff Bryson was moved in his heart to tell me about his team's shoe-signing moment and their dedication of the season to my father. Yes, it happened in a matter-of-fact manner, but I find it interesting my mother and I had originally decided to decline the invitation to attend the reception, the exact place I ended up receiving the news. Had we followed our original line of thinking, I doubt I would have become aware of the incredible connection between my father and the Logger's latest championship. But I came to Darrington, and then I ended up spending about an hour at the reception, just long enough to get one last moment with Coach Bryson to hear him share the story about tradition and tennis shoes. Why did I need to hear that story? After all, I was happy just to have been there to honor my father and I would have been quite content to walk away that night without hearing the inspiring news from Jeff. But I was given more than I could ask or imagine and blessings were piled on my already overflowing plate. And I also believe God knew my mother and I wouldn't be the only ones encouraged by this story, but its life-changing message would travel far outside the city limits of Darrington.

Third, and finally, my wife had it on her heart to encourage me to write a book about these events. Again, you have to remember I had no plans to come to the banner celebration. I had no idea about the team's dedication of their season to my father and, even after the banner night was officially over, I had no idea whatsoever a book about these events would be written. Thankfully, God had the idea! And with the unveiling of this third and final championship banner, I set out to bring you this story. I hope reading it has been a banner moment in your life.

Section III

The Synopsis

Chapter Twenty-Six

The Next Generation

Much of our society is quite fascinated with heroism. In truth, most of us are caught up in it as well. Deep down in our heart of hearts, we greatly admire those who are considered heroic in some way, and most of us would love to be involved in some type of valiant activity before our days are done. We pay good money to see heroic activity lived out on the big screen. Whether it was *Superman* in the 70's, *Batman* in the 80s and 90s or *Spiderman* in the present day, movies about heroes are typically the highest grossing films, by far, in any given year. But it's not just the cartoon figures we flock to watch at the movie theater—it's war heroes as well. Movies like *Braveheart, Glory*, *Saving Private Ryan* and *Blackhawk Down* all had a way of forcing us to examine our lives for evidence of bravery and heroism. In addition to receiving inspiration from superheroes and war heroes, we love a good story about a sport's hero as well. From Rocky Balboa's rags to riches character in the *Rocky* series, to Jimmy Chitwood's game-winning shot in *Hoosiers*, we're easily inspired by heroism in the athletic arena and it, too, has a way of temporarily bringing out the best in our lives. We also enjoy listening to songs about heroism and we seem inspired, upon hearing them time and again, to perform greater deeds of service for our fellowman. Whether it's Bette Midler famous line of, "Did you ever know that you're my hero?" in her number-one hit of the 80s, *Wind Beneath My Wings*, or Mariah Carey's reminder to each of us that *A Hero Lies in You*, song-lyrics that attempt to inspire us to heroism seem to strike a cord in our hearts that calls us to be our absolute best. We're greatly touched when we hear reports of men and women putting their own lives in harm's way to save another human being, whether it's rushing to rescue an injured soldier on the battlefield or running to pull an unconscious driver from a burning vehicle. Usually these heroic individuals make the morning talk-show circuit, sharing their stories alongside the ones they've rescued and often bringing tears to those of us watching.

But in reality, we can watch Superman, Batman and Spiderman on an every-day basis and still never acquire X-Ray vision, access to the Batmobile or spider webs in our wrists to put us in a better position to rescue our planet from the bad guys. Most of us will never have an opportunity to save someone's life on the freeway or from a frozen lake. It's highly unlikely we'll ever get the chance to hit a game-winning, grand slam-home run in the bottom of the ninth to win the seventh and deciding game of the World Series. And, prayerfully, none of us will have to be called to war and get the opportunity to become a hero on the battlefield.

While all these "you-too-can-be-a-hero" possibilities will probably never be within our reach, a tremendous opportunity still lies before each of us to inspire a future generation of heroes. To accomplish this lofty goal, we must simply commit to doing a better job of setting heroic examples for the children in our immediate presence. It's scary to think about, but most of the choices young people make when they finally reach adulthood (both good and bad) are often determined by what they hear and see in the adults they come in contact with during their upbringing. So, whether you live in a small town such as Darrington, a bustling metropolis like Los Angeles or somewhere in between, remember there are millions of heroes in the wings, all of them waiting to discover the appropriate way to conduct their lives by the example you set.

I'm fully confident young people in Darrington have a better-than-average chance of living heroically as adults, simply because of their opportunity to be influenced by people like Jeff Bryson. Most of these kids will be in Bryson's immediate presence a few hours a day, five days a week during junior high and high school, and they'll undoubtedly have other opportunities to see him conducting a practice, coaching a game or cheering on other young athletes at one of their games. While I'm certain his influence will be positive in many ways, each of those youngsters will need other heroic adults besides Bryson to model the qualities of humility, hard work and a heart to help others so their chances of being heroic someday can be greatly increased.

I'm a firm believer it doesn't take much to impress the children of our world in a positive way, and that kids are, by far, the best imitators amongst us. My personal desire for the children spending time with me is for them to be able to look at my life and simply say, "I want to be like him when I grow up." I have no desire whatsoever for these kids to make that statement in regard to my choice of employment, my selection of entertainment or my athletic abilities. I want them to desire it when it comes to my character as a human being. I want my own two children to say it more than anybody, but I'd like the list to be somewhat longer than that. And this is my hope for you as well concerning the children observing you in your every-day affairs of life. In order for this to happen, you'll need to choose humility, hard work and a heart to help others as the primary focus-points of your life. But the opportunity for you to make a positive impact on children is ripe because your life, at this very moment, is in full view of so many of them, probably a lot more than you even realize. With this in mind, let's consider a few places where "adult watching" takes center stage.

The first and most important place to begin taking advantage of the opportunity to influence future heroes is right in your own home. If your children don't respect you but your co-workers do, what have you accomplished? If your kids aren't the beneficiaries of your energetic and fun-loving spirit, how important is it your Friday-night poker-playing partners think you're an absolute riot or your Saturday-afternoon shopping sisters have a ball just trying to keep pace with your uninhibited, store-to-store routine? It's incredibly easy, isn't it, to put your best foot forward when you're outside the home and dealing with people who don't see you on a day-to-day basis. On the other hand, it's very easy to let your guard down and example slip when you're around those in your immediate family who know you best. While there's nothing wrong with putting your best foot forward with your boss, your buddies or the Bible-believing folks you see at church, when it comes to how you act in front of your children, you should be very concerned about displaying two of the greatest looking feet they'll ever see! Granted, your children will see your weaknesses more than anyone else. But with a greater focus on being a better example to those you've brought into this world, they'll also see your strengths more than anyone else. And even when you do blow it in their presence, there's nothing more important and powerful than setting an example of humility and repentance in regard to your failures as a parent. With those thoughts in mind, here are a few questions to ask yourself about whether or not your activities at home are heroic.

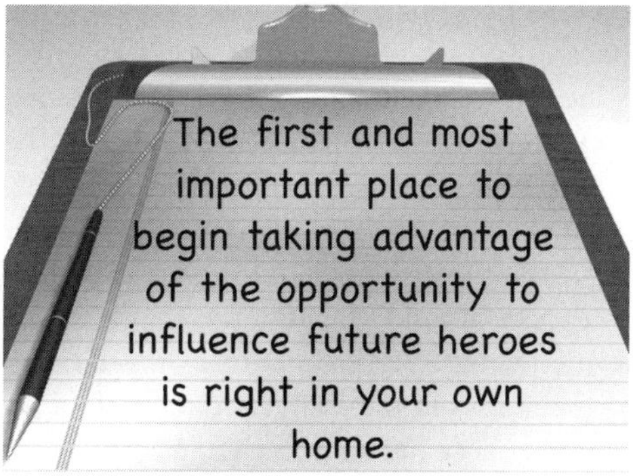

How much humility do you display in your home? Are you willing to admit your mistakes and apologize to your children once you realize you've made them? Do you seek help from other parents about how to raise your children, or are you certain you have it all figured out already? Do your children perceive you to be a hard worker in your life's pursuits? Or is laziness and half-heartedness woven into their character by what they observe in you? How would your kids say you treat them on a day-to-day basis? Do they feel valued, listened to and loved? Or do they feel more of your anger than your acceptance, as though they can never measure up to your expectations or be good enough regardless of their efforts? Do they see you treating other people with love and respect, especially when it comes to your spouse or your significant other? Do they see you displaying kindness toward your neighbors on a regular basis, regardless of how annoying you perceive them to be? How do you talk about your boss, your co-workers and your relatives in your children's presence? What do they see and hear while you're driving in bumper-to-bumper traffic and in a big hurry? How about when you're standing in a long, slow-moving line at the grocery store or the bank? What type of example are you setting for your kids when it comes to showing respect toward those in positions of authority? If you're constantly putting down the President, the local police and other people in public office who create and enforce laws for you, what are the odds your kids will respect their teachers when they establish rules in the classroom?

While the home is the number-one location for future heroes to receive excellent training, let me suggest a few other places you'll have an opportunity to develop a child's character in a positive way. The following information is extremely important, as a high percentage of youngsters unfortunately find little, if any, heroic activity taking place in their homes. The good news, however, is they still can be dramatically changed for the good by the positive adult influences they come in contact with outside the home. But here's the scariest scenario of all—if children see little or no heroic activity taking place in their own home, and if they can't find it in any of the other adults they're around consistently, they're likely headed for big trouble, as are the people they'll be influencing one day. Sadly, this is the reality for so many kids in our world today. Now here's the best news of all—if children can spot heroism in their home, and if they're fortunate enough to see more examples of it outside their home, chances are unbelievably good they'll enter adulthood with heroic qualities of their own. Even if nothing positive or heroic is happening for a child on the home front, yet they're fortunate enough to be in the path of heroic adults in other settings, a good chance remains for them to become heroic adults. Since most of us will have some sort of contact in the immediate future with a number of children, consider some of the following areas as leadership laboratories for future heroes.

The schools our children attend should be full of adults worthy of imitation. Whether you're a teacher or a tutor, a principal or a playground monitor, a superintendent or a secretary, a coach or a cook, you're spending considerable amounts of time around young people. And whether you like it or not, you're molding their hearts and characters by the actions you display in their presence. In many cases, these young people will spend more time with you than their own parents, especially if you teach at the elementary level. So if you happen to work in one of these academic settings, humble yourself and ask these tough questions.

First, how often is the value of humility brought to the attention of the children in your classroom? Yes, the lessons you teach in math, science, spelling, language, history and geography classes provide valuable information for your students in helping to prepare them for certain facets of life. But little, if any, of the material you teach in those classes has ever taught a child how to walk away from a silly or senseless argument or how to, in a practical way, consider other people more important than themselves. But they can learn a lot about those two challenging life-skills simply by watching how you relate to them, their classmates, their parents and the other teachers and administrators at your school.

Continue with the questionnaire, teachers, and be completely honest in your answers, just as you wish your students to be on a difficult test you put before them. Do your students see you working hard or just expecting it from them? Do they have a general sense you're prepared and doing your best to keep things interesting in the classroom? Do your students' parents sense you're pouring yourself out for their children's welfare, or do they see in you a general apathy? Are you willing to go out of your way and stay late after school to keep a struggling student from failing or help one get the first 'A' of their life? Are you willing to give out your e-mail address to parents and work together on their child's behalf? While your students won't be able to possess an entire photo album of the real you in regard to your work ethic, they will walk away from your classroom with a few clearly-developed pictures.

Lastly, do you have a genuine interest in the welfare of your students? Do you really care about their lives outside the school walls and how they'll manage them in the years to come? Do your students feel like you respect them? How would they rate you in the areas of kindness, gentleness, self-control and love? How do you talk to your students? What is the tone they hear in your voice when you're explaining a difficult problem? Do they sense you have a concern for them beyond the borders of the classroom? Could they come to you with a problem and feel you would listen and look to get involved?

In my opinion, teachers have one of the most important positions in the world. But a powerful opportunity to change a child for the better can quickly become counterproductive if the wrong individual is left in charge of a classroom. As I stated in the opening chapter, if you're a teacher, you are in many respects a heroic individual already. Few people in the working world feel the pressure you feel with so little income to show for it. Few people work more overtime than you and yet are so often underappreciated for it. Few employees outside the classroom setting work eight hours a day, five days a week with the daunting challenge of training moldable minds, all while encountering issues like puberty, problems in the home, attention deficit disorder, outward rebellion, social dysfunction, physical and sexual abuse, sadness and grief. Who, more than a teacher, has to figure out how to help dozens of individuals with various levels of intelligence, social skill and confidence get the best shot at success, all in a fair and friendly environment? If that's not challenging enough, add to all that the unpleasant 21st century challenges of gangs, drugs, open sexual situations, little or no ability to enforce discipline, fears of being stabbed or shot by a disturbed or disgruntled student and possible terrorism plots against the school. If you're a teacher, I applaud your efforts. But you must realize the tremendous responsibility you have to set a good (not perfect) example for students in your classroom.

If you teach a Sunday school class at your church, what are your students learning? Yes, the Bible is the greatest book ever written, containing the most important information in mankind's history. And, yes, the stories of Noah's ark and David's dead aim with his slingshot are wonderful and true. But the kids you teach will benefit a whole lot more from experiencing your kindness and patience than they ever will from memorizing the Ten Commandments, knowing how many pairs of pigs and possums came on board with Noah or being able to calculate, to the nearest inch, just how tall Goliath really was.

For those coaching Little League Baseball or Youth League sports of any kind, are you more into training young people to be a great athlete or a good human being? Keep in mind the chances are sky-high none of the little guys and gals you're now teaching the skills of base-running, basket-making and blitzing will ever don a college or professional uniform. Chances are very good, however, they will one day choose a profession, get married and raise children of their own. And they will likely be offered drugs at some point in their lives, and they'll probably have more than one opportunity to steal from their employer. Doesn't it make sense, then, that fair play, having fun and forgetting about the referees rotten calls are a lot more important items to teach your kids than the right technique and timing on their jump shot, how to turn the double play as quickly as possible or how to properly tuck and spin during a platform dive? In the few hours a week you have with these heroes-in-the-making, don't you have a much better chance of helping them thrive in our harsh and hectic world than helping them develop the athletic expertise that could, if they're incredibly lucky and loaded with talent, turn into a prolific career in professional sports? And I've never quite understood how learning how to snap off a curve ball to fool a batter has ever been helpful in knowing how to deal with someone who all of a sudden snaps on you. Most of the Roger Clemens and Randy Johnson wannabes you're coaching right now will end their pitching careers at age 18, or long before. They will, however, be dealing with rude and obnoxious people until the day they die—on the freeway, on the phone or on the first day of a new job. And while the proper way to execute scoring a goal on a power play is of prime importance to all junior hockey coaches, it's nowhere near as important as teaching the second-coming of Wayne Gretzky how to respond if someone makes a power play on him at work someday. How you deal with an official's blown call that ends up costing you the game, or how you respond to a play-dirty strategy employed by the opposing coach are two issues of much greater significance than a trip to the playoffs or protecting the winning record you've had for the past 15 years.

If you're an older sibling, a regular babysitter or a participant in the Big Brother or Big Sister programs, remember a hero is waiting in the wings and watching to see how you do it. It's not just a matter of spending time with these kids—it's much more a matter of how you conduct yourself while you're spending time with them. If you're a piano teacher, while helping the future Mozart learn how to effectively manipulate those 88 keys, don't forget to model the three keys of success—humility, hard work and a heart to help others. Have you ever thought about preparing your students for a recital on any of those?

And what about those kids running wild and crazy in your neighborhood? What do they think of you? Are you thought of as a mean, Mr. Wilson to the menaces on your block? Or are you the one who brings out the cookies and milk when you spot them playing in the street, or the one who grabs a glove and joins their game of home-run derby? Are you the one they can count on for a sale (and a really nice tip!) when they set up their yearly lemonade stand? Are you a grump or the goofy guy who gets down on all fours occasionally and takes them for a thrilling ride? Or are you just too old to hang out with the kids anymore? Do you feel justified in avoiding them because, hey, you raised children of your own, thus fulfilling your obligations to the younger generation? Or could these children possibly learn a thing or two from the six or seven decades you've spent in gaining valuable insights into what constitutes real success?

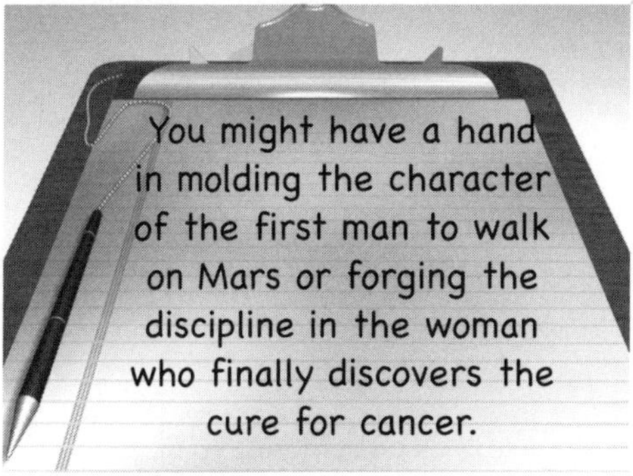

Who knows, the good example you set for a child might just help produce the National Teacher of the Year in 2030 or the new president of the United States in 2048. You might have a hand in molding the character of the first man to walk on Mars or forging the discipline in the woman who finally discovers the cure for cancer. You may be influencing the head coach of the Darrington Loggers in 2040 or the coach of the Dallas Cowboys in Super Bowl 70. Or, more likely, you might be leaving the needed inspiration for the hard working cleaning lady who'll have more influence at the office complex she daily beautifies than all the CEO's working there combined, simply because of her constant smile and charismatic spirit, the same qualities she saw in you in her younger years.

Never underestimate your importance to the next generation. These kids will soon grow up and enter the adult world, the exact same world you could be living in for many more years. May your example of heroic living inspire a hero in the wings, and may all of our combined examples be a spark to ignite an entire generation of them.

Chapter Twenty-Seven

A Boy, A Ball and A Big Need

On a cold and drizzly Saturday afternoon, eight-year-old Jimmy emerges from the sliding-glass-door on the back porch of his parent's modest home, situated on their 24-acre farm just outside of town. Underdressed for the occasion and carrying an under-inflated rubber basketball with both hands, Jimmy races down the porch steps, then down the steep hill of grass just beyond the deck of his home, making his way to the 30 x 15-foot cement basketball court that's been there since he was three. His simple plan for the next few minutes is to get in as many shots as possible before his mother calls him to the dinner table. You can almost always see him shooting at some time or another during a typical day, a routine he imitates from what he's witnessed in his two older brothers. Jimmy's oldest brother is 14, the middle brother is 11, and they both love the game of basketball. Like Jimmy, both boys put in plenty of time shooting and practicing their drives to the basket on their home court, looking to hone their skills and improve their chances of playing varsity basketball at the high school they'll soon be attending.

On this day, Jimmy missed most of the shot attempts he put up on the 10-foot regulation rim that is usually just out of range for his skinny, eight-year-old frame. But the low percentage of made shots has never really mattered much to Jimmy. Just making one shot out of 100 keeps him coming back for more. And he's not interested in getting a lower rim, or even an adjustable one he can raise when he gets bigger and stronger. After all, his brothers didn't use one when they were his age, so why should he? Nobody has to tell Jimmy he needs to get outside to the court and practice more. And almost every time he's there, he'd like to stay and play a lot longer than his mother allows.

Jimmy has been to a number of basketball games at the high school gymnasium located a few miles from his home. He dreams of the day when he (like his brothers are now able to do) can watch the excitement while sitting next to someone other than his mom and dad. He attends all the eighth grade contests in town his brother plays in, and he can't wait to get his first shot at organized ball in the school system.

Basketball is in Jimmy's blood. His father was a two-year starter on the varsity team two decades ago and his uncle is still known all over town for his game-winning three-point shot that catapulted the school into the state tournament for the first time. Jimmy plans to play on the team as well, and his parents have no reason to disagree with him or dampen his ambitions. They have no plans to move away from the small town this side of death, and they both believe basketball is one of the best opportunities the small-town environment affords Jimmy for learning discipline and developing a strong character.

In addition to basketball, Jimmy knows quite a bit about farming, and he just started doing a few chores entirely on his own. He's been taught and reminded numerous times about appropriate manners at the dinner table, being polite to everyone who comes by the house to visit, respecting authority figures in his life, having compassion for the elderly, enjoying the simple things in life, working hard, having faith in God and, of course, the ins and outs of basketball.

Jimmy is one of the many young boys living in small towns across America whose lives revolve around basketball and being all you can be as a person and player, great training for life beyond the high school hallways. In Washington, you'll find hundreds of boys such as Jimmy in places like Reardan, Oakesdale, Washtucna, Peshastin-Dryden, Ritzville, Curlew, Chimacum, Skykomish, Napavine, Onalaska, Klickitat and Kittitas, just to name a few. It's a very high probability Jimmy and most of the boys in the aforementioned towns of Washington won't play college basketball anywhere. They may even decide not to attend college and work in the woods or with their fathers on the family farm instead. But they'll grow up with a set of beliefs and a respect for life many other kids in bigger spheres won't get the opportunity to develop, and they'll have a pretty good understanding of important information the state university can't teach them, no matter how many degrees they earn there.

Like all these boys, Jimmy will rise and fall a number of times in his young life while playing basketball. He will succeed and fail. He will feel exhilarated and awful, and he will learn many valuable lessons along the way. He will probably score a game-winning basket at some point in his career, and he will likely make a turnover to cost his team a victory. On certain school days, Jimmy will bask in basketball victories from the night before, and he will thoroughly enjoy the moments when he receives the royal treatment. A few times before he graduates, he will absolutely hate the thought of going to school after a loss because he'll believe he's contributed to bringing down the spirit of the entire school. At some point in Jimmy's high school basketball career, his coach will chastise him for poor play or lack of effort, and he will more than likely be heralded as the example everyone should follow at other times. He will probably spend some time sitting on the bench in his early years, itching for a few minutes just to show off his abilities. And at some point, he will perform on center stage at the end of a big game, sinking two free-throws with one second remaining to lead his team to victory. And through each of these and many other basketball scenarios, Jimmy will learn about life. Hopefully, he'll be receiving guidance along the way from a heroic individual he calls Coach. Besides Jimmy's mother, father, older brothers and a few of his relatives who live nearby, this one man will have a tremendous amount of influence in Jimmy's very impressionable life, influence that will undoubtedly have a lasting affect on him.

Basketball coaches in small-town America are more than just men and women putting up X's and O's on locker room chalkboards to point their teams toward success. While they will most likely know the game quite well after a few years of coaching, they also must realize there's a lot more of life to be lived for the kids they're coaching, far beyond their days of playing basketball. While these coaches bark out instructions from the bench, they'll be teaching their highly-impressionable players many lessons on the more important game of life. At times they may be a player's biggest supporter. At other times they may be their biggest critics. Throughout their tenure of coaching high school basketball, each of these men and women will be given a number of opportunities to model the kind of character that can give their players a much better chance of succeeding in life once their sneakers are put away for good.

The two basketball coaches you've been reading about are prime examples of the kind of men and women we need in our country to get involved and stay involved in high school sports, small town or big city. One is no longer alive, but his heroic example, both on and off the court some 50 years ago, still resonates in the hearts and minds of many of the teenagers who once played for him, men who are now in their mid to late 60s. The other man is still involved in the training-boys-to-be-men business. He's been doing it since 1991 and he, too, has helped shape the characters of many young men. These men are now out on their own—going to college, making plans to get married, raising families, starting their own businesses, working the graveyard shift at the local factory or trying to emotionally bounce back from a recent tragedy. Each of them is clinging to the many lessons they learned from Jeff Bryson while playing Darrington basketball—lessons that will help them in the day-to-day drama of maintaining sanity and surviving the many challenges of life. Bryson and my father exemplify the importance of having appropriate adult role models for the younger generation, and they illustrate the important part all adults play in trying to keep the next generation from succumbing to fatalism or failure.

While Jimmy has no idea at the moment what he will need in life (right now all he can think about is being in a uniform and having people wildly cheer for him), one day he will be introduced to the high school world, the final frontier and training ground before independent living is finally upon him. If he's fortunate enough to be under the direction of a small-town hero, he will likely be better prepared for what lies beyond the last stanza of pomp and circumstance. If he should miss out on the blessing of being tutored by heroic men such as these, he will one day be more likely to quit an important project, quit his job, quit in his marriage or, saddest of all, quit on life altogether.

For 20 minutes on this day, Jimmy shot baskets, putting in a mere five shots out of the 100 or so he attempted. His mother finally called him in for dinner, and he sat down, as always, to a healthy meal—on this night it was pork chops, mashed potatoes, a salad he played with more than he ate, a homegrown glass of milk and chocolate cake for dessert. Jimmy went to bed a few hours after dinner, excited, as usual, about the new day ahead. In less than 10 years, nearly all of his beliefs, convictions and character will have been shaped and reshaped by the adults living in his small town, and his basketball coach will be one of the most influential.

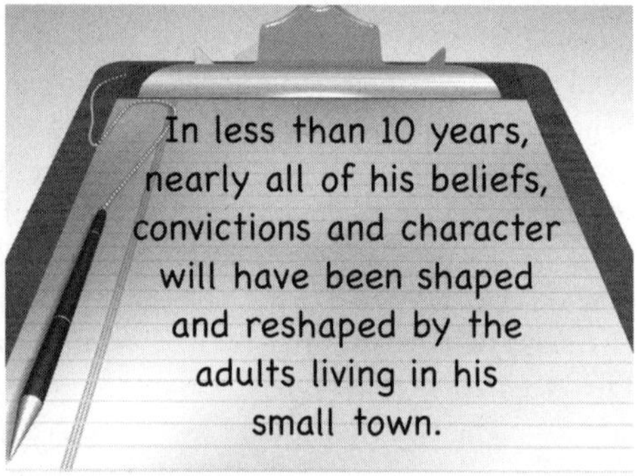

You were a child, too, just like Jimmy. Oh, perhaps at the age of eight you spent more time playing with your Tonka bulldozer or your Easy Bake Oven than you did playing basketball. And as you were growing up, maybe you ran the courts with a large group of kids on the playground in the inner city instead of in a small town like Jimmy. Maybe in your days of youth you weren't all that interested in playing organized sports, but you spent a lot of time doing things like memorizing lines and rehearsing for an upcoming play, hunting and fishing whenever you could find the time with some of your best friends or practicing in your garage with other members of the band trying to better your chances of making it big someday. However you chose to spend the bulk of your time from eight to eighteen, you played and you played and you played—and you loved it! And, suddenly, you were all grown up. In that process, you developed your character, primarily by what you saw in the adults who spent the most amount of time around you.

What were your mentors like? What did you learn from watching them? Who is the one person who helped steer you the most in the best direction? Or what leader in your life do you wish had never been there because what you gleaned from them had nothing but negative ramifications for your life? More than likely, most of us can answer all of these questions without much hesitation. It's good to think about those things and ask those questions from time to time, but it's far more crucial to realize those days of youth are over and that now, in many ways, you're the teacher.

Can you see another eight-year-old such as Jimmy (or Jaclyn) heading out to the court to work on becoming the next LeBron James or Lisa Leslie? Maybe it's your son or daughter, or maybe it's the neighbor kid whose parents just got a divorce. Maybe it's the boy who will be tempted one day to experiment with alcohol and drugs and he just needs a good role model to lead him away from that lifestyle. Maybe the child isn't heading outside to shoot hoops, but he's walking to the corner grocery store to get a candy bar. Maybe she's building a snowman or just heading home from school and trouble awaits her once she steps foot inside her house. Whoever these youngsters are, and wherever it is they're going, what kind of encouragement and example will they receive from you along their way? What things can you do to invade their space and change their destiny from bad to better or okay to outstanding? How can you convince them to spend more time in the classroom than in the streets? What can you do to encourage them to say "no" to the gang lifestyle and "yes" to the after-school program that will better prepare them for college? What can you do to inspire them to greatness in their own world? Whether it's an hour a day, an hour a week or a moment in time to make a difference, what legacy will you leave that child and how will you help them to grow up and make a vital and lasting contribution to society?

May these sobering questions enter your mind, and may they remain there for as long as you live. You don't have to coach basketball or play basketball to be a hero. You don't even have to like basketball. But you do have to be willing to embrace your role as an adult of influence. And you can't minimize your responsibility to step in and help when you can. Why not live out the remainder of your life with the realization you have a golden opportunity and a great responsibility to be a hero? If that should become your way of thinking, you too will be crowned champion in every sense of the word.

Chapter Twenty-Eight

Lessons Learned

My original plan for writing this book was simply to tell an inspiring tale of high school basketball and the importance of sports in small-town America. But the more I researched the facts of the story and discovered some additional information about its central characters, the more I realized there were a number of valuable life-lessons to be learned by telling it. I've tried my best not to be too preachy in my writing (that's extremely hard for a preacher), but the behind-the-scenes information that made this story possible really does need to be preached, whether it's done at a church, a community center, a championship banquet or a child's bedside. I hope this information has caused you to think about your own life, and it will end up being useful to you in your day-to-day activities. As we near the end of the book, allow me to be a little preachy and share with you a few lessons I've learned in the past two years. Hopefully, they'll be a benefit to your life as well.

The first of these lessons has nothing to do with the actual story, but plenty to do with me telling the story. It's a lesson that took me way too many years to learn, the lesson of honoring your father. For many years, I've considered myself a staunch believer in this traditional value. But I've come to realize I could have done a much better job in this area with my own father. Despite living in an era where independence is heralded as a virtue and breaking away from the grip of dad can't seem to happen soon enough, the value of honoring your father is still one of the most important lessons the younger generation needs to learn. Like so many have said in their post-adolescent days, "It's amazing how smart my father became the older I became!" I wholeheartedly agree! We would all do well to listen a whole lot more to the old man's wisdom, because it works such a high percentage of the time. (King Solomon had a few things to say about this topic as well.)

I believe if we took a little more time to analyze some of the qualities our fathers displayed to earn our honor, we could probably come up with a fairly long list. While making a list of his honorable behavior is a good beginning, the bigger need is making sure they feel the honor. Does yours? How do you know? Have you told him and, if so, how often? Have you ever written a letter to express gratitude to your father for all he has done for you and the sense of pride you carry from being his son or daughter? Have you ever apologized for the dishonoring episodes that may have crept into your relationship? How might the encouraging words you express to your father, along with the ongoing honoring you can give him from this day forward, make the remaining years of his life more enjoyable and satisfying?

Now I know some of you will have to search long and hard for an appropriate way to honor your father, since many of his efforts (or lack thereof) would be classified as dishonorable. But that's exactly what I'm encouraging you to do—search carefully until you discover an item or two you can put on your list and follow that up by expressing your appreciation to him in an appropriate way. Who knows what your search-and-find exercise might do for his heart? And it certainly won't do any damage to yours.

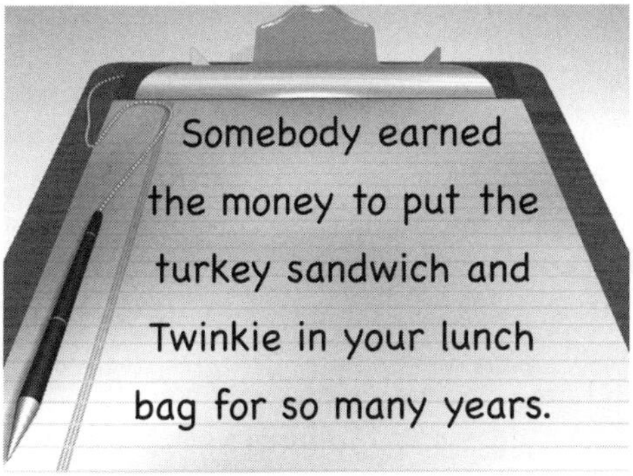

If you weren't fortunate to have a father growing up, think of the one individual who occupied that role more than anyone else and apply this suggestion to him. My point is this—somebody was there to show you the ropes of life. Somebody told you to stop when you really wanted to go, and now you're incredibly glad you stopped. Somebody made sure you had a privilege taken away when needed due to bad behavior. Sure, it made you stew on the inside, but it ultimately saved you from ending up as the meat. Somebody earned the money to put the turkey sandwich and Twinkie in your lunch bag for so many years. Somebody declined to buy a nicer car so the money saved could be used to put you through another semester at the community college. Sure, he was far from perfect and he probably hurt you a few times along the way. Just remember, in whatever leadership role (or roles) you find yourself in at the moment, you don't have it all figured out either! And, especially, to all parents and parents-to-be—how will you want to be treated when your biggest blunders are laid bare before the child who's expected to honor you?

A second lesson I've learned is the importance of being a hero to someone. Are you anybody's hero? Are you looked up to and greatly admired by another individual? Does anybody want to grow up and be just like you? Now I'm not suggesting you stand at a busy intersection, wait for the light to turn red, then display your "I Really Want to be Your Hero" sign to all the stopped cars. I'm not suggesting you express this desire to anyone. Simply realize people need hero figures in their lives then do your best to model for them the three heroic qualities we've focused on in this book.

The third lesson is to be careful who we select as heroes in our lives. We mustn't allow ourselves or our children to settle for the athletic star, rock star and movie star being the primary people we idolize and look to imitate. We've got to do a much better job convincing each other a hero doesn't have to be on the cover of Glamour or GQ, and they certainly don't have to be famous, worth millions of dollars or really talented in anything. As a matter of fact, we'll usually have to remind ourselves of just the opposite. Here's a sampling of those reminders:

A true hero is someone who's proud to associate with the elderly and puts their needs and comforts above everybody else's, not the 25-year-old musician who slammed his parents and encouraged rebellion in his latest CD.

A hero isn't the multi-millionaire living in his mansion of many rooms who, instead of gladly housing his aging and ailing mother, sees his financial surplus as the perfect opportunity to put her in the nicest nursing home across town. No, the true hero is the middle-class man who works a second shift at his job a few days a week just to get the extra monies needed to build an addition onto his house so his mother can spend her final years with the ones she loves the most.

Let's give homage and praise to the woman who volunteers her time at the Veteran's Hospital, not the veteran ballplayer being paid $15 million dollars a year for his ability to hit home runs who then donates a mere $100,000 dollars of it to his favorite charity. If your current hero happens to be a big league ballplayer, just make sure his off-the-field qualities are worthy of imitation, especially in regard to his family and the less-fortunate.

Another lesson I've come to learn in a deeper way is the lesson of taking full advantage of the opportunities before you—being more spontaneous and open to taking a few risks. Now, I'm not talking about hopping on an inner tube without a lifejacket and floating down the most dangerous section of the Colorado River. Use your brains on that one! But use your heart a lot more often than you're doing right now. Listen to it talk to you about going back to college and pursuing the career you've always wanted. Listen to it communicate with you about how you need to communicate your love to someone for the very first time. Listen to it dream as it tells you to go after the dream you've always thought could become a reality if only you pursued it with all your heart. Listen to it tell you to go ahead and do the right thing, even if it might set you back a bit financially or distance you from a valued relationship as a result. Maybe your heart is crying out for you to take up a new sport. Maybe you should skydive. How about running for public office or organizing an event in your community? Maybe you could write a book—even if nobody else ever reads it, you will! Why not try out for the team? Send in that letter to the President. Start your own business. Travel to the part of the world you've always wanted to see. Tell the girl you really love her. Ask her to marry you. Stand up to your boss the next time he encourages you to lie. Go to your 20-year class reunion and be totally secure in the person you've become. Disagree with the person who intimidates you the most when you believe your way is better. Retire earlier than planned and devote more time to your church or a charitable cause. Paint the picture you've thought about painting since you were in school, then frame it and proudly display it in your living room.

Perhaps I got your attention with this list, or maybe it doesn't include your heart's biggest desire. But I'm pretty sure you're already thinking of a few things that fit this description. Whatever you decide to do with those thoughts, make sure you leave no room for regret. Who knows, the next decision you make may be the most heroic thing you've ever done and you'll attract a following the Pied Piper couldn't even rival.

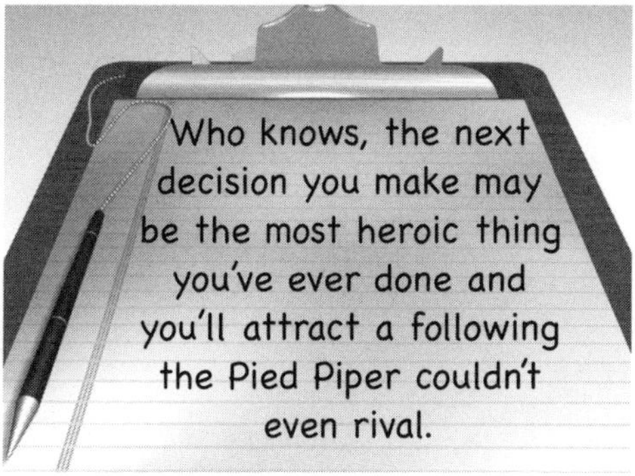

To close this chapter, allow me to once again mention the three heroic qualities I've been highlighting throughout the book. This is the one lesson I've come to learn in a much greater way—the lesson of just how important it is to model humility, hard work and a heart to help others. Let me encourage you to become known for these qualities, experts in each of them you might say.

Display humility on a consistent basis. None of us know-it-alls know it all or even close. We all have a lot to learn about a lot of things and we all have a long way to go before we can be considered an expert in any area of life. Just admit it.

Work hard. In basketball terms, whether you're playing, coaching, refereeing, cheerleading, scorekeeping or sweeping the gym after the game, do your very best and put in an honest day's work.

Have a heart to help others and care deeply for people. Cut people some serious slack when they blow it. Apologize first. Forgive faster. Smile more. Say good morning to a stranger. Be kind to the waitress who gets your order completely wrong. Attend a funeral. Write a card of encouragement to someone. Let the other guy go first when you're hustling out of the stadium parking lot. Visit a nursing home, even if your relative isn't a resident there. Drop by an orphanage. Adopt a child. Say "thank-you" more often than you think you should. Get to know your neighbors. Call an old friend you haven't talked to in years. Ask more questions about how someone is really doing. Send some of your hard-earned money to a local charity. Volunteer there. Donate blood. Take a homeless person out for dinner at a nice restaurant. Give up your aisle seat on the plane to the person in the middle looking a bit cramped and uncomfortable.

Along with gaining the desire to get reconnected with my small-town roots then remembering to imitate the positive qualities I learned while growing up in that environment, those are just some of the lessons I've learned since I started working on *Small-Town Heroes*. I'm quite certain I've missed a bunch, but at least it's a start. Yet with just these on my current list, I have plenty of things to work on improving the rest of my life.

Chapter Twenty-Nine

The Clark Kent Club

I'd like to leave you with one final suggestion as to how we can best multiply the number of heroes around the world. Yes, it's just a suggestion. But from personal experience in regard to how a positive, small-group setting can greatly aid in radically changing your life for the better, I have to believe the following plan will have a similar affect on those of you who choose to participate.

Though he's merely a make-believe figure, Clark Kent had it going on! Nobody displayed the three heroic qualities we've been discussing quite like Clark. Talk about humble! Nobody else in town (or the world for that matter) was accomplishing the feats he managed to display on a daily basis as Superman, yet not a single soul was aware of the true greatness of this mild-mannered man with the dark, thick glasses. Whenever a desperate call for help was brought to his attention, Clark quietly slipped away to the nearest phone booth for a quick change, all without drawing any attention to his whereabouts or intentions. And after performing his latest heroic deed, Clark just as quietly returned to his desk at The Daily Planet, not wanting to take any of the credit for the amazing rescue story appearing on the paper's front page. What a guy! Oh, that more of us would have the heart of Clark Kent when it comes to the "I'm-here-to-help" missions on which we embark. Whether it's letting someone know of our next great plan to help a needy soul or hoping at least a few people acknowledge our selfless and sacrificial efforts once they've been accomplished, most of us have a hard time doing anything behind the scenes, and even fewer are content with staying there.

While humility definitely described the bookends of Clark's many life-saving operations, he was quite familiar with hard work as well. Have you ever tried changing clothes in less than a minute in a phone booth? Have you ever had to work as hard as he did just to keep the positives in your life from going public, or go so far out of your way just to keep one person from finding out about all the wonderful things you've been doing? Have you ever had to take on a powerful and persistent troublemaker like Lex Luthor and work super hard to stay on top of your good-guy game for so many years? And though I've never done it before, flying all over the world can't be all that easy, especially when you're carrying someone in a complete state of shock! And surely, stopping a speeding locomotive headed for certain disaster or entering a burning building to save a young damsel in distress must require a person to exert a ton of physical energy. But Clark was doing those things and a whole lot more on a regular basis. He didn't just have a day job, he was on-call for much tougher assignments than any newspaper reporter would ever encounter, 24 hours a day, seven days a week. Even hard working doctors get a break from the blinking pager every now and then! Even a construction worker gets a well-deserved lunch break and can look forward to the five o'clock hour when he can finally rest his sore and weary body.

Though he excelled in the ever-so-difficult areas of humility and hard work, Clark's greatest attribute was his heart to help others. Forget the incredible and unmatched power he possessed and the humility he always carried to keep his efforts incognito. Without a love and genuine concern for the people he encountered in harm's way (not only Lois Lane, but every individual in need of Superman's power), he would have ignored the many desperate cries for help he heard and bypassed every last phone booth in his path. Having the ability to fly in on a moment's notice and catch someone falling over Niagara Falls is nice. But unless you care about the individual about to be devoured by the rushing water, you'll probably just let them die their appointed death and allow the tragedy to be a lesson to every other careless human trying to get to close to the waterfall's edge. Sure, he was faster than a speeding bullet, but since that was the case, he could just as easily have sped away from anybody in need of his heroic activity. Yes, Clark Kent was a hero and one we all admired. Why did we like Clark so much? Why did he have such longevity in his comic book career and why do we still glamorize him? Could it be because he displayed the qualities of a true hero—those of humility, hard work and a heart to help others?

So here's my suggestion for keeping Clark Kent alive and well in our hearts—a simple plan for producing a lot more of his type, only this time it will be real people doing real deeds that have real significance. Start your own Clark Kent Club. If one has already been started in your area by the time you read this, find out about it and ask someone if you can place membership. Whether this group consists of individuals from your workplace, your church, your neighborhood, your high school, your college dormitory, your fraternity or sorority, your sport's team or your most immediate circle of friends, that's completely up to you. It doesn't really matter where it happens and with whom it happens as long as members of the group are committed to the cause of heroism and the main function of the group is to sharpen one another in that pursuit.

Here's a sample schedule for your Clark Kent Club. Once a week, twice a month, once a month or however often the group chooses to meet, gather for an hour or so and discuss how you're doing in the pursuit of heroism. How's your humility at work? How have you been modeling it at home around the spouse and the kids? Did you see it when you were driving in traffic, looking for a parking spot, standing in a long line or talking with a customer service agent who wasn't sounding real cooperative or sympathetic about the item you were trying to return without a receipt? How did you respond when receiving correction from your boss or your spouse? When and where in the past week were you tempted to lay humility down for a short nap and pick up with the pride instead? Who did you find it most difficult to be humble around and why? These are just some of the questions you'll be asking each other and, most importantly, answering honestly. Encouragements and practical suggestions from other members of the group can then be brought forth, giving each of you more of the necessary equipment for living a life of humility until you meet again. You could even choose to have partners within your group, and those two individuals will make a commitment to call each other every few days just to check up on each other's progress.

Not only will humility be on each meeting's agenda, hard work will be a topic of discussion as well. Many of the same questions you ask each other in regard to humility can be repeated in this area as well. What has your work ethic been like the past few weeks at your place of employment? Would your boss agree with that assessment? How about when nobody was watching compared to when everyone was watching? How has hard work been displayed in your home? Did you take the necessary steps in disciplining your child or did you let their bad behavior slide one more time because you were just too tired to deal with it decisively? Husbands, have you done the dishes lately? Did you put the dishes away where your wife said they should go or where you decided they would go? How about vacuuming? Did you really reach way under the coffee table to suck up those last few pieces of dirt? When your wife asked you to finish the backyard project, did you do it excellently? Did you really get all of the weed's roots this time, or did you leave a remnant that will rise again? In your personal relationships, how hard did you work to get closer to people this week? In your efforts to lose weight or gain strength, did you really push yourself or decide to plateau? Did you check deep enough into that dirt-cheap insurance plan to see if it really could save you money in the long run as advertised? Once again, each member of your group will take turns discussing how they feel they're doing in this area and, most importantly, each of you will welcome any input (positive or painful) the other members of the group provide.

And finally, you'll use the group to better determine how you're doing in the most important area of all, having a heart to help others. How much time did you spend thinking about the needs of others? Did the people in your home feel a sense of security and protection from you? What were your first thoughts about the person being a thorn in your side? What did you ultimately do with those thoughts? When was the last time you surprised somebody with something significant? How much of your money is being used to help people besides yourself or your family? How many sick people have you talked to or visited recently? Is there a card, letter or e-mail you need to send someone just to let them know you're thinking about them? How have you been doing as far as returning your phone calls? Whose calls did you screen and why? How would you rate your friendliness this past week—with people in your own home, with people in your office, with people working in retail and even with complete strangers who shared the same space with you momentarily? These are pretty probing questions that are sure to elicit some strong emotions, both positive and negative. But asking them and answering them will prove to be quite beneficial in your desire to be heroic.

If this type of discussion takes place in your Clark Kent Club on a regular basis, what kind of heroic individual might you become? And how might your input to others in the group help them to reach their highest levels of heroism? There's no way of knowing the answer to these questions unless you do it, and do it consistently. If there isn't a group like this in your area at the present time, start one yourself and share your plans with a few others you think might be open to the idea. All you really need are two willing people to get the group started. It won't be long until word starts spreading (you won't be spreading it of course) and more people will want to be included. And once the ball gets rolling, watch out. When your tiny group finally grows to the size of ten or twelve, it's probably time to divide and conquer. Break into two groups of five or six and keep up the heroic activity.

In addition to these general group guidelines, there are a number of other activities that could prove to be very productive for your group. Perhaps you could all read the same autobiography of someone heroic. Maybe each member could do their own research on one of their heroes then present their findings to the group. A group project to help someone in need could go a long way in encouraging someone at your workplace or in your church. Have a time of discussion each week about the biggest needs you're aware of, list them in their order of significance and create a plan to meet all those needs in the next number of months. Have a night devoted to the homeless where one person hosts a party at their home and each member of the group sets a goal to bring a homeless person to the festivities. At the party, create the greatest spread ever known to man and make those without a home feel like they're the most important people on the planet, at least for a few hours. Go watch a movie together and afterward discuss the different characters and their heroic qualities, or lack thereof. Rent the Superman series and watch Clark Kent like you've never watched him before. Have a different person facilitate the meeting each week. (This will be a great test of humility for those in the group with the most obvious leadership skills!) Invite different people to your meetings just to observe and ask for their input. Bring in a newspaper and look through the local section to see if there's a pressing need your group could meet. Then go to the national section and ask the same question. In either case, don't be concerned about your small status and the rational train of thought that will expose your inability to meet most or all of the need. Almost all great efforts to change the world or change one person's life have started small. Even if nobody else is planning to assist you in your efforts, at least you're doing something positive. And don't underestimate the possibility of a power greater than yourselves kicking in to supply the remaining need. Go on a weekend getaway together and have some fun (even Clark Kent needed to let loose once in a while!), but spend a few hours discussing ways to make the group more cohesive and productive. Talk about your heroes growing up and why you considered them such.

The first place to begin displaying these three heroic qualities is right there within the group. Make sure you're being humble with each other, you're working hard for each other and you're showing genuine care and concern for each other. It's great to help your next-door neighbor with his plumbing problems, but if a fellow member's confidence at work or cohesiveness with his wife is going down the toilet, he's going to need your time and expertise just as much. But while you're focused on caring for each other, don't allow the group to become self-focused. Always keep looking outward so you don't become exclusive. Nothing is more unattractive to an outsider than feeling ignored by members of a certain group, or when they think the group views them as someone belonging in a lesser league.

A positive group dynamic with some form of accountability can boost production and pizzazz in many important areas of our lives. This truth is recognized by successful athletic coaches from peewee to professional leagues, CEO's in the fastest-growing Fortune 500 companies and churches that are expanding their borders and making an impact on their communities. Organizations and individuals who ignore this valuable training tool will consistently lag behind those who submit themselves to a group and surround themselves with like-minded individuals with a similar passion to be their best. So I hope many of you embrace this idea of a Clark Kent Club and garner the many benefits awaiting you. And I'm quite certain those of you with a large quantity of creativity in your genetic makeup can take this idea and make it even better than what I'm proposing. Go for it! Call it by a different name (perhaps the 3H Club or Solomon's Subjects), come up with a different schedule and create a better dynamic by using your own ideas. But whatever you do, may it be done with humility, may you work hard to make it as excellent as possible and may your participation in it bring about a deep desire in you and the fellow-members of your group to help others in need.

Chapter Thirty

My First Heroes

There are so many people to thank for being heroic figures in my life. I probably didn't put most of them in this category when I was younger and going through adolescence, but the longer I think about what's really important in life, and the more I think about the qualities these individuals modeled for me, the more I realize they really were heroes.

My sixth grade teacher Gary Jensen is the first individual who comes to mind. He made learning interesting and even fun at a time when school was about the last item on this 12-year-old's list of things I wanted to do. We read lots of books together as a class, my favorite being *Charlie and the Chocolate Factory*. He brought his guitar to class on a number of occasions and taught us through music. I can still remember singing Peter, Paul and Mary's, *"Puff the Magic Dragon"* and Bob Dylan's, *"Blowin' in the Wind"* and actually enjoying it. He organized a class trip to the big city in Portland, Oregon where we watched a movie together. He produced and directed a mock trial on the dangers of smoking for our health class that we actually got to perform for the community, and I have to believe this anti-smoking enactment made a significant contribution to my avoidance of the habit. Though my fellow sixth-graders and I may have considered him a bit corny at times, he definitely brought out the best in us and I'll always be grateful for his influence in my life.

Dick Kretz was a neighbor, a good friend of my father's and one of my coaches in Little League baseball. But more than a coach, he was a caring human being who was liked by all. He led our Little League team to the championship when I was 12, and made both practices and games an absolute blast. Though he loved to win, I never felt as if it was his goal in coaching. He was an incredible humanitarian and his life ended in his mid-40s while displaying his big heart to help other people. On returning home from work, he came upon a fire and stopped to help extinguish the flames. He was a volunteer fireman in our town and wanted to use his abilities to assist others whenever he could. Unfortunately, a live telephone wire had fallen in the earlier efforts to put out the fire and he was electrocuted in his efforts to secure safety for those nearby. I have often used his zest for life and concern for others along the way as a model for how I need to live out my remaining days.

Bob and Dodie Read were the parents of my first serious girlfriend during my freshman and sophomore years in high school. While I'm sure they had great concern about the amount of time I was spending with their daughter, they always treated me with such incredible kindness and did what they could to include me in their family's schedule. While neither of my children have had a serious dating relationship as of yet, when they do I will recall how I was treated by Bob and Dodie and do my best to treat their opposite-sex interests with great kindness and respect.

Ruth Rodin was a second mother to me for about three weeks in 1969. While my brother was in intensive care about 50 miles from our home, I was able to spend the majority of that time in her home while my parents stayed by his side. Her son, also named Curt, was one of my best friends and I don't know how I would have survived those difficult days without her willingness to welcome and care for me. Though the Rodin's home was quite small, and though I'm sure my presence caused a financial and emotional challenge to their household of five, she always made me feel like one of the family.

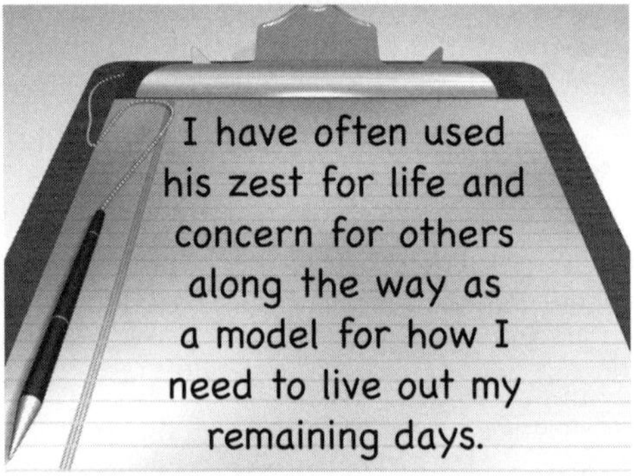

Tim Frandsen was a neighbor and good friend during my growing-up years. We had lots of fun together racing our Hot Wheels, playing a form of home-run derby using a tennis racquet for a bat and some rolled-up tin foil for a ball, playing tackle football in his front yard and wrestling with his St. Bernard named Tom. But his heroic activity was best lived out in the religious conviction he displayed in high school. After going through some very painful episodes in his own family, including the death of a stepfather he dearly loved, Tim began seeking out spiritual matters his sophomore year. Though he admittedly had his share of problems living up to the higher standards he sought, Tim was genuinely excited about the new direction his life was taking and wasn't ashamed to share that excitement with others. He did what he could to encourage me to seek out a spiritual path, taking me to a few events where I would be encouraged to address my need for greater spirituality. But I had little or no interest at the time in changing my view of God or changing any aspect of my misguided life. Though, at times, I privately persecuted him and the other religious people in our high school for what I thought was their missing-out status, I will always remember Tim and his willingness to stand his ground and stand out for what he believed.

Brad Cooper was another hero figure of mine in high school. Brad was two years ahead of me in school and, without a doubt, one of the best athletes to ever play sports at Toutle Lake High School. He was quarterback for the football team, leading scorer and All-State selection on the basketball team and an incredible track-and-field athlete who broke numerous school records. But it wasn't his athletic achievements I remember most, but his humility. Brad was better, by far, than most of the athletes he competed with and against in every sport, but you never would have known it unless you saw him play. He wouldn't talk about himself or his many accomplishments, he didn't draw attention to himself—before, during or after any sporting event in which he participated—and, though intensely competitive, he was always polite, both on and off the court. Though he was someone I definitely wanted to imitate on the basketball court, I now realize how fortunate I was to have had an example of humility like him during my first two years of high school.

Dennis Oman was our high school's varsity basketball coach from the time I was in seventh grade through my junior year. Coach Oman was a standout basketball player himself at Ilwaco, Washington, and he brought his playing success to the coaching corner where he led Toutle Lake to three consecutive state tournaments from 1974-1976, a 19-1 record in the 1973-74 regular season, an undefeated regular season in 1974-75, culminating in a fourth-place finish at state, and a renewed pride in Fighting Ducks' basketball. The most important things I learned from Coach Oman were intensity, hard work and a no-excuse mentality. My natural character as an athlete and human being was to be too soft, too whiny and too interested in passing the buck when it came to addressing my mistakes—three non-heroic qualities that often led me to settle for second best. Coach Oman helped to drive them out of me. I often think back to pre-season practices and in-game admonishments with Coach Oman and how tough they were, but just how important those episodes were in driving out the laziness and take-it-easy tone I would have played with if not for his influence. He gave up coaching in 1977, my senior year, but his heroic influence during his days at Toutle Lake has had great impact on my life to this very day.

But perhaps the two most important individuals in my high school days were Mary Brown and Margaret Woltjer. Miss Brown taught English, Writing and Drama, and Miss Woltjer taught German while also serving as the school's librarian. Unfortunately, I think I gave the two of them more grief than any other teachers in the school. But they were always able to shrug it off and granted me unconditional mercy and grace on a regular basis, though I'm sure, at times, they desired to do the exact opposite. I brought Miss Woltjer to tears on a few occasions with my sarcasm and all-around class-clown demeanor, but she never allowed it to distance herself from her main goal of teaching me and treating me with kindness, as I'm sure she chalked much of it up to my high levels of immaturity and insecurity. I was a student in many of Miss Brown's classes and acted in a few of the school plays she directed, and she always tried to make each activity as fun as possible, even while we were in the exceedingly-painful stage of reading Shakespeare and trying to figure out what in the world Bill the Barth was talking about. I haven't seen or heard from either of these women in more than 28 years, but I think of them occasionally and how they were used to show me some very important qualities for appropriate daily living. Though I haven't spoken a lick of German since I graduated, and though I've never spent one minute with Shakespeare since I was 18, I have had numerous opportunities to imitate these two women in areas of life the textbooks never covered. (Not to mention I became a writer, I've performed in a few theatrical productions as an adult and I love reading books.)

And I would be remiss not to mention the individuals whose names I heard on numerous occasions while growing up, and I will always be grateful for what these Darrington basketball players meant to my father and me. They were, and still are, heroes to me, and my father was blessed to have them under his authority serving as Darrington's head coach. Little brought light to his eyes and excitement to his voice more than a recollection of the young men he was privileged to coach in his three most successful years in Darrington—1955, 1957 and 1958. They were heroes of mine growing up and will remain on my heart for as long as I live.

Thanks to all of you who were a part of the first Darrington championship in 1955. You surprised the entire state of Washington and your exploits will not soon be forgotten. Members of that team include Roland Mount, Gerald Green, David Edwards, Ken Estes, Daryl Edwards, Duane Sanford, Darryl Smoke, Jack Bates, Dick Noble, Bill Green, Harold Haga and Larry Gilbert.

My gratitude also goes out to each member of the "Darrington Demolition" team and your conquest of the competition on your way to a state title in 1957. You gave my father one more opportunity to bask in the sunlight of basketball supremacy. The players on that championship squad were David Edwards, Dan Bates, Randall Phillips, Gary Sweeney, Roger Buchanan, Dick Hitchcock, Daryle Whittall, Dwayne Whittall, Lyle Edlund, Bob Green, John Tanner and David Andrews.

My sincere thanks go out as well to each member of my father's 1958 team. Though you can all probably still remember that game against Yelm as though it happened yesterday, and though you can no doubt think of one or two things you could have done differently to turn the tide of that disappointing upset loss in the semi-finals, your efforts both on and off the court brought great joy to my father and you went down to defeat with class. Your victory in the consolation game the following night proved what type of players and people you were. The members of that third-place squad include David Edwards, Roger Buchanan, Randall Phillips, Cecil Parris, Gerald Howard, David Andrews, Ken Fox, Gordon Hyde, John Peterson, Jerry Hayter, Terry Reece and Bill Bethard.

My heartfelt appeciation is sent to each of those men, as well as to every individual player under my father's leadership during his 17-year reign of coaching in Darrington, Rochester and Toutle Lake. In a real way, your exploits provided me with hours of unforgettable conversations with my father for many, many years, long after you hung up your sneakers, and you granted so many wonderful moments for my father to look back upon, moments that lived in his memory until his final days.

There are others, I'm sure, but these are the ones, in addition to my parents, who paved the way for me until I graduated from high school. After that period in my life, so many others have provided heroic contributions in my life via their words and wonderful examples, all of them helping to mold my character into what it is today. The two simple things I've done through the years have been to watch their lives closely and allow them to wield their swords of correction in my direction whenever necessary. Their heroic lifestyles and loving words have pierced my heart and pushed me in the proper direction on many occasions, as a husband, father, minister, writer, friend, neighbor and man of God.

I hope you have your list of heroes as well. If not, take some time and write one out, and by each name list the specific things you learned from that individual. As I plan to do, you could give each of them a call and express your gratitude, or maybe write them a note of thanks. Many heroic people have stood in your presence, and I'm certain some are still there. They live in small towns, medium-sized towns and large cities all across the country, and they've been put there to point all of us in a better direction. First and foremost, recognize their efforts. Then do what you can to contribute your own heroic qualities to a world in desperate need of the good things living in your heart.

Don't get bogged down thinking your efforts will have little or no impact on a planet occupying almost seven billion people, or that your available gift to society is too plain, poorly wrapped and perhaps best suited for placement under a Charlie Brown Christmas tree. If the small package you're offering contains any trace of humility, hard work or a heart to help others, it may end up being the biggest and best gift ever opened by another individual, one that could create a ripple affect to eventually flood our world with heroes.

Epilogue

It's late December of 2005, a little more than three years since my father passed away and the moment twelve young men decided to carry his memory and legacy throughout their basketball campaign. Just five months after that decision, they were crowned state champions for the first time in 46 years. Following that storybook season, the Loggers qualified for the state tournament in 2004, placing seventh. In 2005, the Loggers failed to qualify for the state tournament for the first time in seven years. And projections for the 2006 Loggers indicate a time of rebuilding in the basketball program. Jeff Bryson is still in Darrington, displaying similar qualities to the ones I've documented in this book, qualities I firmly believe led to the 2003 championship. He remains committed to Darrington basketball and bringing his teams back to the state tournament year after year with a legitimate shot at winning the title. How long that process will take is simply a guess, but Bryson is determined to do all he can to bring a fourth title to the town he grew up in and still loves. And Bryson's players from his first championship team, while hopeful about the future of Darrington basketball, stand firm on what it will take to win again.

"Everybody in Darrington realizes it (a championship) can be done. But they (the team) will have to do it the way we did it, or it probably won't happen."

The "way" will involve people like Kevin and Randy Ashe taking personal responsibility for boys at an early age, working with them for a number of years on the basic fundamentals of the sport, entering their teams in tournaments that will pour out their competitive juices to the max, planting a vision of greatness in their minds and preparing them for the challenges that await them once they begin playing high school basketball in a highly-competitive atmosphere. And, as the Ashe brothers were fortunate to experience during that eight-year training program, an incredibly supportive and sacrificial group of parents will complete the winning equation.

The "way" will involve a dedicated group of ballplayers with a high level of commitment to excellence and each other. It will include making and keeping promises to one another—promises to keep basketball success at the forefront of their minds and promises not to allow distractions and temptations to turn them away from their desired destination. It will involve a united resolve and recommitment to certain goals at some point during the season, as every championship team will likely face an obstacle or two on the season's road to greatness.

And the "way" will also involve a united coaching staff with a deep level of respect for tradition, a regular acknowledgement of success achieved in the program before their arrival and a humble spirit to learn from the winning ways of the past as well as those in the present.

Should you ever get the chance to visit Darrington in the next few years, evidence of the "way" should be fairly easy to find. Stop by the IGA grocery store and spend a few minutes with Kevin and Randy Ashe talking about what they believe brought basketball success to their town. Among the many things they'll express, they will be most adamant about the need for a few good men to pick up the championship baton the two of them left behind in 1999 when Kevin's son Jason moved into the high school ranks—someone willing to work with and train a team of young boys from first grade until the final buzzer sounds ending their junior high competition. And they will be more than willing to offer their wisdom and expertise to anyone willing to learn all they did those eight years while honing young boys' basketball skills.

After you've finished chatting with Kevin and Randy, head over to the public library about three blocks away. You're likely to run into Clarence Caspers there, a 79-year-old man who was in Darrington to witness the championships of the past and present. Caspers spends a few hours at the library almost every day of the week, and he would love to offer you his insights into basketball success in the small town he's called home for more than 52 years. Caspers was one of my father's roommates in the 1950s when both were bachelors and beginning their teaching careers. Caspers moved from a much larger school district to teach in Darrington in 1952, and he still believes the quality of basketball was better in Darrington during the 50s than what he had seen in the larger schools. Caspers knew my father quite well and he's very familiar with Bryson and his brand of winning basketball. He will tell you their personalities and coaching styles are eerily similar and he isn't surprised at all Bryson has brought back a sense of pride to Darrington residents about their basketball team and a great amount of respect for the Logger's program around the state. Caspers still enjoys attending some of the Darrington home games, and from time to time he can be seen tooting his horn in the stands along with the younger members of the high school band. That, too, he says, keeps him connected with the past. Caspers served as the music teacher and band director for Darrington from 1952-1984 and directed the band during both of my father's state championships in 1955 and 1957.

About one mile south of the library is Darrington High School. If you decide to visit, make sure you check out the trophy case in the main hallway. There you'll find a 20 x 20-inch board with the signatures of all the players and coaches from the 2002-2003 team, strategically placed alongside the championship trophy of the same year. It will remind you that dedication to a plan, teamwork and maintaining focus on a goal are all valuable tools of the championship trade.

After spending a few minutes there, take a short walk over to the Community Center. After marveling at the mint condition of the old, all-wood gymnasium, spend a few moments looking at the championship banners hanging on the east wall and remember the connection between the two championship coaches who won it all nearly five decades apart. Visualize the deep level of respect Jeff Bryson had for my father and think about how his humility to include my father in his season's plans helped him to win a title.

If you're there on a weekday around noon, you probably won't get a chance to talk with Bryson and hear what's in his heart concerning success and championship seasons. That's because he'll be eating lunch with his mother, Bettie, a long-time librarian at the high school, just like he's done almost every school day for the past few years. If you finally catch up with him and he has a free moment from his duties of husband, father, teacher and varsity basketball coach, he'll be more than willing to tell you about the many magical moments of his 2003 title run. And in that conversation, I'm almost certain my father's name will come up, that he will be spoken of in the highest regard and that Bryson will probably point to his accomplishments more than his own as the biggest reason why he's the proud owner of a state championship ring.

If you're hoping for a conversation with any of the players on Bryson's championship squad, your best bet is to come during the summer or one of the holiday breaks. That's because nearly all the players from that team are currently attending college somewhere, looking to better prepare themselves for life beyond the textbooks. Should you get a chance to speak with any of them, they'll be more than happy to share their most memorable experiences on the way to a title—the pre-season pact, the practice sessions, the decision to write a hero's initials on their tennis shoes, the wins and losses, the friendships, the frustrations, the doubts, the determination, the emotions of helping a good friend and teammate through the loss of a close family member, the late-season slump and subsequent shirt-burning, the 10-game winning streak that culminated in the first state title for their town in 46 years and the coach and championship choreographer they will always respect for his humility, hard work and heart to help them, not only as ballplayers, but as human beings.

On your way out of town, you can find one last piece of evidence for basketball success should you stop for a moment at the southwest corner lot of the Darrington Cemetery. There you will discover on a tombstone the name LaVerne Simmons. Buried beneath the headstone are the remains of the man many Darrington residents believe put their town on the map, and the one who provided so many wonderful moments and memories for the community during his incredible run of basketball success in the 50s. Your time spent at the cemetery will be a tremendous reminder to you about the vast importance of displaying humility, hard work and a heart to help others on your road to success, three qualities my father's peers and former players said they saw him display on a regular basis.

But even with the abundance of evidence for what must happen to usher in more championship seasons to the town, nobody really knows what lies ahead for Darrington basketball. Who knows how many years will pass before the town can celebrate another title? Maybe, to everybody's surprise, it will come this season. It may be a decade before the Loggers claim the top prize again. Or, it could be another 46 years from the time of their latest title, or sometime in March of 2049. If it happens sooner rather than later, you can certainly count on humility, hard work and a heart to help others being the main ingredients in that championship season. If it happens later, rather than sooner, and Bryson is no longer directing the Loggers from the sidelines, another coach will have to humble himself and do all he possibly can to bring traditional values to the forefront for his players, and Bryson's heroic deeds will need to be made available for public consumption. If the Loggers still haven't returned to the winner's circle by 2049, Bryson will be 84 years old by then. If he's still alive, chances are real good he'll be in attendance at the Community Center for a number of games during the course of the 2048-2049 season, watching his great-grandson or another relative sink a game-winning shot or make a key steal to secure a victory. And it's highly likely he'll also make the trip to Spokane for the state tournament later that year should the Loggers qualify, and he'll probably be one of the first to congratulate the current coach should he lead them to their fourth title. And the hundreds of Darrington fans who attend basketball games during the course of that year will no doubt greet Bryson each time with great enthusiasm and honor him with tremendous respect while recalling stories of the incredible championship season he directed in 2003.

If Bryson were to already have passed by that time, I would hope the initials JB could be found on each of the player's tennis shoes, in honor of the man who believed in upholding tradition and paved the way for his own tradition of success to be heralded in Darrington. If his initials are on those shoes, I'm inclined to believe a number of extraordinary things will fall into place throughout the season, enabling the Loggers, once again, to hoist the hardware of state champions.

And whether it happens tomorrow, ten years from now or in the year 2046, should this small-town story's model for success become descriptive of your day-to-day activities, you, too, will be well on your way to becoming a hero.

Other Books by Curt Simmons

The Revealer: The Man,The Majesty, The Model, helps us take a trip back to the first century and discover the one who claimed that he alone was the Word made flesh, the only way to the Father and the only flawless example when it comes to victorious living! This book will help you to understand the son of God in new ways, to see his humanity, to understand his divinity, and to realize how Jesus is the model for our own dreams, hopes and lives.

DETAILS
Author: Curt Simmons
ISBN: 0-9745342-5-0
264 pages. Paperback
Price: $15.00

The Unveiling, exploring the nature of God. Written in a unique and refreshing style, this book will be hard to put down. Author Curt Simmons blends insights into contemporary culture with an invigorating look at biblical wisdom to show us the real God of the Bible and how he influences, impacts and changes our lives.

DETAILS
Author: Curt Simmons
ISBN: 1-884553-59-1
208 pages. Paperback
Price: $12.00